# RESURGENCE AND REFORMATION

This concise study by an eminent scholar clearly relates the political dynamics of the sixteenth century to the subsequent course of English history. In the 118 years of Tudor rule, England underwent changes that led it from the Rome-dominated Middle Ages into a new era of national expansion and sovereignty.

*The Tudor kings first crippled, then abolished, the power of the Church in England; society was secularized, the Reformation begun. The rule of a strong central government brought peace to the land and allowed the prosperous pursuits of trade and industry to thrive as never before. Growing cities broke beyond their medieval walls. With the increasing security of society, popular arts flourished: it was the age of Shakespeare. And, in the New World, English explorers planted the seeds of colonization that were to blossom into the greatest empire since Rome.*

Fascinating as well as enlightening, Dr. Woodward's history recaptures the color, crisis, and drama of this vigorous period, the book supplies brief biographies of notable personalities of the sixteenth century, together with reading lists and illustrations.

# Other MENTOR Books on English History

**A Short History of 17th Century England: 1603-1689** *by G. E. Aylmer*

A study of the most crucial period in English political history: the struggle between Crown and Parliament during the eighty-six years between the accession to the throne of James I and that of William and Mary. Includes full comparative date chart, maps, and eight pages of photographs.          (#MT512—75¢)

**A Short History of 18th Century England: 1689-1793** *by R. W. Harris*

A survey of the forces in England that brought about the triumph of Parliamentary government, the rise of great statesmen, and a growing vitality in commerce and overseas trade that was to make eighteenth-century England into a great world power. Includes bibliography of suggested readings and eight pages of photographs.          (#MT515—75¢)

**A Short History of 19th Century England: 1793-1868** *by John W. Derry*

A study of England under the impact of the Industrial Revolution, which transformed her from a rural to an urban nation, brought about heated debates on reforms, and posed new questions in areas of politics, philosophy and religion. Includes chronological table of events, comprehensive bibliography and eight pages of photographs.
          (#MT516—75¢)

**A Short History of 20th Century England: 1868-1962** *by T. L. Jarman*

England's most catastrophic years, as she passed from a position of unrivaled strength through two wars that threatened her existence and led to the emergence of Russia and the United States as greater powers. Includes chronological table of events, comprehensive bibliography of suggested reading, and eight pages of photographs.          (#MT517—75¢)

# A Short History
## of
# Sixteenth-Century
# England

by G. W. O. WOODWARD

*A MENTOR BOOK*
PUBLISHED BY THE NEW AMERICAN LIBRARY

Published as a MENTOR BOOK
by arrangement with Blandford Press Ltd.,
who have authorized this softcover edition.

FIRST PRINTING, JULY, 1963

This book is published in England under the title
Reformation and Resurgence, 1485–1603

MENTOR TRADEMARK REG. U.S. PAT. OFF. AND FOREIGN COUNTRIES
REGISTERED TRADEMARK—MARCA REGISTRADA
HECHO EN CHICAGO, U.S.A.

MENTOR BOOKS are published by
The New American Library of World Literature, Inc.
501 Madison Avenue, New York 22, New York

PRINTED IN THE UNITED STATES OF AMERICA

# Contents

# List of Illustrations

*(Plates will be found between pp. 128-129.)*

## Acknowledgements

Photograph number 6 has been reproduced by gracious permission of Her Majesty the Queen.

The remaining photographs have been reproduced by permission of the following:

1, 2, 3, 4, 5 and 13   The Trustees of the British Museum

7, 8, 9, 10, 11 and 12   The Trustees of the National Portrait Gallery

# *Preface*

HAVING FOR many years been obliged to concentrate my attention, both as a student and as a teacher of history, upon the comparatively narrow limits of a single century, it is pleasant, and rewarding, to be given an opportunity to leave for a short while the minutiae of the Tudor period and to view it as a whole, at the same time attempting to assess its contribution to the general course of English history. This is the kind of exercise which helps to keep one's own work in perspective, and is therefore both chastening and encouraging. For the invitation to perform this exercise, and for much encouragement and helpful comment during the performance of it, I am greatly indebted to the general editor, Mr R. W. Harris. I should also like to set on record my further very great indebtedness to my friend and colleague, Dr R. Ashton of the University of Nottingham, without whose unselfish assistance much of this book would have been much harder to write, and whose kindly encouragement has at all times been a great stimulus. I must, however, absolve him of all responsibility for any of the statements made or opinions expressed in the following pages.

*University of Nottingham*
*September 1962*

G. W. O. WOODWARD

# 1

# *An Introductory Survey*

IN 1485 THE FIRST of the royal Tudors gained the Crown of England on the field of battle. In 1603, on the death of his grand-daughter, that same crown passed, in peace and without opposition, into the hands of the ruler of the neighbouring kingdom, England's ancient enemy Scotland. In this, the first and most obvious contrast between the events of those two years a little more than a century apart, can be seen some measure of the changes which had been wrought upon England in the Tudor period; and in our endeavour, during the course of this book, to evaluate the contribution made by this particular period to the whole course of English history, it is with these changes that we shall be primarily concerned. And yet, though change is the essence of history, and though a society which during a long period remains substantially unchanged in its forms and manner of life can scarcely be said to have a history, there remains nevertheless a considerable element of stability and continuity in even the most active periods of change. And so it was with the period when the Tudors governed England. There were many changes. There was also much that remained unchanged.

## The Element of Continuity

English society was still in 1603, as it had been in 1485, predominantly rural. London had grown substantially, it is true, but few of the provincial towns had followed suit, and some had in fact decayed. The predominance of country dwellers over town dwellers remained unchallenged. The village community continued to be the typical social unit, and in many villages the yearly cycle of sowing and reaping ran its accustomed course, untroubled by the activities of enclosers and improving landlords who were, in some districts, so busy. Perhaps the village community in 1603 had rather more contact with the "outside world" of national affairs than in earlier days, for royal officials and Crown commissioners were more plentiful and more active than they had been a hundred years before, and the Tudor government, with its ambitious social and economic policies, naturally needed more frequently to make its will known and its authority felt, even in the remotest parts of the kingdom. But this was a difference of degree rather than of substance, and village life in the England of the sixteenth century experienced, as a general rule, no change comparable with those produced by the impact of agricultural improvements in the eighteenth century, or by the revolution in transport and communications in the nineteenth and twentieth.

English life remained rural. It also remained decidedly aristocratic. The aristocracy itself underwent a change of considerable magnitude and importance, but the aristocratic principle remained firmly embedded in the foundations of society. There were still those who were born to rule and command, and those who were born to obey and serve. Every man knew his place in the ordered ranks of society, and those who succeeded in pushing themselves forward to a place nearer the front, those who, despite humble birth, attained an exalted station, still attracted to themselves the jealousy and disapprobation of those whose equals they aspired to be. There was no democracy. There was little equality. Indeed in 1603 there were probably fewer opportunities than there had been in 1485 for the ambitious man to improve his status in society. That avenue of advancement which the church had provided for men of ability whatever their origins was still open, but the entrance to it was narrower and the prizes attainable far fewer in number. Whatever shift in political power the Tudor period had witnessed had concerned the ruling class alone. Parliament might now speak with a louder voice, but that voice was the voice of the peers and of the gentry. Lesser Englishmen still had no share in the government of their country.

Nor is it only in rural life that we must stress the element of continuity. In the towns, and in the ports, there was also much that did not change. English industry altered its organisation and methods hardly at all. Some new manufactures were introduced, some capitalisation of industry did take place. There were even attempts to set up large workshops something after the manner of a modern factory, but still the bulk of English manufactures was produced by independent operatives like the yeomen weavers who worked at their own looms in their own cottages. English ships were larger, probably more numerous, and certainly better designed, but still built of wood and powered by sail. English roads were still as full of ruts and potholes, and generally impassable for wheeled traffic in wet weather. The packhorse remained the principal form of inland transport in regions beyond the reach of the navigable rivers. English towns remained as crowded and insanitary as ever, and, as timber was still the material most commonly used in urban building, were still as liable to visitation by fire as well as plague.

And so we could go on, pointing not to the contrasts between England in 1485 and in 1603, but to the similarities, for there were so many facets of English life that changed remarkably little between the day of Bosworth and the day of Elizabeth's death. The 118 years of the Tudor period were by no means so revolutionary as some subsequent periods of equal length. A man who had lived in the England of Henry VII, could he have returned to live again in the reign of James I, would have found himself less of a stranger to his country than a man from 1785 dropped suddenly into the England of 1903, so much more dramatic were the developments of the nineteenth century than those of the sixteenth. The rate at which change takes place, not only in England, but in the world at large, has accelerated very considerably in the four centuries which separate us from the England of the Tudors, and it continues to accelerate so rapidly that it requires no great prophetic vision to predict that the England of 2003 will be even more radically different from that of 1885.

## The Element of Contrast

Compared then with the rate at which modern developments are changing the face of England and the lives of Englishmen, the sixteenth century seems a placid, if not a static age. And yet, of course, there were important changes taking place in the Tudor period. Some of them were to be of considerable consequence in their own day. Others were not to be so immediately effective, but are still worthy of our attention because of their great importance to subsequent generations. Some of these changes, notably in the realms of government, religion and commerce, have been for many years regarded as sufficiently significant to mark off the Tudor period from its predecessors as the first to which the epithet "modern" should properly be attached to distinguish it from the "medieval" periods which went before. But most present-day historians are dissatisfied with this conventional division which has been enshrined in so many textbooks and examination syllabuses, and would like to see it abandoned. Viewed from our mid-twentieth century standpoint, the developments in scientific thought in the seventeenth century, or in industrial processes in the eighteenth, or in communications in the nineteenth, seem more clearly to mark off our modern scientific and technological age from the era of horses, handcrafts and hagiology which preceded it, than do the development of governmental efficiency, the outbreak of religious controversy, or even the discovery and exploitation of the New World. So perhaps we should give up thinking of the sixteenth century as the first century of modern history and regard it rather as the last century of the Middle Ages. But this does not mean that the changes which took place in the Tudor period have suddenly lost all significance for us. They remain important, vitally important, to the proper understanding of the processes which created the modern England which we know. All that the changes of the sixteenth century have lost is their primacy of importance when compared with some of the changes which belong to the centuries which follow.

And so let us return to our point of departure, and enlarge a little upon the significance of the contrast which we drew between the manner in which Henry VII and James I in turn attained the English throne.

Henry, we said, fought for his crown at Bosworth. He fought for it again at East Stoke in 1487, and had, for the greater part of his reign, to be constantly on the alert against his rivals' attempts to dethrone him. James, on the other hand, succeeded to his throne in peace, and, except for the momentary menace of the Gunpowder Plot, enjoyed un-challenged possession of his kingdom to the end of his days. The contrast is plain enough, but is it anything more than the difference we should expect to find between the career of a usurper with a very slender claim to the throne and that of a legitimate heir of the blood royal? A little closer exami-nation will, I trust, show that the difference goes deeper than that. There is no need to enlarge upon the well-known weakness of Henry Tudor's dynastic claims.[1] The fact that his father's mother had been the widow of an English king is quite irrelevant. The only link that Henry could claim with the blood royal of England was through his mother, Margaret Beaufort, who was a descendant of John of Gaunt. That is to say (leaving on one side the question of the legitimacy of the Beauforts about which there was room for doubt), Henry's claim depended upon a female link. But once it was admitted that the title to the English throne could descend through female heirs as well as male (and that was one of the big issues of the day), then there was no challenging the superior-ity of the Yorkist title with its link, through Anne Mortimer, to Lionel, Duke of Clarence, the third son of Edward III. Any Lancastrian title, legitimate or otherwise, could only descend from John of Gaunt, the fourth son of Edward III, and was therefore inferior. And so Henry Tudor had no clear title by descent, and had to supply the deficiencies of his claim by force of arms. James I, on the other hand, could claim not only to be the direct heir to the doubtful Lancastrian title of Henry VII, but also to the far firmer Yorkist title of Henry's queen, Elizabeth, eldest daughter of Edward IV. James' great-grandmother had been the elder daughter of that politic Tudor marriage. Henry VIII had been the only son of Henry VII to attain maturity and beget heirs, but none of those heirs had left a child to carry on the royal line, and when the last of them, Elizabeth I, died in 1603, the King of Scotland was clearly next in order of succession and entered into his legitimate inheritance.

And yet it is a mistake which is too commonly made to assume that James' title was indisputable. By our modern

[1] For these, and for what follows, see the genealogical tables Nos. 1 and 2 in Appendix B on pp. 232 and 233.

rules of inheritance it was, but those rules were by no means established beyond question in 1603. Indeed it is one of the little ironies of history that the repeated attempts of Henry VIII to abolish all doubts about the law regulating the succession to the English Crown had only resulted in the creation of further difficulties. By calling Parliament to his aid in a series of Succession Statutes the second Tudor King had hoped to ensure that, despite the complications created by his various marriages and separations, there should be no doubt about the order of succession after his death, and so no chance of a renewal of that dynastic civil strife which had bedevilled the fifteenth century. But the very number of Acts of Succession which eventually proved necessary did a great deal to weaken the principle of inheritance and to establish the rival principle of parliamentary regulation of the succession. The last of Henry's succession statutes, that of 1544, stood unrepealed in 1603. This Act had, it is true, accepted the hereditary principle in so far as it had devolved the Crown in the first place upon Henry's own children and their heirs. But, failing these (an eventuality unlooked for in 1544, but which had come to pass by 1603), the statute departed from strict heredity in empowering the King to make further provision for the succession in his will. This Henry had done, and in doing so he had deliberately passed over the descendants of his elder sister, the Scottish royal house, in favour of the offspring of his younger sister Mary, Duchess of Suffolk. In 1603 this Suffolk line was represented by Edward Seymour, Lord Beauchamp, who had therefore (though there were some doubts about the validity of his parents' marriage) on the basis of King Henry's statute and will, as good a claim to succeed Elizabeth as James had by heredity. Indeed the claims of Beauchamp's mother, Catherine, Countess of Hertford (sister of the unfortunate Lady Jane Grey), had been most actively canvassed in the crisis of 1562 when Elizabeth I had almost died of smallpox, and had not been entirely forgotten since. Thus what is chiefly remarkable about James' succession is that although there were grounds upon which it could quite reasonably have been contested there was no one in England prepared actively to contest it. The proclamation of the King of Scotland passed unchallenged and James made his leisurely way south to his new capital amidst the encouraging enthusiasm of his new subjects. There was no party or faction in the state sufficiently dissatisfied, or sufficiently ambitious, to put up its own candidate. The days of kingmakers and pretenders, of aristocratic faction and dynastic strife, were over. The troublesome times of the fifteenth century would not recur. The fears of Henry VIII, that if he died without a son to succeed him there would be a renewal of the anarchy which his father had so recently ended, now seemed to have been so much anxiety expressed in vain. The house of Tudor had petered out in the third generation but there was no succession dispute. For this the chief credit must go to the Tudors themselves for their effective disciplining of the country, and for their exaltation of the power and prestige of the monarchy and the council which governed in its name. The supreme office of government, the kingship, was no longer a prize to be contended for by the great noble houses. It was already a semi-divine trust to be exercised only by those called to it by the God-guided accidents of birth and death. So high had the Tudors raised the Crown that it was now beyond the reach of even the most exalted of subjects. The peaceful accession of James I is in this way evidence of the great change in the status and power of the monarchy which the Tudors had brought about.

## The Diplomatic Revolution

The unopposed accession of James I was also, in another way, a testimony to the profound alteration in Anglo-Scottish relations which the Tudor period had witnessed. For centuries before and for many years after the accession of Henry VII, England and Scotland had been enemies. The sharing of a common land frontier with the almost limitless opportunities for border clashes that this entailed, was in itself almost a guarantee that this should have been so. But there were of course other reasons too for this long persistent hostility; the claims to overlordship over Scotland which English kings had made from time to time since the reign of Edward I; the periodic attempts, with varying degrees of lack of success, to enforce these claims; the stubborn Scottish defence of a highly prized independence; the reliance of the Scots upon the assistance of England's other ancient enemy, France.

This anti-English Franco-Scottish alliance was still very much alive in the earlier part of the sixteenth century. The Scots were as little loved in England as the English were in Scotland, and the royal line of Scotland, the house of Stuart, was certainly no exception to this rule. If England ever found herself obliged to accept a king from abroad, the royal line least likely to be acceptable would be that of Scotland. This much was made abundantly clear in an Act of Parliament of the reign of Henry VIII which referred to the then King of Scotland (James V) as one

> to whom this realm hath nor ever had any affection; but would resist his attempt to the Crown of this realm to the uttermost of their powers.[2]

This anti-Scottish prejudice was kept alive by the wars of Henry VIII's reign, and in all probability was taken into consideration by that monarch when, in his will, he attempted to cut the Scottish line out of the succession to the throne of England. And yet in 1603, England and Scotland, the ancient enemies, had been living for many years at peace, and the people of England, peacefully, and even joyfully, accepted as their own the Scottish king. How this radical change of sentiment had been brought about we shall discuss more fully in a later chapter. For the present we must just take note of it as one of the significant developments of the sixteenth century, and one of which the unchallenged and peaceful accession of James I should be a constant reminder.

But is the peaceful accession of the Scottish king to be explained solely in terms of the factors we have so far mentioned; the better internal discipline of England, the exaltation of the monarchy, and the improvement in Anglo-Scottish relations? It must also be borne in mind that when Elizabeth I died England was at war, and at war with that country which was by general repute the most powerful in Europe at that time, Spain. In the external crisis of the war could England have afforded the luxury of a succession dispute which might have opened the door to foreign intervention? Might it not be that fear of giving advantage to the common enemy would deter from action men who in time

[2] 28 Henry VIII cap. 24.

of peace might well have sought to advance their own fortunes along with those of a suitable candidate for the throne? This sort of question is incapable of answer, but in asking it we must not allow ourselves to exaggerate the extent of the danger from Spain. In the Spanish war the year of supreme crisis had come in 1601 with the landing of Spanish forces at Kinsale in the south of Ireland. Had Ireland then fallen under the control of the Spaniards and their allies the Irish rebels, the turn of England would have come next, with the chances of Spanish success far higher than they had been in the Armada year of 1588. But the Battle of Kinsale had been fought and won, and the Spaniards had been compelled to withdraw. The English forces under Mountjoy* had restored the Queen's authority over wide areas of the Irish kingdom, and in 1603 the rebellion was all but over. Indeed, only a few days after the death of Elizabeth, the Irish arch-rebel Tyrone* laid down his sword. Meanwhile, in the sea war with Spain, England continued to hold her own, and was in no immediate danger from her adversary. Although Philip II of Spain (who claimed descent from John of Gaunt) had had his own candidate for the English throne in the person of his daughter Isabella, his son Philip III took no active steps to support her claim, and there was, at Elizabeth's death, little for England to fear from Spain. In these circumstances it is hardly likely that fear of Spanish intervention could have deterred potential English rivals from challenging the claims of the King of Scotland.

And yet if we are to discount the Spanish war as a factor in securing the Stuart succession, we must still take note of it for what it was in itself, a sign that England had broken away from her traditional alliances and embarked upon a new period in her diplomatic history. The improvement in Anglo-Scottish relations which we have already noticed was only part of a more extensive international realignment which is sometimes called the "diplomatic revolution" of the sixteenth century. The detailed examination of this change in alliances must be kept for a later chapter. Only the bare outline need be set down here. The commercial and diplomatic

* Brief biographical notes upon persons marked thus in the text will be found in Appendix A on pp. 200–231.

links between England and the Netherlands' provinces had, even in the sixteenth century, a very respectable history. The alliance, in the fifteenth century, between the Burgundian dukes who then ruled the Low Countries and the Lancastrian kings of England, had suffered interruption from time to time but, being based very firmly upon an extensive commercial traffic very profitable to both parties, it had always been revived and handed down, first to Yorkist, then to Tudor kings. But as the descendants of the Burgundian dukes had come to inherit ever wider dominions,[3] so the Anglo-Burgundian alliance had become first an alliance with the Imperial house of Habsburg, and then, through them, with Spain as well. The counterpart to this Anglo-Habsburg alliance was English enmity with France, the chief rival of the Habsburgs, and towards Scotland, the ally of France. This was the normal diplomatic alignment in the earlier Tudor period. There were departures from it from time to time, as we shall see, but until the reign of Elizabeth I these departures were never more than temporary and of little significance. The last occasion upon which the Anglo-Habsburg alliance went into action against the French was in the war of 1557–9 when Calais was lost.

By the end of Elizabeth's reign England had quite changed sides, and had become the ally of France, the friend of Scotland and the enemy of Spain. This change was not one of allies alone. The ends which the alliances were designed to serve had also changed. The wars of England against France and Scotland in the earlier Tudor period had been wars of dynastic ambition and royal rivalry, wars between neighbours arising easily out of border incidents. The Spanish war of Elizabeth's reign was the first of a different kind of contest, a war into which commercial and colonial competition entered, a war between rival naval powers for the control of the wealth of distant lands. The Anglo-Spanish war of 1588–1604 was closer in spirit and in nature to the Anglo-Dutch wars of the seventeenth century or to the later Anglo-French wars of the eighteenth century than to those earlier Anglo-French wars of the fifteenth and sixteenth centuries.

[3] See the genealogical table No. 4 in Appendix B on p. 235.

War was no longer the sport of kings. It had become the business of nations.

## The Enlargement of Physical and Mental Horizons

This Anglo-Spanish rivalry at sea was both a symptom and a consequence of another significant development in English activity in the Tudor period; the increasing interest displayed in overseas exploration, in trade in distant waters, and even in the colonisation of far-away lands. England in the sixteenth century lifted her eyes to wider horizons. At the beginning of our period English overseas commerce was almost exclusively concerned with the North Sea and the English Channel. Though English merchants were also to be found in the Baltic and the Mediterranean they were not very influential in those waters. By 1603, on the other hand, English ships were trading regularly not only with the Baltic and eastern Mediterranean ports, but with the White Sea coast of Russia and the Atlantic coast of Africa, and the first steps had been taken towards opening up to English ships that route to India round the Cape of Good Hope which the Portuguese had pioneered over a century before. On the other side of the world, the American coasts and Caribbean islands were now well known to many English captains, and the way was being prepared for the planting of English settlements in those regions. But not only had English trade increased its range, it had also increased significantly in volume, and in the proportion of it which was carried in English ships. England was well on the way to becoming a formidable maritime power.

All this rapid expansion of English overseas activity had been assisted by, and in turn had stimulated, a great expansion in the Englishman's knowledge of the world beyond the shores of his own little island. With new lands to be discovered, new ocean passages to be explored, and new features to be added every year to the map of the world, it was an exciting age to live in, and one which encouraged the exploration not only of distant waters and unknown lands, but also of every aspect of the physical universe. The writings of the ancient Greeks no longer provided entirely acceptable answers to all the questions men were prompted to ask. The authority of the ancients was therefore yielding place to that of contemporary scholars and scientists who were piecing together the new discoveries that they and others had made, and were constructing new systems to replace those that were now found to be wanting. Though the greatest advances were made in those branches of knowledge which were of most immediate interest to the voyagers and explorers (e.g. geography, astronomy, navigation and magnetism), human curiosity was turning in other directions too, and the way was being prepared for the great intellectual advances of the following century. In this beginning of an expansion in the frontiers of knowledge we can see yet another way in which a great change had come over England in the sixteenth century.

## The Tudor Peace

But the greatest change of all upon which so much else depended was the change which we have already mentioned in connection with the unchallenged accession of James I, the change from an England rent by civil strife in which the reputation and the authority of the Crown were both of very little account, into one governed by a strong and respected monarchy whose servants and agents reached out to every corner of the kingdom and kept it in peace and in subjection to the law. Internal peace, security of life and property, good order, and the rule of law, these, which were commonplace commodities in the England of 1603, had been rare luxuries in 1485. That this gift of internal discipline which the Tudors gave to England was no legal abstraction but a practical reality with tangible consequences may be readily seen by looking at the changing fashions in the domestic architecture of the dominant class, the gentry. As late as the reign of Henry VIII the needs of defence could still play a big part in the design and construction of a manor house. Though spacious windows might be permitted to overlook the internal courtyard, the outer walls would be lofty, battlemented and forbidding, pierced only by narrow windows little more than loopholes, the gateway would be well defended, and the whole external appearance would be more suggestive of a fortress than of a residence. But in the reign of Elizabeth I no gentleman would have dreamed of building in this manner, or thought it either desirable or necessary. Some features of the old defensive exterior, such as the battlements, might be retained, but only as decoration and often in a very fanciful and quite impracticable form. The differences between an Elizabethan mansion and its fortified predecessor are far more striking than any minor similarities such as these. The protective curtain wall, for instance, has disappeared. Large windows, well glazed, dominate each elevation, and even the internal court, that last remnant of the primitive defensive enclosures of our prehistoric ancestors, has vanished from the plan of all but the largest houses. The Elizabethan squire, though he still quarrelled with his neighbours and engaged occasionally in violent frays, no longer built his house to withstand a siege, and was, on the whole, more dedicated to the arts of peace than ever his great-grandfather had been. The Englishman's home no longer had to look like a castle.

## The Rural Scene

This defortification of the manor house was only one of the great changes in the appearance of the English country-side that an Englishman returning home late in Elizabeth's reign after a very long sojourn abroad would have noticed. Had such a traveller gone overseas before 1536, he would also have observed, upon his return, that the monasteries and nunneries, which had been so familiar a part of the medieval landscape, were no more. Some would have disappeared entirely, the stones pulled from their walls to use in other buildings. Some would still be faintly recognisable in their new guise, converted into palatial residences for the local squires. Some would stand roofless and desolate, at the beginning of that long road of neglect and decay which has made them the tumbled ruins that they are today. Our returning traveller would also have noticed how the natural forests which had once covered so much of the island, but had been steadily in retreat for many centuries, had now almost disappeared in many parts of the country. England which had once been a sea of woodland dotted with islands of cultivation and habitation, had now become an almost continuous tract of farmland studded here and there with still shrinking areas of timber. The process of deforestation had been greatly accelerated in the sixteenth century as the expanding population had brought more and more land under cultivation, and as the demands of industry and shipbuilding had made inroads upon the remaining woodland. Indeed so far had this process gone that the nobles and gentlemen who delighted in hunting, as most of them still did, could no longer count upon finding sufficient wild game in its natural habitat, and had taken to fencing in and stocking with deer wide acres of parkland round their country mansions.

Nor was this making of parks the only type of enclosure that had taken place. In some parts of the country, in particular in the Midlands, the whole pattern of village agriculture had undergone a radical alteration with the breaking up of the ancient open fields and the creation instead of separate and unified holdings. Hedges and ditches were beginning to be a familiar sight where mearing stones, baulks and headlands had formerly sufficed. All this was, of course, a long-term process, one that had been in train long before the Tudors had ascended the English throne, and one which was to continue for many years after the death of Elizabeth, and yet the sixteenth century was a critical one in the process. It was in this century that the new pattern of agriculture, with its emphasis upon the separate enterprise of the individual farmer, acquired respectability and came to be favourably contrasted with the older methods of intermixed holdings and common labour. It was in the sixteenth century, too, that the enclosed village ceased to be the exception and became an accepted part of the English landscape.

## The Towns and Churches

All these changes in the outward appearance of the countryside would have been readily observable by our imaginary returning traveller. He would not have been struck so immediately by changes in the towns unless he had been sufficiently familiar with early Tudor London to have appreciated how extensively it had grown during his absence. He might also, here and there in the provinces, have found the town walls crumbling through neglect and the houses beginning to spread more boldly outside the ancient boundaries. But on the whole, he would have found the external appearance of the towns little changed. There would still be the same crowded rows of timber-framed buildings leaning towards each other across the narrow streets. There would still be the same multiplicity of church spires rising above the house-tops. But inside these churches, as inside the village churches too, he would have found great differences. He would at once have missed the former wealth of decoration and ornament. The ancient frescoes would now be whitewashed over, the images and holy pictures gone, all altars but the principal one taken away and even that replaced by a readily movable communion table. Dominating all, and exemplifying the character of the changes, he would have found the royal arms set up in the rood loft where formerly had stood the image of the crucified Christ. And if our traveller had entered a church at service time he could not have failed to notice the very different nature of the form of worship now observed. No rich vestments clothed the minister, but only a plain white surplice, and even that he might remove before entering the pulpit to preach. Even the language of the prayers would at first have struck his ears as strange until he realised that it was English instead of the once universal Latin he had been expecting to hear.

On leaving the church and observing more carefully the people as they went about their daily business, our traveller would soon have become aware that the change which had come over the religion of Englishmen had not been confined to the churches and their interiors. He would have found, for instance, that most people went less frequently to church. Attendance every Sunday was still the common practice, indeed it was required by law, but that was now the limit of most people's church-going. There were few who kept up the earlier practice of dropping into church for a few minutes' devotion at the beginning or end of a working day. And even the Sunday attendance laws were being defied by a considerable number of people, some because they deplored the departure from the old ways, others because they held that the changes that had been made had not been sweeping enough. Criticism of the church was more common and more outspoken than it had been. The church in England was no longer the church of the nation, although a still very extensive and predominant majority adhered to it.

Finally, our returning exile would not need to be particularly observant to have noticed yet another change in the position of the church in English society. The most obvious symptom of it would have been the considerably reduced number of persons clothed in clerical garb to be seen in the streets of the towns and on the roads of the countryside. But it was not only in their numbers that the English clergy had, during the course of the sixteenth century, suffered a drastic reduction, but also in their power and status in society. They no longer held the key positions in government. They no longer possessed a virtual monopoly of education. The greater among them no longer controlled the vast riches their predecessors had enjoyed. Instead, the laity had come into their own. It was the laymen who now filled the chief governmental offices. It was laymen who predominated in the councils of the monarch. It was laymen who took the limelight on the local as well as the national stage, and even exercised, as royal commissioners, ecclesiastical authority of a kind that had always formerly been the preserve of bishops and their delegates. Moreover, with their increasing power the laity had acquired also an increased confidence in their own capabilities, and a correspondingly diminished respect and reverence for the clergy.

This secularisation of society and emancipation of the laity exerted so important an influence in so many ways that if we are to have a proper understanding of the nature and significance of the political, religious, social, economic and other changes which we have sketched in such brief outline in this chapter we must first attempt to understand the nature and importance of this key development. It is to this task that the next chapter will be addressed.

Emma
Nichols

1 own bell ruled 17
1U 41 Runble
H. S

MOCK POLITICAL CONVENTION

## 2

# The Emancipation of the Laity

THERE CAN BE little question but that in the Tudor period the English clergy lost a large measure of the power and influence which they had been wont to exercise in former centuries. A simple comparison between the place they occupied in society before the reformation and that which they still retained in the closing decades of the reign of Elizabeth should be sufficient to make this point clear.

### Fewer Clergy

Take first the question of numbers. In this respect there was little change as far as the higher clergy and the parochial incumbents were concerned. The number of English and Welsh bishoprics in 1485 was 21. As a result of the creation by Henry VIII of six new sees (Peterborough, Oxford, Gloucester, Bristol, Chester and Westminster), the endowments of which were found out of the spoils of the monasteries, the number was for a short time raised to 27, only to be reduced to 26 in the following reign by the suppression of Westminster, and at 26 it remained for the rest of the period. The number of deaneries, and of cathedral prebends, was also increased in the same proportion, but this was not a very remarkable expansion in number, and could, in any case, do little to compensate for the much greater loss in numbers suffered by the clerical estate as a result of the suppression of the monastic orders. The 8,000 to 10,000 monks and canons who were turned out of their cloisters by Henry VIII did not, it must be remembered, cease to be clergy, nor were their services entirely lost to the church, for a considerable proportion of them found their way into parochial livings. But the availability of this large body of

27

"temporarily unemployed" clergy did affect very seriously the chances of promotion for a new recruit to the priesthood, and a marked falling off in the number of entrants to the ministry can be detected in the record of ordinations in the bishops' registers in the years immediately following the dissolution of the monasteries. Thus, though somewhat indirectly, and only progressively, the suppression of the monastic orders did have its effect in reducing by a very considerable figure the total number of clergy in the country.

The parochial clergy, however, felt the consequences of change the least of all. Whatever the religious viewpoint of the government in power it was necessary to provide for the spiritual welfare of the parishes, and the number of livings available did not alter appreciably either way at any time during our period. And yet the number of auxiliary clergy available in the parishes was very seriously reduced by the dissolution of the chantries in 1547. Though the chief function of the chantry priest had been to keep up a regular round of masses for the health of the soul of the pious founder of the chantry, he had also performed a variety of other tasks, as assistant to the parish priest, as local schoolmaster, or as chaplain-secretary to the guild that contributed to his maintenance. The seizure by the government of the endowments of the chantries had, in some cases, therefore, the indirect consequence of depriving the vicar of his curate, or the children of their teacher. In any case it removed from the active list a further very considerable body of clergy who went to swell the pool of unemployed priests with the consequences which we have already noticed in connection with the monastic clergy. Certainly by the time that all the ex-monks and ex-chantry priests had been absorbed back into the church or been claimed by death, the total number of clergy of priestly rank in England must have been reduced by more than half.

## The Minor Orders and "Benefit of Clergy"

The bishops, cathedral and parish clergy, monks and chantry priests, with whom we have so far dealt, do not by any means complete the list of those who in the earlier years of the sixteenth century were entitled to the name and privileges of clergy. The close and very ancient association of the church with education made it natural that many men engaged in occupations which we should nowadays regard as secular professions chose then to offer themselves for admission to one of the lesser orders in the church. The special legal standing, or "benefit of clergy", which even those in these minor orders enjoyed, added a further incentive for the taking of this step, for the man entitled to this "benefit" was exempt from punishment by the secular courts. However serious the offence with which he was charged, he could only be sentenced in the church courts whose powers of punishment did not extend to the infliction of the penalties of death or mutilation. And so, as a species of insurance policy, many men whose profession we should describe as that of teacher, civil servant, secretary or even land agent, were, before the reign of Henry VIII, also clergy, though they might be content always to remain in one of the lesser orders and not wish to rise to the priesthood. The words "clerk" and "clergy" have the same root and were, in early Tudor times, interchangeable, because the great majority of men who, by acquiring the skills of reading and writing, had qualified themselves for "clerical" occupations, had also taken orders and were therefore "clergy".

Of course this clerical legal privilege was open to abuse, and it is quite clear that many an able scoundrel saved himself from the scaffold by successfully "proving his clergy". There was little objection to the enjoyment of this special status by men whose vocation was clearly priestly, for the priesthood set men apart from their fellows, and it was thought undesirable that they should at any time be subjected to sentence by earthly judges who did not enjoy a similar or superior status. But there was common complaint among the laity at the granting of this privilege to men in minor orders who had no priestly vocation and whose way of life was hardly to be distinguished from that of laymen. And so there was considerable pressure from the laity for the restriction of this privilege, and during the course of the sixteenth century it was progressively curtailed. The early parliaments of the reign of Henry VIII gave expression to lay opinion on this subject, and that of 1512 actually passed an Act (4 Henry VIII cap. 2) restricting the operation of this privilege in certain cases of murder and robbery. But

the Act was temporary in duration, and in the fury of
the controversy aroused by the death of Richard Hunne
in December 1514, it was not found possible to renew it.

## The Case of Richard Hunne

Hunne, a London merchant, allegedly an associate of men
of heretical opinions, and a man of litigious temper who
would not leave his adversary alone while he had a shred of a
case against him, after a protracted legal argument with his
rector, was imprisoned on a charge of heresy and found
dead in suspicious circumstances in the Bishop of London's
prison. His jailers said it was suicide, but the coroner's in-
quest jury preferred to lay an accusation of murder against
the Bishop's chancellor and those of his subordinates who
had had charge of Hunne. The Bishop, Richard Fitzjames,
was anxious to save his chancellor from being brought to
trial. He therefore appointed to preach, at the opening of
convocation in January 1515, Richard Kidderminster, Abbot
of Winchcombe, who had been one of the English delegates
to the Lateran council of the previous year. At this council
the Pope, Leo X, had reminded the clergy throughout Europe
of the extent of their legal immunities, and had issued a decree
claiming that benefit of clergy exempted the clerk in holy
orders not only from punishment by the secular courts, but
even from trial before them. The current practice of the
English courts, which was to try clerical offenders and only
to permit them to plead their clergy after conviction, was
clearly incompatible with the law of the church as declared
by the Pope. Abbot Kidderminster was careful, in his
sermon, to draw the attention of his clerical audience to this
conflict of authority, and argued that the statute of 1512,
and the English practice of trying clergy in the secular
courts, were both contrary to the law of God and the
liberties of the church. His sweeping claim for clerical privilege created quite a stir, and for a time distracted public attention from the particular case of the Bishop's chancellor. Dr.
Horsey, by raising an important point of principle. When
there was a conflict like this between the long-established
practice of the king's courts and the terms of a papal decree,
which was to be observed in England? This very question
was long and hotly debated before the King, his council

and the judges, and eventually, despite the urgent pleas of the clergy that the matter should be submitted to the Pope's judgment, decided in favour of the practice of the secular courts. Then Dr. Horsey, after this long delay, was brought to trial. But Henry VIII was still sufficiently the loyal son of the church not to press his clergy too far. Once Horsey had accepted the jurisdiction of the court of King's Bench the case against him was dropped, and his plea of "not guilty" was accepted. The laity had scored an important point in bringing Horsey to trial, but they lost the game when the Act of 1512 was not renewed in Parliament.

In the rather different circumstances of 1532, when the King had come to have a little less respect for the authority of the Pope, Parliament was to succeed once again in imposing restrictions upon the operation of benefit of clergy. This time all those in minor orders who committed murder or certain types of robberies were to lose their privileges (23 Henry VIII cap. 1). In 1536, when the authority of the Pope was no longer recognised in England, Parliament was able to extend the terms of this Act so as to include offenders in major orders as well (28 Henry VIII cap. 1). But the real blow to the clerical estate and its legal privileges was not dealt out by any of these statutes, but by the issue of the new English Ordinal in 1550. Because its new forms provided only for the ordination of priests and deacons and for the consecration of bishops, their acceptance by the English church meant the end of the minor orders. In future only those with a clear vocation to the priesthood would be admitted to orders and enjoy what was left of the benefit of clergy. Already, before the issue of the ordinal, the progressive curtailment of the legal privileges of the minor orders had contracted recruitment to them. Now there could be no more admissions to these lesser degrees, and a clear distinction was henceforth made between those called to the ministry, or "clerkship in holy orders", and those whose clerkship was of a purely secular kind. The number of Englishmen who could call themselves clergy was thus further, and quite drastically, reduced.

## The Secularisation of Government

It is not only the great reduction in the numbers of the

clergy that we must notice in the Tudor period. Though this in itself would result in a greater secularisation of society, what is more significant is the corresponding loss of power and authority by the reduced body of the clergy. Of course the two processes went hand in hand. The fact that laymen began to appear in greater numbers in the civil service may have meant no more than that, with the curtailment of the privileges attaching to minor orders, the clerks in the government service no longer considered it worth their while to seek ordination. But at the highest level of government the change was more significant than that, and is seen at its clearest in the succession to the office of Lord Chancellor. This, the most important office of state until Thomas Cromwell* made of the Secretaryship something even greater, had for many decades been the preserve of the episcopate. All Henry VII's chancellors, Rotherham, Alcock, Morton and Warham, were bishops, but, in the following reign, Wolsey,* who replaced Warham in 1515, was the last, and in some ways the greatest, of this continuous succession of episcopal chancellors which can be traced back, with only two brief interruptions, to the early years of the fifteenth century. Archbishop of York, Lord Chancellor and the King's right hand man, Thomas Wolsey was the medieval ecclesiastical statesman *par excellence*. For a decade and a half he dominated both church and state, and was so continuously occupied with the business of the nation that the functions of his episcopate had to be discharged by deputy. In this latter respect, however, he was no exception. It was expected of a bishop in Wolsey's day that he should be employed in the service of the state, either at home, or on embassy abroad. The close connection which existed between the royal service and the higher ranks of the clergy was maintained in two ways. Sometimes men who had shown their ability in rising through the ranks of the church were selected by the King for his service, but more frequently it worked the other way round, and men who had shown their worth in the service of the state were rewarded by the King with promotion to a bishopric or archdeaconry. Either way the result was the same, and the system produced a secular-minded bench of absentee bishops who had little time to spare for their dioceses, save when they fell into disgrace at Court, as did Stephen

Gardiner* for a short time in 1532, and Thomas Wolsey in 1529.

After the dismissal of Wolsey from the chancellorship, Henry VIII made a significant departure from custom by appointing a layman to succeed him. Admittedly the man selected, Sir Thomas More,* was exceptional in his generation. A scholar and writer, a controversialist of international repute, and already a tried servant of the King, it comes as something of a surprise to realise that almost alone among his great contemporaries, Erasmus, Colet, Fisher, Tyndale,* Tunstall, Luther, Melancthon and Zwingli, More was not in orders. And yet the fact that he was not was symptomatic of the newer way of regarding the priesthood, not as a status to which every man of learning should naturally aspire, but as a calling to be followed only by those charged directly with the care of souls. More's promotion to the chancellorship was a sign that the hold of the clergy upon the higher offices of state was being broken. More's successors in office in the reigns of Henry VIII and Elizabeth I were all laymen. Only at the end of the reign of Edward VI, and in that of Mary, was there a temporary return to clerical chancellors in the persons of Goodrich, Gardiner and Heath (1552–8). From the accession of Elizabeth I to the present day, with the single exception of Bishop Williams in the reign of James I, the Lord Chancellor has always been a layman.

In the same way, the office of Keeper of the Privy Seal passed into lay hands in 1530 when Cuthbert Tunstall, then Bishop of London, and soon to be Bishop of Durham, surrendered it to Anne Boleyn's father, at that time Earl of Wiltshire. Wiltshire was not quite the first lay Lord Keeper, for Lord Marny had held the office for a few months in 1523, but Tunstall was certainly the last clerical one. In similar fashion the office of King's Chief Secretary passed from clerical to lay hands when Thomas Cromwell took over from Stephen Gardiner in 1533.

As Thomas Wolsey was the type, and almost the last example, of the great clerical administrator, so Thomas Cromwell who so shortly succeeded him in the chief confidence of the King, was the pattern, and among the first examples, of the great lay administrator. The power which he came to exercise when holding the offices of King's Chief Secretary and Lord Privy Seal was every bit as great as that which Wolsey had exercised as Lord Chancellor, for it was the closeness of a man to the confidence of the King rather than the tenure of any particular office which gave him power. And the power which Wolsey had enjoyed over the church as papal Legate was soon to be matched by that of Cromwell as Vicar-general for the King in his newly proclaimed capacity as Supreme Head of the English church. Here is the measure of the rise of the laity when not only the chief authority in the state, but even that in the church was given into their hands.

The position which Cromwell enjoyed in the 1530s was exceptional, and he had no successor as royal Vicar-general. Instead of continuing with this revolutionary expedient of giving supreme ecclesiastical power to a layman, Henry VIII, and Edward VI and Elizabeth I after him, tried to keep both clergy and laity each to their proper sphere, and to rule the church through the one and the state through the other. This was particularly true of Elizabeth who, while keeping the clergy out of state offices, tried to ensure that the bishops and clergy had undisputed authority in all church matters. Yet even she, when she appointed delegates to exercise the ecclesiastical powers with which she was vested, did from time to time join laymen with clergy in her commissions.

## The Statute of Praemunire

In their struggle to free themselves from clerical domination the English laity had in their hands a very potent weapon of which they made, on several occasions, most effective use. This was the Statute of Praemunire, or, more correctly, the series of statutes of provisors and praemunire which culminated in the Act of the sixteenth year of Richard II, commonly known as "the great Statute of Praemunire". To understand the nature and purpose of these acts it must be remembered that, down to the time of Queen Victoria, the Canon Law of the church, and the church courts which enforced it, were not merely concerned with the lives and behaviour of the clergy, but dealt also with many matters which touched the laity too. For example, until 1857 all disputes about the validity or invalidity of marriages, and all arguments over the administration of wills, could only be settled by the church courts according to the laws of the church. In the Tudor period, and before, the jurisdiction of the church courts was very extensive and they concerned themselves actively with such matters as heresy, blasphemy, defamation and the payment of tithe, as well as with marriages and wills. At the same time, as we have seen, they had jurisdiction over all clergy whatever their offence. There were also, of course, the king's courts, which existed to administer the Common Law of England, and to enforce obedience to the statutes enacted in Parliament. Naturally, with two sets of courts enforcing two distinct systems of law which were not always in agreement, there were plenty of opportunities for dispute, generally over the question which of the two types of court had jurisdiction in any particular case. The preamble to Henry VIII's Statute in Restraint of Appeals (24 Henry VIII cap. 12) endeavoured to draw a general line of distinction between the two jurisdictions when it declared that the church courts should act when "any cause of the law divine happened to come in question" whereas the jurisdiction of the temporal courts should be invoked:

> for the trial of property of lands and goods and for the conservation of the people of this realm in unity and peace

but these definitions were couched in terms too general to meet every case.

It is at this point that the Statute of Praemunire comes into the picture. Though originally designed as a specific remedy for a specific grievance which the English king and his higher clergy believed they were suffering at the hands of the contemporary pope, the Act of 1393 had come, by the reign of Henry VIII, to be regarded as much more general in application, and was held to empower the king's courts to take action against and to inflict severe punishment upon any person who acted in any way that tended to deprive the king or his courts of any part of their rightful jurisdiction. Now, as the king's courts were the interpreters of statute, including this very Statute of Praemunire, it was left to them to decide just what was the extent of their own rightful jurisdiction and what kind of act could be considered an attempt to deprive them of any portion of it. This meant that in effect the king's courts claimed that the Statute of Praemunire gave them the power to define the limits of the jurisdiction of their rivals the ecclesiastical courts. Pressed to its fullest extent this could mean that the church courts in England exercised their jurisdiction only by permission of the king and his temporal judges.

Not all the clergy were prepared to accept without protest the inferior position which was prescribed for them by this reading of the Statute of Praemunire. The first answer of convocation to the criticism of them known as "the Supplication against the Ordinaries" which was passed to them from Parliament in 1532, made a determined effort to defend their claim to a truly independent power to make law and to sit in judgment without being beholden to the temporal power, or even to the king, and Stephen Gardiner wrote to Henry VIII:

> if it be God's authority to us allotted, though we cannot use it condignly, yet we cannot give it away.[1]

But in the end the clergy submitted, and accepted in principle that the existing corpus of Canon Law would have to undergo revision to purge it of any matter which might conflict with the rights of the king and the jurisdiction of his courts, and that for the future the king must enjoy the power, if necessary, to veto acts of convocation.

It is little wonder that the clergy submitted, for hanging over them all the time was the very real threat of praemunire, and the penalities of life imprisonment and forfeiture of all their possessions which the Act prescribed. In 1515 it had been the threat of praemunire proceedings which had brought the clergy literally to their knees, and put a stop to the argument about the trial of Dr Horsey. In 1529 it had been the threat of praemunire which had brought Wolsey down, though it had been with the king's permission and connivance that he had obtained and exer-

[1] Muller, *The Letters of Stephen Gardiner* (Cambridge University Press), p. 49.

cised that legatine authority which was later held against him. In 1531 the even more sweeping allegation had been made and sustained that all ecclesiastical judges, from the highest to the lowest, had infringed the Statute of Praemunire countless times in the exercise of what they had thought to be their normal and perfectly legitimate jurisdiction. There seemed then to be no limit to the reach of praemunire. In vain the clergy asked for some closer definition of the nature of their offence so that they might avoid it for the future, but no satisfaction was given them. The answer of the laity was that given by Lord Chancellor Audley (Thomas More's immediate successor) to Bishop Gardiner:

> we will provide . . . that the praemunire shall ever hang over your heads . . .[2]

The threat was enough. It was not found necessary to use the Act again after 1532. The clergy for the future tacitly recognised that the temporal power had the upper hand, and were content to exercise such of their former jurisdiction as the King and his courts did not wish to claim for their own.

## The Layman and Education

We have seen, thus far, how the English clergy, during the course of the sixteenth century, declined in numbers and in authority, and found themselves increasingly subjected to the over-riding control of the temporal power. And, of course, what the clergy lost, the laity gained. But the laity could never have taken over the seats of authority from the clergy, or asserted their supremacy in the state had they not at the same time been making an effective assault upon the former clerical monopoly of education. Of course the educated layman was no new phenomenon in the Tudor period. Examples of his kind, though rare, can be drawn from nearly every century, and the study and practice of the Common Law had for long been as much the monopoly of the layman as that of the Canon Law had been the property of the clerical estate. What was, however, a new development in the sixteenth

---

[2] Muller, *The Letters of Stephen Gardiner*, p. 392.

century was the increasing respect for and interest in education displayed by the general body of the laity, and in particular by the gentry. In earlier years, and even in the earlier part of the sixteenth century itself, the politically and socially dominant class of the country landowners had tended to despise book learning, and even the elementary skills of reading and writing, as fit for clerks alone and not for those of gentle birth. The pursuits proper to a gentleman, so it was believed, were those associated with war and the chase. Skill on horseback, proficiency in arms, hardihood, courage and endurance, these were the arts and the qualities which the gentleman should set himself to acquire if he wanted to attract the admiration of his fellows. If the management of his estates required a knowledge of figures, or the protection of his property a knowledge of the law, his chaplain, whom he kept for such purposes as well as for the health of his soul, could deal with such matters which were not worthy of his master's personal attention.

But already in the fifteenth century the first breaches were being made in the walls of this gentle complacency. Although the original impetus for the founding of endowed schools came mainly from the clergy, and though the intention of the earlier founders was to provide educational opportunities for the sons of the humbler ranks of society rather than the offspring of the gentry, and although the aim of most of the earlier schools was to prepare boys for admission to the universities where they would almost inevitably take orders, those who in the end were to profit most from the new foundations were the gentry themselves. The example of the Court was important here. The Tudors were all great believers in education and saw to it that their own children were well provided with instruction in languages and letters. Henry VIII, though he excelled in all the manly accomplishments of the age, was also proficient in Latin, French and Italian, fancied himself, and not without cause, as a theologian, was well versed in mathematics, and was a competent musician both as performer and composer. He saw to it that his three children followed in his footsteps, and secured for them the best tutors available. The example of the Court was catching. The king was the fount of all honours and preferments. Those who wished to make their way into the favour of a cultured king could not now afford to play the bluff and hearty knight and seem to despise that learning upon which their monarch prided himself. The sons of the gentry began to go to school. The gentry took to rivalling the clergy in the matter of founding new schools. The poor scholars for whom the earlier foundations had in so many cases provided, found themselves being shouldered out of their places by the sons of the squires. The monastic-like routine of Oxford and Cambridge colleges, with its early rising and long hours of study, began to break down under the impact of a new generation of aristocratic students who took unkindly to such a discipline, but were anxious to acquire the reputation which a few years' residence conferred, even if they were not in many cases the prelude to the taking of a degree.

The fruit of this revolution in the attitude of the aristocracy towards learning can be seen in the brilliant Court of Elizabeth I. Poetry, music, painting, drama, each of the arts now had its patrons and devotees among the circle of Elizabeth's courtiers, and some not only their devotees, but practitioners. Sir Philip Sidney,* the gentle poet and accomplished sonneteer who perished heroically on the field of Zutphen, was outstanding, but not exceptional, in his age. The ideal combination of man of letters with man of action which he exemplified was the ambition of many of his contemporaries who sought to wield the pen as ably as the sword. The Court of Elizabeth had no place for the man who had no place in his life for books.

Nor was this revolution in attitude confined to the immediate circle of the Court. It spread its influence outward from that centre until in some measure the whole of the squirearchy was affected by it. Thomas Elyot, in his *Boke named the Governour* (1531) was the apostle of the new movement, emphasising as he did that the education of a gentleman must prepare him for the discharge of magisterial responsibilities, and that for the performance of these duties something more than the skills of knighthood was needed. By the closing years of Elizabeth's reign it would have been a difficult task to have discovered an illiterate gentleman, and certainly impossible to have found one who was proud of his illiteracy, so far had the old notion that "clerks' learning" was beneath the notice of a gentleman been left behind. This improvement in the educational standards of the ruling classes we shall have occasion to refer to again when we come to discuss the changing character of Parliament in a later chapter. For the present let us be content to notice it as partly a cause, and partly a consequence, of that emancipation of the laity from clerical domination which was so important a feature of the Tudor period in England; partly cause, because without learning the laity would not have been fit to fill the positions of authority and responsibility once monopolised by the clergy; partly consequence, because the curtailment of the powers and privileges of the clerical orders made a career in the church so much less attractive to the educated and ambitious man who was now prepared, and able, to make his way in the world without its help.

# 3

## The Exaltation of the Monarchy

IN OUR INTRODUCTORY chapter we made brief mention of the increasing respect for the authority of government, and of the exaltation of the power and prestige of the monarchy which England experienced during the Tudor period. Our purpose in this chapter will be to examine rather more closely the way in which this improvement in the discipline of the nation was brought about. Three closely related factors were involved in this development. In order to win respect for its own authority the monarchy had to build up its own strength, it had to enlarge its own reputation, and it had to keep in check the pretensions of would-be rival authorities.

### The Resources of the Crown

The strength of any government in the latter part of the fifteenth century rested primarily, and almost entirely, upon the resources in men and money at its command. The Crown had not yet become the focus of that semi-mystical cult of monarchy which was to reach its climax in the widespread acceptance of the Divine Right of kings, and to give to the crowned heads of Europe an additional and very potent hold upon the hearts and loyalties of their peoples. Instead, the loyalties of most men tended to be to their immediate lord rather than to the king who was little more than the greatest of the lords. The strength of the monarch could, of course, be reinforced by the addition to his power of that of his noble supporters, but, as Edward IV had found to his cost when the kingmaking Earl of Warwick had turned against him, such noble props to royal power were as dangerous as they were valuable. It was therefore wise policy on the part of Henry

VII, who, before his defeat of Richard III at Bosworth, had been but one of the nobility himself, to dispense as far as possible with the support of the great lords, and to devote himself instead to the building up of his own resources until the authority of the Crown, even unassisted by noble supporters, could successfully dominate all possible rivals. And so, though Bosworth was followed by the expected forfeiture of the titles and estates of the defeated party, it was not followed by any noticeable redistribution of those estates and titles among Henry's supporters. Of course, those who had shared the exile of Henry Tudor in France and Brittany, and who had fought at his side in the overthrow of Richard III, had to receive something in recognition of their services, but the new King bestowed such customary favours with an uncustomarily stinting hand. It was with the hope of further favours rather than by the immediate satisfaction of all expectations, that Henry kept men loyal to him.

This caution in the matter of grants was also displayed by Henry's successors. Henry VIII dispensed largesse with a freer hand than did his father, but even he did not give much away, save perhaps to such intimate associates as his brother-in-law Charles Brandon, Duke of Suffolk. Henry VIII's repeated need of money to finance his military adventures made him as careful of his estates as political necessity had made his father. Indeed, in his reign the value of the lands retained in the hands of the Crown became so great that a new government department, the Court of General Surveyors, was established to take over the management of them. The monastic lands, which the Crown acquired in the years 1536–40, were not for the most part rashly bestowed upon favourites but sold at a fair market price. Henry VIII was also the inaugurator of that cunning Tudor policy of exchanging with bishops and other clergy poor manors for good, to the financial advantage of the Crown but to the detriment of the endowments of the church, a policy which his daughter Elizabeth I was also to find convenient.

Not only did the Tudors take care to maintain the position of the Crown as chief landowner in the realm, they also followed the example of Henry VII in keeping the administration of their estates up-to-date, and in exacting the maximum profit from them. In the sixteenth century the Crown lands still accounted for a very substantial proportion of the monarch's revenue, but estates meant not only wealth but men, tenants and servants whose loyalties were not divided between king and lord and who could be relied upon to answer the call to arms in times of emergency.

Another very substantial proportion of the royal revenue in the Tudor period was derived from the duties imposed upon trade, and this fact very largely accounts for the abiding interest of the Crown in the state of commerce. In this respect it was once again Henry VII who set the example with his many commercial treaties, such as the *Magnus Intercursus* made with the Netherlands in 1496, designed to encourage trade between England and her neighbours. Even Henry VIII, though probably the least interested in trade of all the Tudors, had to take note of the complaints of the merchants in 1528 when his war against the Emperor threatened to interrupt their traffic with the Low Countries. Edward VI's council, Mary and Elizabeth, continually displayed an active, and by no means disinterested, interest in plans for the development of new trades, for when trade flourished the Crown shared in the prosperity of its merchant subjects.

## Additions to Royal Income

The dissolution of the monasteries and chantries fits into the picture here too. The immediate consequence of these two acts of nationalisation was to increase very substantially the landed property in the possession of the Crown, so substantially indeed that a new government department, the Court of Augmentations, had to be created to deal with it. Here, in the former church lands, the Tudors had a capital asset of very considerable value. Had these properties been as carefully managed as undoubtedly Henry VII would have managed them, or as Thomas Cromwell would probably have managed them had he not been sent to execution only a few months after the last of the monasteries had fallen, the revenue from them would have increased the power of the Crown to such an extent as to have made it virtually independent of other supports. However the French and Scottish wars of Henry VIII in the closing decade of his reign, the disastrous monetary policies of the same period and the increasingly heavy defensive military expenditure found necessary in the reign of Elizabeth I, all made it very difficult not to adopt and to continue the less far-sighted policy of disposing of church lands for the sake of the cash in hand rather than that of remaining content with the income which they could provide. Yet even when the monastic lands passed out of royal ownership the Crown did not lose all pecuniary interest in them. Most of the major estates sold were to be held in "knight service" of the king, that is to say they had imposed upon them all the irregular, though often substantial, obligations of a feudal tenancy-in-chief. Of these, reliefs, payable upon the succession of an heir (a species of death-duty), and wardship (the right to administer and take the profits from the estate of a minor) were the most onerous to the tenant and profitable to the Crown. Another of the new government departments established in the reign of Henry VIII, the Court of Wards and Liveries, was found necessary to deal with the administration of this greatly increased source of revenue.

Finance was one of the recurrent problems of the Tudors. The ordinary revenues of the Crown (that is to say the revenues to which the monarch was entitled by right, and for which he was not dependent upon a grant by Parliament or any other body) were considerably augmented during the course of the sixteenth century by many devices, the chief of which we have already touched upon. Yet all the best efforts of the officials of the courts of Augmentations, Wards and General Surveyors could not raise the monarchy to the level of financial independence. Henry VII came the nearest to achieving this goal. After the dismissal in 1504 of what was to be his last parliament, he managed, by economy in expenditure, and by that ruthless exploitation of every source of revenue with which both his contemporaries and succeeding generations have linked the names of Richard Empson and Edmund Dudley, to make his budget balance and to lay by a considerable surplus. But Henry VIII's wars soon squandered that surplus, and no subsequent monarch, Tudor or Stuart, ever again enjoyed the financial good fortune of Henry VII. Elizabeth I, surprisingly enough, came close to success. Even at the very end of her long reign she still had a small annual surplus on the ordinary account, that is to say her ordinary revenues were more than sufficient to meet the ordinary expenses of peace-time government. But Elizabeth was not at peace, and the very considerable cost of the Spanish war and the concurrent Irish rebellion was not by any means covered by the parliamentary grants she received, so that her great deficit on the extraordinary account swallowed up her small ordinary surplus and left her with an overall adverse balance, to meet which she had to resort to selling Crown lands. Yet, taking a comparative view, the financial position of the Crown was far stronger in 1603 than in 1485. Not even the resources of the greatest of her subjects could for a moment compare with those of Queen Elizabeth. As money meant strength, and as strength meant the ability to enforce its authority, so the authority of the Crown was significantly enhanced by the augmentation of the royal revenues during the course of the Tudor period.

## The Reputation of the Monarchy

Money was not, however, the only thing that counted. The strength of the Tudors and their ability to impress their authority upon their subjects did not depend solely upon their power to provide "coat and conduct money" for the men they summoned to their banner in time of danger. The reputation of the monarchy, the image of it retained in the eye of the subject, the prestige, the splendour, the appearance of power, all these played their part in establishing the Tudors in the affections of their subjects, and in strengthening the bonds of duty and devotion by which they were held obedient. In this respect it was the reigns of Henry VIII and Elizabeth I which were the most significant. As Henry VII was the ablest manager of the royal finances, so his son and grand-daughter were the ablest propagandists for monarchy in general and their house in particular. Henry VIII was, from the start, a kingly King. The great state with which he surrounded himself, the splendour of his public appearances, the fame of the knightly tournaments in which he in person, in his younger days, displayed his skill, the climax of the year 1520 when the Holy Roman Emperor, the greatest prince in Europe, came in person to England to seek an alliance with her King, and when Henry in turn met the King of France on equal terms of brilliance at the Field of the Cloth of Gold; these

extravagant struttings of the royal peacock evoked no mur-
murs of dissent from indignant taxpayers, but rather the
respectful adulation of adoring subjects proud to claim a
share in the glory of their King, for it was a commonplace
of the day that the reputation of a prince was but the reflection of the reputation of his subjects. Only a proud and
prosperous people could maintain so splendid a Court and
King without feeling the strain.

But this spontaneously awakened affection for a royal
prince who raised the reputation of himself and of his subjects
to such heights was not left to flourish unattended. It was
constantly cultivated by astute propagandists who hammered
home the object lesson of the civil strife of the previous
century. Those wars between the white rose and the red which
had torn English society apart so bitterly had ended, as the
chronicler Edward Hall put it, in the "Union of the two noble
and illustrious families of Lancaster and York" of which union
King Henry VIII was the "undoubted flower and very heir".
More credit was thus, by implication, given to the marriage
of Henry VII to Elizabeth of York than to all the highly
successful efforts of that King to sustain his usurpation against
all comers and to pass on the throne in peace to his son.
This propaganda, of course, obscured the real weakness of
the Tudor claim in the male line, and emphasised the link
with the house of York. It was, however, a subtle propaganda
which had the effect of making the remnant of the Yorkist
faction, the Poles and the Courtenays,[1] appear as traitors
even to their own cause, for the true Yorkist heir was Henry
VIII himself. The Tudors, by their double inheritance, signi-
fied heraldically by the double Tudor rose, had brought peace
to a faction-torn England, Those who now sought to trouble
their rule or to dispossess them could have no right on their
side, but were mere raisers of faction pursuing their own
interest in preference to that of the realm. References to the
"troublous" times of the previous century abound in the literature of Henry VIII's reign. The widespread fear of a recur-
rence of civil strife is played upon to encourage men to
support the ruling house. Even the King himself is haunted

[1] For their relationship to the Tudors see genealogical table No. 3
in Appendix B, p. 234.

by this fear which underlay so many of his matrimonial difficulties.

In the reign of Elizabeth I it was foreign rather than domestic dangers which formed the main theme of Tudor propaganda. The Queen was seen as the heroic defender of her country and of its reformed faith against all its foes, sharing fully, in a very personal way, the dangers which threatened the realm, for it was against her life that all the conspiracies and plots of her reign were directed. And yet, though she shared the risks with her subjects, she made sure, by her careful cultivation of the *mystique* of monarchy that she stood on a plane above that of even the greatest of her people. She was not simply one of them called to a position of power and responsibility. She was a creature apart, of royal blood and royal birth, called by God to her throne and anointed in His name. Elizabeth never let even her most intimate advisers forget her, or their, station. This constant emphasis upon the sanctity and separateness of monarchy, which was reiterated in all her many public appearances, tended to exalt still further the position of the Queen in the eyes of her subjects, and to encourage the growth of a loyalty to the Crown which was of a different nature to, and over-rode, any other loyalty to lord or patron. The encouragement of the cult of monarchy by the Tudors materially strengthened their position in relation to their subjects. In Henry VII's reign a de la Pole or a Stafford[2] might think himself as good a man as the ruling Tudor, and claim a better right to the throne. In the reign of Elizabeth I even the Seymours and the Stanleys[3] who were closely linked by blood with the royal house would not have thought to aspire to replace or even to succeed the Queen. Monarchs had become a race apart from other men. Mary Tudor had made it clear to those who had wanted her to marry an Englishman that in taking a subject for her husband she would disparage her royal estate. Elizabeth I, though she may in her earlier years have entertained thoughts of marrying Leicester, later came, like her sister, to regard a marriage with a subject as out of the question.

---

[2] See genealogical tables Nos. 1 and 3 in Appendix B, pp. 232 and 234.
[3] See genealogical table No. 2 in Appendix B, p. 233.

## The Enforcement of the Law

Both in wealth and in reputation the Crown thus stood considerably higher at the time of Elizabeth's death than it had done when tumbled under a thorn bush on the field of Bosworth. But a rich and exalted monarchy will not for long retain the affections of its subjects if it does not dispense good government, and good government, in the sixteenth century, meant above all the just and impartial enforcement of the law of the land. The good king was the just king whose courts brought speedy and effective redress to the aggrieved and swift retribution upon the malefactor.

The routine exercise of the judicial powers of English kings had, for centuries before the accession of the Tudors, been delegated to the judges of the courts of Common Law, and over the course of the years elaborate procedures had been developed to ensure that substantial justice was done. But though kings had delegated their judicial powers to their judges, they had not abdicated them. They still retained every right to sit in judgment in or through their council, that organ of government most intimately associated with the person of the monarch. The jurisdiction of the king's council was not in origin, whatever it may have become later, a rival to that of the Common Law, but was supplementary to it. In cases where the normal machinery of justice had failed to function satisfactorily, appeal could be, and was made regularly, to the king for redress, and most of such appeals were handled by the council. There were two principal ways in which the courts of Common Law might fail to give the litigant satisfaction. In the first place, though the law might take its course without improper interruption, the special circumstances of the case might still lead to a failure of justice. In the second place the proper course of the law might be interrupted or interfered with by outside pressures. Cases of the first kind, in the fifteenth and later centuries, were generally dealt with by the Lord Chancellor, who developed precedents and procedures of his own in dealing with them, which came to be known as the rules of Equity. Cases of the second kind generally arose when the local influence of some magnate, usually exerted upon juries or witnesses or both, by the threat or the actual use of violence, made it impossible for justice to be done in any case which touched his interests. In cases like these only the authority of the king in council could hope to set matters right by introducing a new force which could counteract that of the "overmighty subject", or by retrying the issue in an atmosphere quite free from undesirable local pressures.

This corrective jurisdiction of the king's council was no new invention of the Tudors. It had a long history before the so-called "Star Chamber Act" of 1487 (3 Henry VII cap. 1) gave it a more formal shape. What was new perhaps in Tudor times was the extent to which Henry VII, and after him Wolsey, encouraged men to apply to the council for redress. So rapidly did this side of the council's activities increase in the early years of the sixteenth century that it became necessary to commit the conduct of such judicial business to a specialist group of councillors who remained accessible to litigants in the "starred chamber" of the palace of Whitehall wherever the king and the rest of his council might happen to be in the course of their routine peregrination around the royal manors. This physical separation of two parts of a single institution, the council, was the beginning of the separate existence of the court of Star Chamber, which was to prove so valuable an instrument in the restoration of law and good order after the comparative lawlessness of the fifteenth century. Star Chamber brought the power of the king home to his subjects and taught even the mightiest in the land that the king was mightier than they, and that they could not with impunity interfere with the course of his justice.

Star Chamber was on the whole careful not to interfere unnecessarily with the activities of the Common Law courts. It is clear from the many surviving Star Chamber pleadings that in order to bring a case before the council it was necessary for the litigant either to plead that he had already tried, and failed, to obtain justice at Common Law, or that, because of the potent influence of his adversary and the violence of his actions, he could not hope for justice in the local courts. Plaintiffs who were unable to make and substantiate either of these pleas would as a rule find that the council declined to interfere and remitted their case to the ordinary courts for trial. Star Chamber was also, in its early days, a popular tribunal, and it is clear from the suspiciously high proportion of the pleadings which describe in virtually identical terms how the defendant and his men appeared "riotously with force of arms, that is to say with halberds, bills, staves, swords and knives" and put the plaintiff forcibly out of possession of certain of his lands, that the speedier and more impartial justice of this court was being invoked, by alleging fictitious riots, to settle cases which properly belonged to the Common Law courts. Justice Shallow, in *The Merry Wives of Windsor,* was merely following a course of action to which an Elizabethan audience was well accustomed when, having quarrelled with Falstaff over a matter of debt, he threatened:

> I will make a Star Chamber matter of it . . . the Council shall hear of it . . . it is a riot; knight, you have beaten my men, killed my deer, and broke open my lodge . . .[4]

reeling off some of the customary complaints.

Star Chamber therefore gave the Englishman of the sixteenth century a renewed respect for the majesty of the law, and for the monarchy which upheld it, and so contributed, not only to the power, but also to the prestige and security of the house of Tudor. But Star Chamber, though the most famous, was only one of the conciliar[5] courts. Similar to it in powers and jurisdiction were those regional councils of the North, and of Wales and the Marches, which, though not entirely Tudor in origin, were developed by them into very effective instruments to discipline over those usually troublesome and lawless areas. These councils, though they only very exceptionally met in the presence of the king, and were staffed predominantly with men of non-noble origin, were backed by the full force of the king's authority, and, being above and apart from the many feuds and jealousies of the border magnates, proved in the long run more effective organs of government than would have been either the main body of the council in distant London, or the local lords themselves. The councils of the North and of Wales ex-

---

[4] *The Merry Wives of Windsor,* Act I, scene 1, *passim.*

[5] So called because they originated as offshoots of the council. The alternative name, "prerogative" courts, tends to mislead by implying the existence of a conflict between their jurisdiction and that of Common Law.

tended the authority of the Crown over regions which had hitherto had scant respect for a generally remote authority. The disciplining of the Welsh marches was chiefly the work of Roland Lee, Bishop of Coventry and Lichfield from 1534 to 1543, and, at the same time, president of the council of Wales and the Marches. The taming of the North was the work of the reorganised council established in 1537 after the suppression of the rising known as the Pilgrimage of Grace. Again the chief credit must go to a bishop, in this case Robert Holgate, Bishop of Llandaff from 1537 to 1545 and Archbishop of York from 1545 to 1554.

## The Justices of the Peace

The authority of the king in council was expressed in other ways and through other instruments besides the conciliar courts and regional councils. In every county the chief responsibility for the maintenance of law and order, the apprehension of offenders, the putting down of disturbances and the enforcement of government policies, had for long rested with the Justices of the Peace, drawn from the ranks of the local gentry, and vested with authority by a commission under the Great Seal. The Tudors did not create this office, but they multiplied its responsibilities, and gave it a greater standing in relation to that of other local offices. They also subjected the justices to a much closer degree of oversight. They made sure that they made proper use of the authority delegated to them, and performed the functions required of them. Slack or negligent justices were likely to receive letters of warning from the council, and, if these were ignored, risked a summons to appear in person in the Star Chamber to give an account of themselves. In extreme cases they could be struck off the commission, but this ultimate sanction was seldom necessary. The gentry, far from resenting having so heavy a burden of government work laid upon them with no salary or perquisites as recompense, were proud of their responsibilities and accepted them not merely as a necessary consequence, but as the very badge of their position in society. It was expected of the gentleman that he should play his part in the government of his country. To be made a justice was a recognition of one's social status. To be dropped from the commission was a social disgrace which few would willingly suffer. And so a word of warning usually sufficed to bring a negligent justice to heel, and for the most part the council and the justices worked harmoniously together. The justice was both the eyes and ears of the council, keeping the government in touch with local events and local opinion, and also the hands and feet of the council, acting on their instructions as the agent of government policy. The tasks of the justices were manifold. Not only did they have powers of arrest and petty criminal jurisdiction, they also supervised the maintenance and repair of roads and bridges, the licensing of ale houses, and in Elizabeth's reign they became responsible for the regulation of wage rates and for the administration of the poor law. Lesser local officials, the constables, the church wardens, the overseers of the poor, came under the supervisory eye of the justice who was responsible for their good behaviour and efficient functioning. And yet, varied and extensive though the regular tasks of the justice were, it was from time to time found necessary to issue additional commissions appointing persons to attend to matters which lay outside the scope of the justices' commission. These special commissioners, as they were called, were often, but not always, the justices themselves. Their tasks were usually of a non-recurrent nature, and their commissions of a limited duration. It was special commissioners who, for example, surveyed stocks of grain during times of dearth, who discovered, and seized, the goods of Scotsmen when the neighbouring kingdoms were at war, who made a complete record of the wealth of the church for purposes of taxation and who dissolved the monasteries. Some special commissioners, such as those for Sewers who co-ordinated and supervised land drainage in low lying areas such as the Fens, were reappointed so regularly that they became virtually permanent officials. But, permanent or temporary, these commissioners were in every way as much the agents of the Crown as were the justices, and carried the authority of the king, which was their only warrant for action, into every corner of the kingdom, and into every department of the nation's life. The authority of the Crown was everywhere and at all times increasingly apparent in the multifarious activities of its agents and commissioners, and the subjects of the Tudors were kept continually aware of the active concern of their rulers for their welfare and for good government.

## Military Organisation

Though even by the close of the sixteenth century there was still nothing like a permanent army in England, the military organisation of the kingdom had undergone in the Tudor period a significant reorganisation which also contributed materially to the strength of the Crown. The earlier Tudors had, like their predecessors, relied for their military strength in time of crisis partly upon the rank and file of their subjects who could be summoned to the royal colours, but mainly upon the local followings of their noble supporters, private armies, little to be distinguished from those that had fought in the Wars of the Roses. Contrary to the popular belief, Henry VII did not put a stop to the practice of "retaining" as the keeping of these bands of followers was called, but merely saw to it that this practice was kept within the legal limits which had been prescribed in earlier reigns. He made sure, for instance, that the bond of loyalty created by the agreements into which lord and retainer entered could never take precedence over the allegiance of the latter to his king. Thus, though the retainer was usually bound to follow and support the fortunes of his lord, he could not be compelled to take arms against his monarch. The nobles' bands of retainers, subject to this condition, were allowed to remain as a useful trained nucleus for a company of the royal forces in time of war or other danger.

By the middle of the sixteenth century, however, the system of retaining was breaking down. In more peaceful and settled times the lord had less use for a company of idle armed men, and the Crown had to rely for its supply of soldiers more and more upon the ordinary levies from the shires, men called directly to the king's service in time of danger. There had for centuries been an obligation incumbent upon all subjects to maintain and bear arms when necessary in defence of the kingdom. This obligation had been given a more precise definition by Henry II's Assize of Arms, but with the introduction of new weapons, in particular of the handgun or arquebus, it was found necessary, in the sixteenth century, to bring the whole matter up to date in a new statute, that of 1558 (4 & 5 Philip and Mary cap. 2). At about the same time greater care began to be taken to muster the able-bodied men of the shire from time to time to inspect their arms and to give some opportunity for an elementary military training. To supervise these musters, and to see to local defence, the Crown now delegated its power to lords lieutenant, at first for the duration of a particular emergency, later on a more permanent basis. Through the lord lieutenant the Crown entered into a direct relationship with the local military forces. No longer were troops in an emergency raised through the intermediacy of the nobility and the gentry. Though the lord lieutenant frequently, indeed usually, was one of the great landowners in the shire in which he held his commission, it was solely by virtue of the royal authority delegated to him by that commission, and not by virtue of his estates or title or local influence, that he raised, trained and commanded troops. The change was an important one. The lord lieutenancy was in the gift of the Crown. No longer could a great lord oblige the king to lean upon his support because of the strength of the forces he commanded. Instead the lord was now dependent upon the Crown for the very authority which gave him power to levy troops.

## The Decline of Rival Powers

And so in wealth, in prestige, in reputation and in military strength, the Tudors built up the power of the Crown. This increase in power was at the same time emphasised by a parallel and notable decline in the strength of all rival claimants to power. Chief of these was the church, with which we shall deal more fully in subsequent chapters, for the conflict between church and state is one of the major themes of the history of the sixteenth century. But at the same time as the Crown was successfully asserting its authority over the church it was also conducting a long-term and generally successful campaign against the areas of private jurisdiction known as liberties. Many of these had fallen into the possession of the Crown as a result of forfeitures during the Wars of the Roses and afterwards, but there were still many in private hands. These were now kept strictly in check and, where possible, the superior rights of the Crown were

asserted. Independent corporations, like the boroughs and
the craft and merchant guilds, were also made to feel the
weight of royal authority and to acknowledge that such privileges as they did possess could not operate against the
Crown, which was the source of all authority. Thus, by the
end of Elizabeth's reign, the Crown stood higher than ever
before, its authority substantially increased, its rivals humbled,
its will given effect by a host of servants and agents throughout the land. England now possessed a competent and effective central government. She was disciplined and obedient.
No longer was the problem for governments how to secure
obedience to their will or how to create an efficient administrative machine. The question for the future was rather
who should control the established machinery, the Crown
alone, or the Crown in partnership with Parliament?

On the whole England benefited from this strengthening
of the hands of government. A stable and well-ordered society
is generally more prosperous and happier than one torn apart
by civil strife and competing ambition. The *Pax Tudoriana*
brought many blessings to England. It was not for nothing
that English poets sang the praises of their virgin Queen
and men spoke with reverence of the King, her father, "of
famous memory". The spectre of civil war seemed to have
been banished. Men could build and plan for the future, and
count upon possessing their inheritance in peace. But this
security had to be purchased, and the price to be paid was the
acceptance of the exaltation of the Crown. In rising trium-
phant over faction, disorder and rival authorities, the Crown
had reached a new peak of power. So much more now depended upon the Crown, so much depended, too, upon the
character and intentions of its wearer. In unscrupulous and
ambitious hands it could easily become the instrument of
tyranny. In incompetent ones it might lead the country to
ruin and undo the good work of the Tudors. There was already a decided tendency towards arbitrary government which
might lead on to the establishment of a despotic autocracy.
That this was not to be England's fate was largely the consequence of the great paradox of the sixteenth century, that it
witnessed not only the rising of the Crown to unheard-of
heights, but also the strengthening and growth of Parliament

to such an extent that it was ready to challenge the Crown for control of government itself. But the development of Parliament under the Tudors is a subject which deserves a chapter to itself.

# 4

## *Parliamentary Progress*

IF IT AT first sight seems strange that the sixteenth century, which witnessed the exaltation of the power of the English monarchy to heights hitherto unattained, saw also a significant and substantial development in the power of the English Parliament, that is only because we are too easily accustomed to regarding "Crown" and "Parliament" as separate and mutually hostile (or at least mutually distrustful) powers. If the one, in any period, gained in power, we tend to think that it could only have done so at the expense of the other. This habit of thinking of Crown and Parliament as distinct institutions is understandable enough when we bear in mind the history of the seventeenth and eighteenth centuries when the interests of the ruling monarchs and those of a vociferous and potent section of the two Houses of Parliament seemed so often to be at variance. And yet this way of thinking is erroneous, for two reasons. The first is the purely constitutional one that the Crown is always an essential part of Parliament. Parliament consists, not of lords and commons alone, but of monarch, lords and commons. Parliament cannot properly be a rival to the Crown, for Parliament is an instrument, and an extension, of royal authority. Just as the king sometimes acts in and through his council, so on other occasions he acts in and through that greater council, his Parliament. The second reason is more practical. Even when relations between the monarch and the two Houses of Parliament were most strained there was always an element of support for the king among both peers and commons. Never has there been a simple and clear division between the monarch and the two houses. Indeed the occasions upon which even a majority of the lower house was prepared to press its point of view against the royal will have been very few

57

in number. The contest which we speak of loosely as being between Crown and Parliament has generally been a struggle of the Crown and certain elements in each of the houses against the rest.

This, then, is the first point to make clear; that because the Houses of Parliament are not necessarily to be found in conflict with their sovereign there is nothing inherently improbable about Parliament enjoying an increase in power and prestige at the same time as the Crown. There is in fact no paradox to explain away. But although, without the spectre of this paradox to haunt us, our task is made easier, we are not altogether absolved from the need to offer an explanation of that most important sixteenth-century phenomenon, the rise of Parliament.

## The Old View Criticised

It is customary in many quarters to place the responsibility for the rise of Parliament squarely upon the broad shoulders of Henry VIII, and to confer upon him some such honorary title as that of "the architect of Parliament". Those who take this view argue that it is plain from what we know of Henry VII's relationship with Parliament that the first Tudor found little use for that body, save as a royal taxing machine, and that, once he was firmly established upon the throne, and possessed of a sufficient revenue, he quite cheerfully dispensed with Parliament as much as possible, summoning only one meeting of the houses between 1497 and the end of his reign. For the last five years of his life, from 1504 onwards, he was able, thanks to economy in the expenditure and care in the collection of his revenues, to ignore Parliament altogether. Now had his son and successor pursued the same policies of economy at home and neutrality abroad, the English Parliament might well have died through lack of use. But Henry VIII not only squandered his father's treasure on extravagant wars, he also found himself forced to enter into an alliance with the lay element among his subjects through their representatives in Parliament when he quarrelled with the church and the Pope. And so Parliament was saved. By calling upon it to endorse the many, and often sweeping, measures necessary to legitimise his "reformation", Henry VIII enlarged its scope and increased its authority and set it firmly upon the road to power. Of course the many changes of the following reigns, the further reformation under Edward, the reaction under Mary, and the final settlement under Elizabeth, which were all carried out through Parliament, provided that body with ample opportunities for consolidating that hold upon national affairs which it had first grasped in 1529. For thirty years, from 1529 to 1559, Parliament was accustomed to dealing with the weightiest matters, the relationship of church and state, the succession to the throne, the very powers and prerogatives of the Crown itself. And so from the reign of Elizabeth onwards there was no looking back. Parliament would never again relinquish that share of power to which Henry VIII had found it politic to admit it. The English Parliament, almost alone of the medieval representative institutions of the greater states of Western Europe, survived into modern times to challenge the very authority of the Crown which had given it birth.

Thus, very briefly, runs a commonly accepted version of the story of Parliament in Tudor times. But this view depends for its acceptance very heavily upon establishing two points; first that Henry VII made it a point of policy to keep the rôle of Parliament to a minimum, and eventually to dispense with it altogether; and secondly, that the use which Henry VIII made of Parliament was unprecedented, and in itself provided important precedents for the future. Let us examine each of these assumptions in turn.

## Henry VII and Parliament

First, was Henry VII anti-Parliament? Did he really regard Parliament as a potentially dangerous rival to be dispensed with if possible? There is, of course, no record of what Henry VII himself actually thought or intended. His intentions can only be inferred from his actions. And so, because he summoned six of his seven Parliaments in the first half of his reign when his position both politically and financially was not so secure, and only one in the second half, when his financial needs were not so pressing, it has been assumed that it was only for the financial support which it could give him that Henry valued Parliament. But this is not the only construction that can be put upon his actions, and does much less than justice to the work of his earlier Parliaments. It is true that these assemblies did a lot to improve the King's financial position, by acts of attainder and resumption, and by grants of tunnage and poundage and other supplementary taxation. But they also devoted a considerable proportion of their time to providing for the better execution of the law (stopping loopholes and improving procedures), and to the regulation of trade and industry. In the amount of time which they devoted to such matters the Parliaments of Henry VII did not differ significantly from those of Henry VIII or from their predecessors. The whole life of the country came under their care, and they were ever ready to regulate and control it, sometimes in the greatest detail. Would a would-be autocrat, anxious to dispense with Parliaments, or at least to use them only as providers of revenue, have had the patience to permit his assemblies to deal with such matters as, for example, the prices of hats and caps? Either Henry VII found himself obliged (as we know Elizabeth I was on many occasions) to wait for his subsidies while his Parliaments raised and dealt with these other matters of their own initiative, or else he recognised the importance of Parliament in matters other than financial and willingly granted it time to attend to them. In either case the picture we get is not that of a strong-minded monarch who used Parliament only for his own purposes, and dispensed with it when it suited him, but of a king who recognised that Parliament had by right an important part to play in the government of the country, and permitted it to play that part.

Henry VII's respect for Parliament becomes the plainer when we consider the rôle he allotted to it in establishing the very foundations of his government after the victory at Bosworth. Very shortly after that battle which had given him the crown, indeed only twelve days after his arrival in London, the new king issued the writs summoning his first Parliament. This assembly, when it met, was to endorse Henry's position on the throne by declaring the Crown vested in himself and his heirs, and by attainting his erstwhile enemies. This Parliament did not, of course, make Henry king, for he had already acted the part of a king in issuing the writs which had brought it into being. Moreover, Henry claimed to have been king by right even before the day of Bosworth. The victory there was a confirmation, and not the foundation, of his

kingship. And so it was with his first Parliament. Their very
meeting in response to his summons was a recognition of his
kingship, for only a king could summon Parliament. The
acknowledgement by Parliament of his right to the throne
was no more than a confirmation of a position he already
occupied. Parliament recognised that he was king, it did
not, and could not, make him king. And yet it is indicative
of the importance which Henry attached to Parliament and
to its pronouncements that he should have sought and obtained this act of recognition. Had Parliament been regarded
by the King and his contemporaries as no more than the
subservient tool of the monarchy there would have been
little point in taking such a step, but if Parliament was indeed
the supreme authority in the land then a parliamentary endorsement of his kingship was something worth having.

Henry VII was no despiser of Parliaments. The long intervals between his later Parliaments were no more than a
natural reflection of the stability of both the domestic and
foreign situations during those years. It was a fairly general
rule in the sixteenth century that the more critical the years
the more frequent were the Parliaments. Henry VII's Parliaments may be crowded together in the first half of his reign,
but those were the difficult years when rival claimants and
pretenders gave the King little peace and the throne was
constantly in danger. The seven-year interval between his
Parliaments of 1497 and 1504, and the five-year gap between
the latter and the end of his reign are not exceptionally
long intervals for a period of external peace and internal
security. The five-year interval between the Elizabethan Parliaments of 1576 and 1581 is generally passed over without
comment, and it is often forgotten that in terms of the
average frequency of parliamentary sessions there is almost
nothing to choose between the reigns of the first and the
last of the Tudors. Elizabeth held thirteen sessions of Parliament in a reign of forty-five years, Henry VII seven in
twenty-four years. In either case the average figure is ap-
proximately one session for every three and a half years of
the reign. Both comparatively, and absolutely, Henry VII's
reputation as a parliamentary monarch is not as bad as some
would have us believe.

*Henry VIII and the "Reformation Parliament"*

What then of Henry VIII? And what about the "Reformation Parliament"? Was Parliament from 1529 onwards called upon to exercise an authority that it had not possessed before? These are questions that must still be answered even if we accept that Parliament under Henry VII had not been on the verge of extinction. What did the "Reformation Parliament" do? Did it assume to itself the powers of a constitution-making body and alter the whole relationship between church and state? Did it trespass upon the territory of the spiritual power in an unprecedented manner? Did it magnify the power of the Crown at the expense of that of the church?

The answer to none of these questions can be an unqualified "yes". In the first place when, in the Act in restraint of appeals of 1533 (24 Henry VIII cap. 12) Parliament declared that:

> this realm of England *is* an Empire . . . governed by one supreme Head and King

or when, in the Act of Supremacy (26 Henry VIII cap. 1) of the following year it proclaimed that the King:

> *is* and ought to be the supreme head of the church of England

it was not, in theory, altering the English constitution at all, but merely declaring what the proper relationship of Crown, church and state was, and always ought to have been. Parliament was not, in these instances, making new laws. These Acts are not legislative, but declaratory, being in nature similar to that Act of the first Parliament of Henry VII which, as we have already noted, acknowledged, but did not create, his kingship. This looking backwards, this attempt to represent the new departure as a return to the past and as a resumption by the Crown of its proper powers, is very marked in the Acts of the "Reformation Parliament"; notice, for instance, the appeal to "divers sundry old authentic histories and chronicles" in the Act in restraint of appeals.

In some of the Acts of this Parliament the reference to good parliamentary precedent is clear and specific. For in-

stance, the Heresy Act of 1534 (25 Henry VIII cap. 14)
quotes those of Richard II, Henry IV and Henry V, and
the Act in restraint of appeals is consciously modelled on
the "great Statute of Praemunire" of 1393. In other cases,
though specific reference is not made there is nevertheless
good precedent; for example, the Act for the dissolution of
the lesser monasteries (27 Henry VIII cap. 28) had a forerunner in the suppression of the alien priories under Henry
V, and that limiting benefit of clergy (23 Henry VIII cap. 1)
in an Act of 1490.

Clearly one cannot accept without considerable modifica-
tion any claim that the "Reformation Parliament" was breaking new ground and enlarging the scope of its activities in
order to assist the royal campaign against the church. Indeed
it is particularly noteworthy that contemporary observers
and writers saw nothing unusual or significant about the proceedings of this assembly. The only contemporary chronicler
who saw fit to make more than a passing reference to this
Parliament, which some subsequent generations have regarded as so important, was Edward Hall, but then he was
a member of the House of Commons at the time and so
quite naturally had a greater interest in its doings.

The only man to challenge the competence of the English
Parliament to pronounce upon the validity of the Pope's
claim to have jurisdiction over the church in England was
Sir Thomas More. It took his clear-sighted mind to grasp
the ultimate implications of what the King, Lords and Commons were doing. But for the great majority of men who
made up that Parliament what they were doing was not
substantially different from what many a previous Parliament
had done. The King-in-Parliament was the supreme court
of the realm, competent to judge upon every issue submitted
to it. The normal recourse of the kingdom in time of crisis
or difficulty was to Parliament. Even the rebels of 1536,
those who took part in the Pilgrimage of Grace, acknowledged this when they called for a Parliament to redress their
grievances although previous Parliaments had been the au-
thors of most of them.

Yet further confirmation of this view that the Parliament
of 1529 was not exceptional in the scope of its measures or
precedent-making in the nature of its Acts is offered by

the notable fact that the Parliamentarians of the reigns of
Elizabeth and the earlier Stuarts, fond though they were of
finding precedents to support their actions and vindicate
their claims, did not attach any greater importance to the
proceedings of this Parliament than to those of any other.
Indeed if they had a preference in the matter of precedents
it was for those of the reigns of Edward III and Henry IV.
Some liked to look even further back, to the Witenagemot
of Anglo-Saxon days!

## The Sovereignty of Parliament

If then Parliament was neither so weak under Henry VII
nor yet so suddenly admitted to new powers under Henry
VIII as it is often supposed, we must re-write the story of
Parliament in the sixteenth century. And that is just the very
task upon which many historians are currently engaged. The
picture that is emerging is that of a Parliament which, if
you like to look back, was not so very different from that
of the reigns of Henry IV and V, or, if you prefer to look
forward, from that of the reigns of James I and Charles I.
There is no waning and sudden recovery of power by Parliament, but rather a steady growth. Parliament, all through the
Tudor period, held an honoured and important place in
the state as guardian and creator of the law. And it was the
law that was supreme, not the king. Even Henry VIII acknowledged that. "We at no time stand so highly in our
estate royal as in the time of parliament", he declared in
1543, for in Parliament he and the representatives of his
subjects met together to regulate the affairs of the kingdom,
to amend the law where necessary, and to provide new laws
where none existed.

It is true that the King also possessed, out of Parliament,
an additional power to make law by proclamation, but this
power was strictly limited in its application, and when doubts
arose about its extent and validity these were set at rest, in
the customary manner, by definition in Parliament by the
Statute of Proclamations of 1539 (31 Henry VIII cap. 8).
This Act, on the one hand, added strength to the King's
proclamations by insisting that they had the force of law,
but, on the other hand, ensured that this royal legislative
power was kept within bounds by declaring that it was inferior

in force to statute law. And though the Act of Proclamations
was repealed in 1547, the principles which it had enunciated
were still observed. There is a long letter written by Stephen
Gardiner to Lord Protector Somerset* in 1547 in which he
cites many examples from the reign of Henry VIII in order
to prove the superiority of statute over any other form of
law, and to establish that even the king may not ignore or
over-ride an Act of Parliament, and, although in this instance
it suited the immediate purpose of the writer to make such
a case, there is little room for doubt that his view was the
one commonly accepted at the time. Now the supremacy of
statute over all other forms of law means the supremacy of
Parliament over all other organs of government, for only
Parliament could make or amend a statute. This supremacy
of Parliament was not the creation of Henry VIII. You will
find it accepted in earlier generations too, and set forth
clearly in the works of that great fifteenth-century constitutional writer, Sir John Fortescue, particularly in his *De laudibus legum Angliae*.

## The Influence of the Crown

But although we may accept all this, is it not still true that
the Parliaments of the earlier Tudors, Henry VII and Henry
VIII, were much more amenable to royal control than those
of Mary and Elizabeth, that in this sense Parliament made a
real and important advance in the sixteenth century? Perhaps, but not as great an advance as some would have us
believe. The chief difficulty here is that we do not know,
and probably will never know, as much about the earlier
Tudor Parliaments as we do about Elizabeth's, because the
records available are so much less adequate. And yet, despite
the limited nature of our evidence we do get hints from time
to time that even the early Tudor Parliaments were not always
amenable to discipline. Sir Thomas More's son-in-law and
biographer, William Roper, speaks of a spirited and partially
successful opposition being offered to the financial demands
of Henry VII in the Parliament of 1504. The early pages
of the Lords' Journals, which commence in 1510, show us
that the House of Commons passed, and sent up to the
upper house, more than one measure designed to limit the
privileges of the clergy at a time when the King and his

councillors were not inclined to encourage or even entertain such proceedings. The Commons' campaign against the clergy succeeded at last in 1512 with the passage of an Act limiting benefit of clergy (4 Henry VIII, cap. 2). The resistance of the Commons in 1523 to Wolsey's demand for subsidies is well known, as is the reluctance of the "Reformation Parliament" to meet the King's wishes over the Bills of Wills and Uses. In 1539 the personal intervention of the King was necessary to bring to an end the debate over the Act of Six Articles (31 Henry VIII, cap. 14). These incidents, and others too, taken separately, do not amount to much, but, taken together, they do suggest that the Houses of Parliament, and in particular the House of Commons, possessed, even under Henry VIII, a good measure of that independence of spirit so much in evidence in some of the Parliaments of Mary and Elizabeth.

And yet we must concede that the relationship between the Crown and the Houses did undergo a significant alteration in the Tudor period. Two things happened; Members of Parliament began to have their own ideas about what sort of legislation was desirable, and became bolder in speaking their minds. In the reign of Henry VIII a word of warning from the King was generally sufficient to silence a member who spoke out of turn (like the one who asked awkward questions about Queen Catherine in 1532), but in the reign of Elizabeth such royal hints and warnings were themselves made the objects of attack, and stronger measures had to be adopted to deal with recalcitrant members. The Parliaments of Henry VII and Henry VIII, though they reserved the right to disapprove of government measures, and were active in promoting the interests of their own localities in Bills of local application, were content for the most part to leave the initiative in national affairs to the Crown. The "liberty of speech" they claimed, and were accorded, was liberty to discuss and criticise, and even to reject, matters laid before them. They were not much concerned as yet whether this liberty of speech extended to the choice of subjects for debate. The Parliaments of Elizabeth, however, though in many matters they were still content to follow the government's lead, and still regarded themselves as partners rather than as rivals of the Crown, generally contained a group of more radical members who had their own ideas about what was best for their country, and were not to be deterred by royal warnings from claiming that they were entitled, by virtue of their liberty of speech, to discuss whatever matters seemed to them appropriate. We must not however over-emphasise the extent of this development. The government's view of the extent of parliamentary liberty of speech, as expressed on many occasions by the Queen and her councillors, was much what it had been in Henry VIII's day, liberty to discuss, but not liberty to initiate. It was only the "opposition group" of Wentworth, Cope, Strickland and the others who pressed for a wider interpretation of this privilege.

## The Increasing Confidence of the Commons

There are signs, however, that under the leadership of this dissatisfied and outspoken group the House of Commons as a whole was changing in character. The members themselves were in social origins still the same sort of men, the majority of them those same country gentry who were also, as we have seen, the mainstay of local government. They sat for most of the boroughs as well as the shires, and though some formal distinction was still on occasions drawn between "knights" and "burgesses", it was largely fictitious, and few of the representatives of the towns were any longer townsmen. And yet, as the class to which they belonged developed new interests, acquired a better education, and began to entertain new ambitions, the Members of Parliament came gradually to take a rather different view of their powers and responsibilities. By the reign of Elizabeth this transformation was almost complete, the boorish country knights who had attended Parliament somewhat reluctantly as a duty (for their journey to Westminster took them away from their estates, their business and their accustomed pleasures into an unfamiliar and not altogether attractive city life), had now given way to eager would-be courtiers and statesmen, competing with each other for places in the parliament house, full of great schemes for the better government of both state and church, and only too pleased to have the opportunity of sharing for a while in the busy exciting life of the capital. Those whose ancestors had, in Thomas Cromwell's phrase, "endured" the five or six weeks of a parliamentary session, and had thought, like the Commmons in 1532, that three sessions of a Parliament were enough for any man, now found the life of Parliament all too short for the amount of business they had in hand, and tried to play for more time by postponing consideration of the government's financial measures. This change in the attitude of members towards Parliament and their duties and opportunities in that assembly, this was the really vital development in the history of Parliament in the sixteenth century. And this change was itself the product of the increasing respect of the laity for education, and their developing interest in national and international affairs. This is what made the real difference between early and later Tudor Parliaments. Naturally the latter were more difficult to manage, less easily warned off undesirable topics, less easily satisfied with vague promises, more conscious of the actual and potential dangers that faced the realm. The practice, increasingly common among members of the lower house, of keeping some personal record of parliamentary business in diary form, is a natural symptom of this new attitude to parliamentary affairs.

Of course it would be stretching the point to try to assert that this increasing self-confidence among the Parliament men, vital though it was, was the only reason for the increasing importance of the House of Commons during the sixteenth century. The peers helped indirectly by becoming stricter about the qualifications for membership of their own house. By refusing full membership to any but the bishops and the holders of hereditary lay peerages they obliged those non-noble councillors of the Crown who had in earlier centuries enjoyed an *ex officio* place in Parliament to seek election to the lower house if they did not want to be excluded from that assembly altogether. The resulting appearance of privy councillors as members of the Commons in the latter part of the sixteenth century did much to enhance the prestige of the lower house. The Commons also began to attract as members an increasing number of men with legal training. Their services to their fellows in searching out and establishing precedents, and in the framing of Bills, were of inestimable value in many ways.

It must not be thought, however, that all this sort of development was confined within the walls of the lower house.

We must remember that the peers were equally influenced by the new currents of thought, and the new respect for education. They also had their schemes for the good of the commonwealth, but, standing closer to the Crown than the Commons did, they usually preferred that their clients and dependants in the lower house should take the initiative in proposing measures.

Elizabeth I had of necessity a profound respect for her Parliaments. They had found their strength, and were learning to make use of it. The Queen never openly flouted their wishes. She did treat them from time to time to well-deserved words of reproof, but she knew too how to win their affection and approval. On some matters in dispute (the prayer book in 1559, the fate of Mary of Scotland in 1587, the question of monopolies in 1601), she gave way, on others (her marriage and the succession), she successfully postponed any decision until it was too late to matter. But she never lost the respect and general approbation of her Parliament. When in 1604 the Commons told James I that they had not pressed certain matters in the old Queen's time out of consideration for her age and sex, they were not being entirely frank. It would have been truer to have said that the Queen had handled them so well that they had not realised how vital to them these issues were. Now that the Queen's magic touch had been removed the day of decision could no longer be postponed. The extent and nature of the change that had come over Parliament so gradually and so undramatically under the Tudors was to be revealed with startling suddenness when it had to work with a monarch who had not grown up with it, and who had had no opportunity of learning the difficult art of keeping it in its place.

# 5

## *Ecclesia Anglicana*

THE SIXTEENTH CENTURY was above all the century of the reformation. We have already had quite a lot to say about Henry VIII's Long Parliament of 1529–36 which is often known as the "Reformation Parliament". But the movement which we call the English reformation merely began with the proceedings of that Parliament, and we shall find that the question of the church, its relationship with the state, its own internal organisation and the form of services to be used, came up again and again throughout the following reigns with such persistence that it is difficult to say when, if ever, the process of the reformation came to an end.

### The English Reformation

It would certainly be misleading to suggest that the English reformation reached its fulfilment in the Elizabethan church settlement, for that would be to discount the very extensive influence of the Puritans in subsequent years. Perhaps the year 1662, when the prayer book was re-introduced after the restoration of Charles II, could be accepted as marking the end of the formative period of the Anglican church, or perhaps the year 1689, with its recognition in the Toleration Act of the inevitability of dissent; but whatever terminal date we choose for the English reformation it clearly must lie well beyond our present period. Down to the end of Elizabeth's reign the English church was still in flux, and so for most of the Tudor period the question of the church remained one of the foremost in men's minds. In the course of this and the following chapters we shall consider the changes that were wrought in the church in England during the sixteenth century, thinking of them, however, not as a complete process in themselves, but only as the first stages of a movement which was to continue well into the following century.

It must, however, be made clear at the outset that the word "reformation" is used throughout this book in the neutral sense which is commonly adopted by historians today, to mean "a change in form" without necessarily implying that that change was for the better. Using the word in this impartial manner we can then enquire without prejudice what changes occurred in the organisation, doctrine and ritual of the English church at the time of the reformation in the sixteenth century.

Leaving aside for the moment the fluctuations between Edwardian protestantism and Marian catholicism in mid-century, we can say briefly that there were three main differences between the English church as it stood in 1500 and in 1600. By the latter year it had acquired a national organisation with the monarch as supreme authority in place of the old international organisation under the supremacy of the Pope; it had adopted a service book in the English tongue to replace the older Latin forms; and it had accepted an English version of the scriptures in place of the Latin Bible. Let us take each of these changes in turn, and examine it a little more closely.

## THE SUPREMACY

Nowadays when one thinks of the position the Pope occupies in the Roman Catholic church, when one thinks of what is meant by "papal supremacy", one probably thinks first of the spiritual and moral leadership of the Pope, of the importance to all Roman Catholics of any pronouncement by him upon a matter of doctrine, or of any papal directives touching upon personal, or even political, behaviour. In this close and continuous guidance of the church of which he is the head, the Pope is in a real sense the pastor of his widespread flock. This is what papal supremacy probably means to most people today.

### Papal Supremacy in the Sixteenth Century

When Henry VIII claimed for himself the headship of the church in England and rejected the papal claim to supremacy, it is most unlikely that he was thinking in terms either of faith or of morals. The need for a continuously acting authority in such matters was not felt nearly so pressingly in the earlier part of the sixteenth century. Western Christendom was still a unity, sharing the one faith and following the one moral code. That faith and that moral law were part of the inherited tradition of every man. It was difficult to believe that there could arise any disputes which could not be quite simply settled in the time-honoured way, by the bishops in their dioceses, by the provincial convocations, or, in trickier points of doctrine, by debate among the theologians in the universities. The wisdom of preceding generations of faithful churchmen was to be found in the records of general and provincial councils, and in collections of papal decrees. The faith was well enough defined. Did it matter much whether a pope or a general council or some other body had the last word, for would they not all be in agreement as to what men should believe and do? The question of authority, which had been important in the previous century at the time of the great councils of Constance and Basle, was dormant until the Lutheran rejection of papal condemnation stirred it into life again.

Now Henry VIII was no Lutheran. He was quite satisfied in his own mind, as were many of his bishops, that Luther was in error on most of the points on which he differed from the authorities of his day. And yet Henry, like Luther, rejected papal authority. But the authority which Henry rejected was of a kind different from that with which Luther was concerned. The German theologian challenged the Pope's right to condemn his opinions on matters of doctrine. The English King rejected the Pope's judicial power, his *potestas juris-dictionis,* his power to act as supreme ecclesiastical judge, and to have his decrees and orders obeyed in England.

What Henry objected to becomes clearer when we bear in mind the nature and scope of the church courts at this time. We have already seen in an earlier chapter (chapter 2) something of their influence. Every Englishman, from the days of the conversion down to the nineteenth century, was subject to two laws, that of the state and that of the church. There was no escaping either, for the church was all-embracing, just like the state, and was not a voluntary organisation to be entered or left according to the individual's choice. You could no more avoid being subject to the laws of the church than you could to the laws of the state. Church and state each had its own courts to enforce obedience to its laws, and each set of courts had its system of appeal for dissatisfied litigants from lower courts to higher. But here lay the difference. In the case of the state, the King was the supreme judge and there was no appeal beyond his authority. In the church courts, on the other hand, appeal lay to the archbishops, and beyond them to the Pope. Thus the state courts were organised on a national basis while the church courts were part of an international system with its centre in Rome. What Henry VIII wanted was to "nationalise" the English church and to make himself supreme ecclesiastical as well as supreme secular judge, so that every authority in his kingdom would be truly subject to him; so that he would be effective master in his own house.

To achieve this purpose Henry had not only to cut the links between the English church courts and Rome by the Act in Restraint of Appeals (24 Henry VIII cap. 12), but also to impose his veto upon the making of ecclesiastical law in England by subjecting the convocations of the two English provinces of Canterbury and York to the same dependence upon the Crown as Parliament already enjoyed. This he achieved by the Submission of the Clergy in 1532.

## King Henry's Marriage

Here we can see where Henry's famous matrimonial troubles came in. His desire to secure a separation from his first wife, Catherine of Aragon, in order to marry Anne Boleyn, whether it sprang from base motives of self-gratification, or from a noble concern for the peace of his kingdom which made it imperative that he should have a son to succeed him, was frustrated persistently by papal indecision for six long years. It was not that Henry was asking for a lot. Several royal personages with cases nowhere near as convincing as Henry's had experienced little difficulty in obtaining the papal verdict they desired. But the intervention of Catherine's nephew,[1] the Emperor Charles V, and the failure of Pope Clement VII to realise how determined Henry was to have his way, led to this frustrating prolongation of the proceedings,

[1] See genealogical table No. 4 in Appendix B, p. 235.

and brought home to Henry how little he was master in his own dominions when his (to him) reasonable desires in the matter of his marriage could be for so long obstructed by a distant Pope. The Aragon marriage question could not of itself have brought about the English reformation but it most certainly acted as the trigger to set it off.

Earlier in his reign Henry VIII had been the self-appointed champion of the papacy. His book against Luther (the *Assertio Septem Sacramentorum* of 1521) had won the Pope's approval and the grant of the title *Fidei Defensor* (defender of the faith) which has been borne by every English monarch since. Later, when Henry split with the Pope, he did not in his own mind cease to be the defender of the faith.

> Though we be slipped from the obedience of Rome, yet we be not slipped *a fide Romana nec a Petri cathedra*. We observe and keep the same faith which from the beginning has been taught in Rome[2]

wrote one of his apologists in 1536.

## The Royal Headship

The general acceptance of this change in the headship of the church in England in Henry VIII's reign was facilitated partly by the fact that it made little practical difference to most people, and partly by the fact that the monarchy already possessed in the eyes of most people certain features analogous to the priesthood. Kings were becoming a race apart from ordinary men. They underwent, at coronation, a solemn ritual anointing and consecration very similar in form and symbolism to the act of ordination by which a man was made a priest. It was, because of this, not too difficult to accept the idea which Henry wanted to foster, that kings possessed, by the gift of God, spiritual as well as secular powers, that they had, as it were, two capacities, being at one and the same time both churchmen and laymen, and supreme over all their subjects of both kinds. The theory of the Henrician state is most clearly set out in the preamble to the Act in Restraint of Appeals to which reference has already been

[2] Thomas Starkey to Cardinal Pole. Strype, J., *Ecclesiastical Memorials*, vol. I, part II, p. 284.

made. "This realm of England is an Empire (by which is meant that no alien earthly power has dominion over it),

governed by one supreme head and king . . . (and) divided in terms, and by names of Spirituality and Temporality" (church and state).

And yet the church was not in consequence subjected to the state. It stood, in theory, on a level with the state, two bodies co-equal in authority and sharing the same head; an ideal arrangement which should have avoided for the future any of those disputes between the two jurisdictions such as that which had led to the murder of Beckett in Henry II's reign. However, the theory was not strictly followed in practice. Henry's manner of exercising his supremacy was inconsistent and variable. Sometimes he kept fairly close to the theoretical division, governing the church through the bishops and convocation and the state through council and Parliament. On other occasions, notably that of the Six Articles in 1539, he let Parliament step in and lay down the law to the church. On yet other occasions, such as the examination of John Lambert for heresy, he intervened in a very personal way. All this variety of method has made it possible for very different views to be adopted about what Henry believed his royal supremacy amounted to. But Henry was a pragmatist rather than a theorist, and was more concerned to get things done than to be sure that he did them in the right way.

To accept an adult king as head of the church was not, for the reasons given above, too difficult for most Englishmen. But to accept the delegation of this royal ecclesiastical power to a layman, Thomas Cromwell, was not quite so easy. Then when Henry died and was succeeded by his nine-year-old son there were many who held with Stephen Gardiner that the headship of the church was so intimately associated with the person of the anointed monarch that it could not be exercised for him by the council during his minority but must remain in abeyance until he came of age. Protector Somerset did not agree with this view, and his use, in the King's name, of the supremacy to advance the cause of protestantism in England, confirmed many of the former supporters of Henry VIII in their misgivings about this power, so that they were quite glad when Mary decided to abandon it and to re-accept the headship of the Pope.

## The Elizabethan Supremacy

When Elizabeth succeeded Mary and chose to re-assert the royal supremacy, yet another problem arose. No woman could be a priest, could a woman, even an anointed queen, be head of the English church? It was the expression of this kind of doubt which persuaded Elizabeth to alter her style and to take instead of the title of supreme head that of supreme governor which was less offensive as it so clearly implied an assertion of the *potestas jurisdictionis* alone, and made no claim to any organic headship. Elizabeth further defined her position in her first injunctions, those of 1559, in which she said that she did not claim:

> authority and power of ministry of divine service in the church

but only that authority:

> which is and was of ancient time due to the imperial crown of this realm, that is, under God, to have the sovereignty and rule over all manner of persons born within these realms.

Of course the situation in Europe in 1559 when Elizabeth reasserted the supremacy was rather different from that in 1531 when Henry VIII had first claimed it. In the interim the quarrel between the supporters and opponents of Luther had widened, and the question of authority had come to the forefront of men's minds. By what test could one choose between the contestants in the great debate? Was Luther right to deny to the Pope the power to speak as the voice of the church in matters of doctrine? Was the voice of the church not most clearly heard in the proceedings of a general council? Was that council which the Pope had eventually summoned (the council of Trent) a true general council, or was it not, because it had been summoned by the Pope, a prejudiced assembly which was bound to give its verdict in his favour? But how else could a general council be summoned, save by a Pope? These were some of the questions men were asking.

In the event England and the Lutherans chose to disregard the council of Trent. Meanwhile a new authority was gaining adherents, that of John Calvin. By the second half of the sixteenth century the prestige of this eloquent reformation theologian had given his thoughts and writings an almost unchallenged supremacy in many parts of Europe, including England. The choice before Elizabeth at her accession was virtually between the rival authorities of the Pope in Rome and Calvin in Geneva, and yet Elizabeth accepted neither. Once she had secured recognition of her supreme governorship over church and state she was concerned only with the "face of religion", that is to say, with maintaining a satisfactory degree of uniformity in practice and observance so that religious harmony might prevail throughout her kingdom. With the finer points of doctrine she was less concerned. The thirty-nine articles, when at last the Queen could be persuaded to enforce them, provided a very broad definition of the faith to which few professing Christians could take exception. Elizabeth's supreme governorship was not authoritarian in faith and morals. It was a regulating power concerned mainly with practices and observances, with order and decency.

Elizabeth was more consistent than her father had been in the manner in which she governed the church. Parliament, though it had been associated with the Queen in the first making of the settlement which was contained in the Acts of Supremacy and Uniformity of 1559 (1 Elizabeth caps. 1 & 2), was thereafter repeatedly warned that it had no concern with church matters. It was through the bishops and convocation and her ecclesiastical commissioners that Elizabeth governed her church, trying at all times to keep her secular and her spiritual powers separate and distinct. For the most part she succeeded and the church in her reign retained its independence of the state. The Puritans and their friends in Parliament did not like this. Having failed to capture convocation in 1563 their constant endeavour was to use the authority of Parliament to remould the Elizabethan church into a shape more to their liking. But Elizabeth stood firm, and with the aid of such bishops as Whitgift* and Bancroft conducted a very successful defence of her supremacy.

## THE PRAYER BOOK

The church order which Elizabeth at all times sought to enforce was that set out in the Book of Common Prayer prescribed by the Act of Uniformity in 1559. This book had its origins in the earlier prayer books of the reign of Edward VI, and they, in their turn, owed a great deal to the older Latin service books.

## The Edwardian Prayer Books

Cranmer's* first prayer book, that of 1549, was not primarily a work of original composition. The archbishop did not sit down to write a completely fresh liturgy. He had certain models before him, and the chief of these was the Sarum Use, the form of the mass and daily offices in Latin first adopted in Salisbury cathedral and from there spread by imitation over the greater part of England.

But Cranmer did not simply translate the Sarum Use into English, though he did follow the pattern of his original fairly closely. He was a reviser as well as a translator, and by his revisions he sought to do two things. First, as he himself explained in his preface (which you may still read in the present prayer book under the title "Concerning the Service of the Church"), he wished to simplify the rather complex succession of services and special commemorations. This he did by reducing the daily offices to two, by rearranging the readings from scripture and by reducing the number of variable portions in the mass.

In the second place, as becomes apparent from a close study of his choice of words, particularly in those places where he was not simply translating from the Latin, he wanted to change the significance of certain services so that they would no longer be capable of being interpreted in what he considered to be the wrong way. Thus, in the English mass of 1549 there is a great deal of emphasis upon the uniqueness of Christ's sacrifice on Calvary. The phrase:

who made there by his *one* oblation of himself *once* offered a *full* perfect and sufficient sacrifice

is Cranmer's own and is not to be found in the Sarum Use. This very explicit statement was directed against those who held that the sacrifice of Christ was in some way repeated in every mass.

It was this kind of verbal revision which aroused most

controversy. There were few who objected to having the prayers of the church in the language of the people, or who complained about the introduction of a less complex scheme of services. Nor was there anything particularly "Protestant" about doing either of these two things. One of the earliest of the sixteenth-century experiments with a simplified vernacular liturgy had taken place in Catholic Spain. But when alterations of substance were made which implied changes in the theology behind the book, then there were more objections, and controversy quickly developed between those who disapproved of the changes, those who accepted them, and those who were dissatisfied with them because they did not go far enough.

Cranmer's second prayer book, that of 1552, contained many more of these significant changes, designed this time to make the use of the book incompatible with belief in any substantial presence of the Body and Blood of Christ in the consecrated eucharistic elements of bread and wine, for Cranmer's theology had now moved in this direction. And further to emphasise that the new communion service (as it was now called) was no mere translation of the mass, though it still followed its main outlines and preserved many of its prayers, care was taken to alter the outward appearance of the service by requiring the clergy to wear plain surplices in place of the more ornate mass vestments, by pulling down the stone altars and replacing them with movable wooden tables, and by ordering the use of household bread instead of the specially prepared wafers.

Thus the 1552 prayer book made a clean break with the old ways which must have been obvious to all who used it or attended services held according to its provisions. It had a decidedly Protestant flavour, and yet even it did not satisfy the more radical of contemporary English Protestants who still found too many relics of the old ways in it. These men, who withdrew to the continent in Mary's reign to escape the reintroduction of catholicism, took the opportunity provided by their exile to make further alterations in the Edwardian prayer books they took with them, and produced the "Frankfort Order" and the "Geneva Order", each more radical than the book of 1552.

## The Elizabethan Prayer Book

When the death of Mary and the accession of Elizabeth brought these exiles flocking back to England, it was one of their dearest ambitions to persuade the new Queen to impose one of their revised liturgies upon her people. But they under-estimated the opposition of Elizabeth herself who would prob-ably have preferred the book of 1549, and in any case was reluctant to introduce a prayer book straight away or to make too many changes too quickly. The exiles did gain an important concession from the Queen when pressure from her first Parliament obliged her to introduce a prayer book at the same time as she re-asserted her supremacy, but they had in turn to make concessions to Elizabeth and to be content with an amended version of the 1552 book in which the alterations were all designed to make it more acceptable to the more conservative of the Queen's subjects who still wished to find the substance of the Body and Blood of Christ in the elements of the eucharist. This 1559 prayer book, which has come down to the present day with only minor modifications, was the real compromise of the Elizabethan church settlement. A Protestant book, modified to accommodate Catholic suscepti-bilities, it has since been capable of being read in the most widely divergent manners.

### THE BIBLE

The third characteristic which we said distinguished the re-formed church of England from the pre-reformation church in England was the possession and widespread distribution of the Bible in the English tongue. As a vernacular prayer book is not necessarily a sign of protestantism, neither is a vernacular Bible, but the close association of Wycliffe's Lollard move-ment with the translation and distribution of the Bible, and the fact that in the fifteenth and early sixteenth centuries virtually the only version of the scriptures available in English was that from the pen of this arch-heretic, tended to make the ecclesiastical authorities of those generations associate translators with heresy.

## Tyndale and the Bible

This being so it should not surprise us to learn that when the

young William Tyndale, filled with a sense of shame because of
the ignorance of the contents of the Bible displayed by most
of the laity and many of the clergy, determined to make it his
life's work to remedy this defect by providing them with an
up-to-date English version, and turned to the scholarly Bishop
Tunstall of London for patronage and support, he met with no
encouragement. But Tyndale was not easily discouraged, and,
finding other patrons among the merchants of London, he
settled down abroad, at Wittenberg and Worms, out of reach
of the English ecclesiastical authorities, to carry out the great
task to which he felt himself called.

Tyndale was a pioneer worker and a good scholar, well able
to go behind the generally accepted Latin version and to work
from the best available Greek and Hebrew texts. He began
with the New Testament, and by 1526 copies of his translation of it were on sale in England. But Tyndale destroyed
whatever chance his work had of acceptance by English authorities by his tendentious notes and comments upon his
text, and by his other controversial writings such as *The Practice of Prelates* which marked him as a man out of sympathy
with the existing ecclesiastical order. Once again an English
version of the scriptures had come from the pen of a heretic
and was circulating among his followers. Tyndale's translation
was condemned. The bishops did their best to buy it up and
destroy it.

## The Great Bible

The men who eventually persuaded Henry VIII to change
his mind and give his permission for the printing and circulation of an English Bible were Cranmer and Cromwell. The
former, who enjoyed the confidence, and even the respect and
affection, of the King, was able to convince him that the only
way to combat what he regarded as the malign influence of
unauthorised versions was to provide an approved translation,
free from such undesirable additions as the notes and com-
mentaries which marred, in official eyes, the work of Tyndale.
Cromwell for his part probably explained the extent of the
demand for such a version, and how much it would bind his
subjects in affection to him if he, the newly proclaimed head
of the church, should be the one to give them what they so
clearly desired. The desired permission was given in 1537, but

delays over printing held up the actual publication of the Great Bible until 1539.

By then there were other versions besides Tyndale's in circulation. To the pioneer's New Testament and part translation of the Old, Miles Coverdale had added his own version of the remaining books, making stylistic alterations also in his predecessor's work, and publishing the result in 1536. Coverdale's Bible had then in its turn been subjected to similar treatment by John Rogers who added his own version of the Apocrypha and published the whole under the pseudonym of Matthew in 1537. The new official version drew upon all these sources, and had Coverdale himself as one of the supervisory editors. Thus the English Bible was the work of many hands, though perhaps the greatest part of the credit should go to Tyndale who first projected the work, whose enthusiasm inspired his collaborators and imitators, and whose very words and phrases have in many places survived all subsequent revisions.

For Henry's and Edward's reigns the Great Bible was enough. Every parish was ordered in 1538 to purchase one and to set it up in the church for all to read. Many persons came in addition to possess their own, and even though the ownership and use of English Bibles was restricted by law in 1543, England was already well on the way to becoming a nation of Bible-readers. With the Bible in his hands the religious-minded layman could feel so much less dependent upon the priest. With the Word of God set out in a language he could read and understand he was able now to chart the course of his life according to his own ideas about its meaning without so frequent recourse to the priestly pilot to tell him what the Bible said. Thus the English version of the Bible contributed in its own way to that emancipation of the laity of which we wrote in chapter 2.

To round off the story of the English Bible in the sixteenth century it is only necessary to notice the appearance in the reign of Elizabeth of three new versions. The first to appear, in 1560, was the "Geneva Bible", so called because it was produced by a group of English Protestants in temporary exile in that city. The second in point of time was the "Bishops' Bible", a revised official version which was published in 1568 and authorised for use in churches in 1571. Last to appear was the "Douai" New Testament which was the work of a group of English Catholic refugees, and was published in 1582. The Douai version of the Old Testament did not appear until after the death of Elizabeth.

All three of these translations were to have their influence upon the compilers of the Authorised Version in the reign of James I, but the one which secured the widest readership in Elizabeth's reign was probably the Geneva version. Coming as it did from the city of Calvin it met with the approval of even the most radical of English puritans. Furthermore it was published in a smaller size more suited to the purses and pockets of private persons than the massive folio of the official version.

# 6

## The Plundering of the Church

IN TREATING OF the English reformation in the last chapter we concentrated our attention upon what might be called the positive side of it, that is to say we concerned ourselves solely with those things which the church in England acquired in the Tudor period (the royal supremacy, the prayer book and the English Bible), and said nothing about the losses sustained by the church during the same period. The purpose of this chapter is to examine this, the reverse side of the reformation, and to see what was taken from the church, and why.

### The Dissolution of the Monasteries

The most obvious loss was in the disappearance of the religious orders, the monks, nuns, canons and friars. We have already mentioned in an earlier chapter (chapter 2) the effect of this in reducing the number of clergy in the kingdom, and in restricting the opportunities for promotion in the church. Now we must look at the dissolution of the monasteries a little more closely, and ask, in the first place, why it took place. Why were the religious orders, which had played so large a part in the life of the English church for so many centuries, so suddenly abolished and their property seized in the years 1536–40? We must be careful in our answer to this question to try to distinguish between the alleged and the actual reasons.

### The Reasons for the Dissolution; Alleged and Actual

Some would have us believe that the dissolution of the monasteries was an act of reform. This is the line that Henry VIII and his ministers took. The Dissolution Statute of 1536

(27 Henry VIII cap. 28) speaks of the "vicious, carnal and abominable" living of the monks and nuns, and the reports of the royal visitors sent out in 1535 to inspect the monasteries support in detail this very general assertion. If the religious orders had so far forgotten the high ideals of their founders and so generally ignored the strict rules of conduct provided for their guidance, if they had become self-indulgent drones living in idleness and vice upon the proceeds of centuries of pious benefactions, was it not better that they should be turned out of doors and their wealth redirected to other and better purposes? So ran the official government line, which was also adopted by such popular pamphlets as Simon Fish's *Supplication of the Beggars*.

But most of our evidence for monastic misbehaviour comes from royally inspired sources, and we are quite at liberty to regard it all as so much anti-monastic propaganda designed deliberately to make easier the fulfilment of the government's plan for the expropriation of the religious orders. Such independent testimony as we have, in the form of the records of bishops' visitations, while it makes it clear that not all the monks and nuns were saints, does not confirm the totally black picture painted by the royal visitors. Clearly, with certain notable exceptions such as the Carthusians, the Bridgettines and the Observant Franciscans, there was room for reform within the religious orders in England (what human institution in any age is so perfect as to need no reform?), but was it really necessary that that reform should take the drastic shape of total extinction?

Others suggest that the attack upon the monasteries was a necessary consequence of the severance of England from the Roman obedience. They argue that, as potential supporters of the papacy in any attempt it might make to recover its authority over England, the religious orders were a threat to the new régime which had to be eliminated if the royal headship was to be secure. Now it is true that a high proportion of those who suffered execution for refusing to accept the royal supremacy were monks and friars, but, on the other hand, those executed were only a handful out of the thousands of religious in the kingdom. And the significant fact is that most of these executions took place *before* the dissolution of the monasteries began. It was in 1534 that the Succession Act (25

Henry VIII cap. 22) imposed upon every Englishman the need, if tendered it, to take an oath accepting the validity of the King's second marriage and, by implication, rejecting the authority of the Pope who had given his judgment against it. It was in the autumn of the same year, and in 1535, that royal commissioners toured the kingdom, tendering and recording acceptance of this oath. Every monk and nun was offered the oath, and the only ones who found any difficulty in taking it were some of the members of those three orders which we have already noticed as the most conscientious in the observance of their rules, and they constituted only a small fraction of the monastic population as they had only a handful of houses between them. The vast majority of the monks and nuns accepted the royal supremacy without demur. They certainly showed no signs of being potential supporters of the papal claims. The argument that it was the papalism of the religious orders which was their undoing is difficult to sustain in the face of these facts.

We are left then with the only reason for the suppression which can hardly be disputed, the financial. The wealth of the monasteries, mostly in the form of land, was, taken as a whole, considerable. This is not to say that every individual monastery was well endowed. Some of the humbler and obscurer institutions, particularly among the nunneries, possessed no more than a few acres of demesne land whose produce could hardly have provided them with more than the most meagre subsistence. But the greater and more famous houses, those whose names are remembered and whose ruins still grace our landscape, were landowners on a large scale, often possessing, in addition to large demesnes, distant granges and even extensive properties in adjacent towns. To a monarch who was finding it progressively more difficult to balance his budget the monasteries were a tempting prize. The reputation of the monks was already under attack, for others besides the King were envious of their wealth. A little astute propaganda could soon destroy what little credit they had left. There would be few to defend the monks, or to regret their passing. Other princes had already shown what could be done. In Sweden, Gustavus Vasa had financed his usurped kingship and purchased the support of the nobility out of the spoil of the monasteries in 1527. Several German princes had already taken advantage of the anti-monastic elements in Lutheranism to do much the same thing. Might not the King of England have a try?

## Dissolution by Degrees

The first step in the process of the dissolution was to despatch commissioners throughout the country to compile an up-to-date survey of ecclesiastical wealth of all kinds. This, the great survey of 1535 which led to the compilation of the *Valor Ecclesiasticus,* devoted particular attention to the income and resources of the monasteries. Then, hard on the heels of the valuation commissioners, went the royal monastic visitors searching out what scandal they could, and conducting a vigorous campaign of denigration. Their activities occupied the autumn and winter of 1535–6. Then, almost before the visitors had finished their work, there passed through Parliament in the spring of 1536 the Act to dissolve the lesser monasteries.

The preamble to this statute had a lot to say, as we have already indicated, about the moral laxity allegedly to be found in the smaller religious houses. This was made the main reason for the forfeiture of their property and the dispersal of their inhabitants. But when it came to choosing between those houses worthy of suppression and those to be left untouched, it was not the visitors' reports that were to be the guide, but the findings of the valuation commissioners. It was not the morally degenerate houses which were to be suppressed, but those which had been valued at less than £200 a year net income. In practice this meant that many a monastery in which the royal visitors had found no evil was dissolved, while others which had been the subjects of the blackest reports were left alone. This inconsistency in the Act itself reveals the hollowness of the official case against the monasteries. Clearly all this talk of wickedness and vice was so much window-dressing. The selection of a purely financial line to distinguish between those to be condemned and those to be spared shows only too plainly in what direction the real interest of the government lay.

In the event the Act of 1536 was to prove to be no more than the climax of the first stage in the process of the Dissolution. And yet there are definite signs that no more than a partial dissolution was at first intended. For one thing, the Dissolution Act gave to every monk and nun who did not wish to abandon the religious way of life when his or her convent was suppressed, the chance of moving to another cloister. There would have been little point in permitting such transfers if it had already been decided to suppress all the monasteries. The decision to make an end of the religious houses altogether seems to have been taken early in 1538, that is about a year after the successful crushing of the Pilgrimage of Grace which had been, in part, a protest against the earlier dissolutions. From 1538 onwards monastery after monastery was persuaded "voluntarily" to yield its properties to the Crown and to accept the dispersal of its inhabitants. Now no monks or nuns were sent to other houses. Instead they all got pensions by way of compensation for the loss of their living in the cloister. By 1540 the process of suppression was complete. Some reluctant abbots, such as those of Glastonbury, Reading and Colchester, had to be hanged before their houses could be suppressed, but most monks and nuns were more ready to co-operate and content to take their pensions and go. By 1540 there was not an abbey left in England. In four short years what had begun as a tentative piece of nationalisation had become a wholesale dissolution.

## The Profit to the Crown

What did the Crown gain from all this? Not as much as at first sight might appear. It is true that all the property of the religious orders became at one stage or another the property of the Crown. But the Crown did not only take over the assets of the monasteries, it also assumed their liabilities. What did these liabilities amount to? In the first place, the payment of all outstanding debts, which might be considerable. In the second place, where appropriate, the payment of pensions for life to the former monks and nuns. In the third place, the continuation for life of the fees paid to the more important lay officers (stewards, receivers and bailiffs) who had been associated with the administration of the monastic estates. Generally these offices were held by local gentry whose vested interest had to be respected if the suppression policy of the Crown was to meet with the approval of the representatives of their class in Parliament. In the fourth place it was also necessary to honour for life all annuities charged upon abbey funds. Normally these annuities were purchased by the making of a substantial single payment to the monks who then undertook to pay the purchaser a lesser sum annually for the rest of his life, the whole arrangement being very similar to that which can be made with most insurance companies today. Despite the careful provisions of the suppression Acts against fraudulent annuities it is clear, from the very considerable sums payable under this head after the dissolution, that many monks, when they knew that their house was condemned, granted their lay neighbours annuities on very favourable terms. Altogether, in debts, pensions, fees and annuities, the charge upon the estates of a particular monastery could often add up to the greater part of the income of the house, and even in some extreme cases amount to more than the house was worth. Thus the immediate profit to the Crown was sometimes very little indeed.

Yet, in the long run, as pensioners, ex-officers and annuitants died off, and the charge upon the estates was reduced, the Crown could have been considerably the richer. Thomas Cromwell, had he lived, might have handled the monastic estates as a long-term investment. While he was in charge there were few sales of monastic lands, most of the property being leased out for a term of years. But after the fall of Cromwell in 1540 this cautious policy was abandoned, and outright sales by the Crown, by which it gained a substantial sum in hand but lost the future income, became the order of the day. This tendency was confirmed by the financial pressure of the French war of 1543–5, and by the end of Henry's reign a very substantial proportion of the monastic estates had been disposed of by sale. The financial difficulties of the following reign assured the continuation of this trend, and the Crown enjoyed no substantial permanent augmentation of income as a result of the suppression, but only a temporary escape from bankruptcy.

These sales, however, were to prove important in another way. Those who bought monastic land for good money (and they were the majority of the purchasers, for there were very few cheap sales to Court favourites), bought also a vested interest in the suppression and, indirectly, in the royal supremacy. Any talk of a return to the Roman obedience made them anxious about their title to their estates, and, even as late as 1829, we can find written into the Catholic Emancipation Act a clause which still reflects this very same anxiety and seeks to protect "the settlement of property" within the kingdom.

The purchasers of monastic lands were not, as you will often find it asserted, for the most part "new men". They were the local landowners who knew the location and value of the monastic estates, and wished to round off their own lands, and had some spare capital to invest. The fact that they often used London merchants as agents in negotiating their purchases has led to some loose talk about "speculators" and "new gentry". Of course genuine cases of speculation can still be unearthed, but, pending further investigation of this subject, we must treat all apparent speculators with caution until we can establish their true relationship with their clients.

What justification, if any, was there for this great act of nationalisation which we call the dissolution of the monasteries? The government's case was that the monks and nuns were not putting their property to its proper use. But was the use to which the government chose to put the proceeds of the dissolution noticeably better? A substantial proportion of the money obtained from the sale of monastic lands was spent on national defence, on strengthening the navy, on improving the fortifications of Calais, Dover and Berwick and in augmenting the coastal defences in other regions. Some part of the former monastic endowments went to found new bishoprics, six in number, and thus improved the strength and internal organisation of the church. But, despite the impassioned pleas of men like Latimer for as much to be spent on education as was formerly spent:

> in pilgrimage matters, in trentals, in masses, in pardons, in purgatory matters

there is no evidence that any noticeable part of the spoils of the monasteries was devoted to the endowment of schools. Wolsey, who had set the King a small-scale example in monastic suppression in the 1520s, had planned to use the proceeds to found a school in Ipswich and a college in Oxford. The school never materialised. The college (Cardinal College it was to have been) was refounded by the King after Wolsey's fall, as Christ Church. No similar educational projects were under consideration in the 1540s. Some purchasers of monastic lands did eventually bequeath a portion of their purchase to the endowment of a school, but there was no deliberate government leadership in this direction. Most of the proceeds of the dissolution were absorbed into general government funds. It would be difficult to establish that the King put to a better use property which had hitherto been abused.

## The Fall of the Chantries

The dissolution of the religious orders, though the greatest, was not by any means the only expropriation which the church had to suffer in the Tudor period. Even before the end of Henry VIII's reign another round of confiscations was in contemplation, for the eyes of the government had turned upon the chantries. The financial mismanagement of Edward's reign sealed their fate.

The case against the chantries was set forth in the same high moral tones as that against the monasteries, and is to be taken with the same degree of caution. Now that belief in the ability of the prayers of the living to assist the souls of the departed along the difficult pathway to heaven was no longer officially approved, the chantry priests had lost their original and most important function, namely the offering up of a continual cycle of prayer for the souls of deceased benefactors. To permit them to continue to officiate would be to encourage beliefs and practices now held to be erroneous. And so the endowments of the chantries must be seized and the priests pensioned or found other employment.

But the chantry priests had never confined themselves entirely to their basic function. While in no way neglecting their daily masses, they frequently served the parish in other capacities. Many of them conducted schools, indeed the keeping of a school was sometimes required by the terms of the original foundation. In other instances where the income from the lands set aside for the endowment of the chantry was in excess of that necessary for the maintenance of the priest it was provided by the terms of the foundation that such surplus should be devoted to some useful secular purpose, such as the upkeep of the local bridge, the support of a hospital or the relief of the poor. In such cases, were the government to seize all the land nominally attached to the chantry, it would create considerable inconvenience, and perhaps even hardship. Consequently it is not surprising to find many local people fighting hard to preserve the chantry endowments from the grasping hand of the government. Some were successful, and saved their schools and bridges, but how many, or even what proportion, we cannot at present say with any confidence. What is clear, however, is that a considerable amount of property passed into the government's hands, and through them fairly rapidly into the hands of councillors and their friends.

## Church Furnishings

Only a few months after the putting into force of the Act for the dissolution of the chantries, the church was to suffer yet another series of confiscations in the seizure of such church furnishings and ornaments as were considered by the Edwardian authorities to be superfluous, or to tend to superstition.

In fairness to the Edwardian government it must be pointed out that this particular campaign had begun in the previous reign with Cromwell's attack upon the veneration of relics and the making of pilgrimages to the shrines where they were treasured. Once again, the alleged intention of the government had been to lead the people out of superstition, but as the attack had been concentrated chiefly upon such famous and richly adorned shrines as those of St Thomas at Canterbury and of Our Lady at Walsingham, it is hard to escape the conclusion that the value of the potential booty in precious metals and rich jewels had been as important as, if not more important than, the putting down of superstition in prompting the government to action.

The further seizures of plate, jewels, precious vestments and illuminated service books in the reign of Edward VI were also alleged to be necessary to prevent the continuance of practices now deemed to be superstitious and undesirable. Anything that might lead the unwary into the pitfalls of idolatry (pictures, images, crucifixes), had now to be removed from churches. Furthermore, the emphasis of the second prayer book, that of 1552, upon the break with the past, and its insistence upon a spartan simplicity in worship, rendered redundant all the vestments and many of the vessels which had formerly been in daily use. Lest the continued possession of these treasures should tempt anybody to an unauthorised continuance in the old ways, they were to be confiscated and deposited in the coffers of the state. There was no word of compensation for the loss of these valuables which represented the accumulation of centuries of pious gifts. There was no suggestion that the now redundant gilt and silver vessels might be melted down and recast in some acceptable form, such as that of an alms-dish. There was to be no alternative to confiscation. The government was, as before, more interested in the proceeds of the confiscation than in the abolition of superstition.

## First Fruits and Tenths

Monasteries, chantries, church goods, all were in succession swallowed by the rapacious jaws of an insatiable government. And yet at the very time that the first of these confiscations was in contemplation, that same government was in process of imposing upon the church a perpetual taxation more extensive than any it had previously experienced.

When we read in the preamble to the First Annates Act of 1532 (23 Henry VIII cap. 20) of the "great and inestimable sums of money daily conveyed" out of the kingdom to be lodged in the papal coffers in Rome, and of the plight of newly appointed bishops struggling to pay off the vast debts they were forced to contract in order to meet their obligation to pay a large proportion of their first year's income to the Pope in the form of the tax known as annates, we can almost shed a tear for the plight of the English clergy under papal financial oppression, and bless King Henry as their deliverer. But we must withhold our tears until we have looked at another Act, the First Fruits and Tenths Act (26 Henry VIII cap. 3) of two years later. *1534*

In 1532 the First Annates Act had threatened to withhold these payments from Rome. In the spring of 1534 the Second Annates Act (25 Henry VIII cap. 20) abolished annates altogether. For a few happy months the English clergy were able to forget all about them. But then, in the autumn of the same year, the bishops in Parliament gave their assent with the rest to a measure which not only revived the payment of annates for the benefit of the Crown, but increased the burden of clerical taxation threefold.

In the first place, papal annates had, in England, been demanded of the bishops alone, and not of the lesser clergy. The new royal first fruits were to be payable by all the clergy of every degree from the archbishops down to the humblest curate. In the second place, to the first fruits, laid upon new appointments, was added an annual tax of one-tenth of every ecclesiastical income. Of course papal tenths had been levied also in the past, and fairly frequently, but not in every year. The new royal tenths were to be annual and perpetual, the only concession being that contained in an Act of 1536 (27 Henry VIII cap. 8) which relieved those clergy who were liable for first fruits from also having to pay the tenth in the first year of their appointment. Even for Henry VIII it was too much to expect the clergy to pay both together. In the third place, whereas the papal tax collectors had been content to rely upon an out-of-date assessment, unchanged since 1292, the royal tax collectors were to begin by making a completely new survey of the wealth of the church so that the tax would really amount to one-tenth of current clerical income. How much greater and inestimable were the sums drawn by Henry VIII in taxation from the church compared with those papal impositions of which the First Annates Act had complained with such passion!

## Exchanges of Property

We have not yet reached the end of the story of the plundering of the church. If you examine the record from the reign of Henry VIII onwards you will see that from time to time the monarch effected exchanges of manors or other properties with some of his bishops or other ecclesiastical dignitaries. On the surface these transactions seem fair enough, as they were generally conducted on a "manor for manor" basis, and it might seem that all that was involved was the royal fancy which had fastened upon some attractive episcopal residence, or some convenient ecclesiastical estate, for the possession of which the King was prepared to give equivalent value. But the manor was not a neat or uniform economic unit, and could vary very considerably in size and profitability. If these apparently innocent exchanges of manors are looked into more closely it is soon apparent that in many cases the Crown was the gainer by the exchange. Queen Elizabeth was particularly adept at this game of exchanges which in the long run augmented the resources of the Crown at the expense of episcopal endowments.

In the reign of Edward VI, however, the secular authorities were not always careful thus to hide their rapaciousness behind a façade of fairness. They adopted the more drastic practice of confiscating the entire endowments of a vacant bishopric, putting the new bishop on a stipend considerably less in value than the income from the former properties of his see. Furthermore, in the case of two bishoprics, those of Westminster and Durham, they did not even bother to appoint a new bishop.

By all these methods then the wealth of the church was, during the course of the sixteenth century, passing into the hands of the government and the laity. The result can be seen in Elizabeth's reign. The princely bishops of pre-reformation times were no longer to be found. The senior clergy were still, it is true, quite well off, but were now completely outshone by the wealthier of the laymen. The fact that the clergy were now free to marry and have families to provide for did not help to improve the financial position of those who did so.

## Clerical Poverty, Impropriations and Lay Patronage

It was among the lower ranks of the clergy, however, that the real hardship was felt. The parochial clergy had never been particularly well off. When Parliament had made an attempt to restrict the practice of plurality (the holding of two or more clerical appointments at the same time) in 1529, it had recognised that the poorer livings in the church would never have a priest to serve them unless he could augment his income by serving more than one cure, and so had exempted from the no-pluralities rule all livings worth less than £8 a year. Between the reign of Henry VIII and that of Elizabeth the value of money had fallen steadily. In terms of what it could buy £8 was worth a lot less in 1579 than it had been in 1529. The poorer clergy were very poor indeed, and it is no wonder that the puritan critics of the church found the standard of education among the parochial clergy far from

<u>satisfactory</u>. Would men of education condescend to accept a country parsonage in return for so miserable a pittance?

Even the better-off clergy found the economic pressure severe. Many a bishop, dean or vicar, in order to get a little cash in hand, was obliged to let out part of the lands of his living, or the right to collect his tithes, on a long lease at a low rent in return for a substantial premium. This might save him from immediate bankruptcy, but made the position of his successor even more precarious. <u>This problem, of chronic clerical poverty,</u> was one which the Tudors passed on to the Stuarts. No real attempt was made to tackle it until the time of Archbishop Laud.

In some places the poverty of the lesser clergy was aggravated by the fact that in some previous generation the ancient right of the parish priest to collect from his parishioners a tithe in kind of each of their crops had been converted, by agreement, into an annual money payment, fixed in amount. With the fall in the value of money in the sixteenth century this put at a grave disadvantage those incumbents who were bound by this kind of commutation agreement when compared with those who could still claim an actual tenth of the produce of their parish.

In other parishes the situation of the incumbent was little better because a substantial proportion of the parochial tithes was syphoned off into the pockets of a lay impropriator. These impropriators were not necessarily the wicked grasping misers that some would have us believe in, but simply the inheritors of a system established long before the reformation as a means of augmenting the income of religious houses in financial difficulties. Such monasteries were from time to time granted the right to collect the tithes of one or more, usually neighbouring, parishes, and would undertake in return to provide for the spiritual care of the parishioners by the appointment of a vicar, who, however, was paid a stipend considerably less in value than the estimated yield of the tithe. The balance between tithe and stipend became part of the regular income of the religious house concerned, and the right to collect the tithe would, at the time of the dissolution, pass with the rest of the property of the monastery through the hands of the Crown into those of the subsequent purchaser. The purchaser, of course, was expected to assume the duties as well as the rights of the former monastery, but until, in the time of Archbishop Laud, the bishops began to remind him of these duties (such as that of keeping the chancel of the parish church in good repair), he was frequently inclined to forget them.

Lay patronage, which is sometimes mistakenly associated with lay impropriation, was not a product of the reformation. From the earliest times it had been the practice that the man who first gave land to the church for the endowment of a living should, with his heirs and successors after him, have the right to nominate the successor to a defunct or departed incumbent. This right to present, or "advowson", was treated in law as a piece of property which could be bought, sold and bequeathed, and many advowsons came in the course of time into the possession of Oxford and Cambridge colleges, and of the Crown.

The Crown, as the theoretical founder of all the bishoprics, regularly exercised, even before the reformation, the power to appoint to vacant sees. The form of election by the cathedral chapter was still preserved, but it was the custom for the king to signify his choice of candidate to the chapter, and for them to endorse that choice. This endorsement was made obligatory by the Second Annates Act of 1534, and the system of appointment then established is that which operates today.

The Crown of course possessed, and still possesses, extensive patronage over lesser church appointments as well as bishoprics, and this patronage is not, and never was, dependent upon the fact that the monarch is supreme governor of the church, but is the consequence of a lay influence in ecclesiastical affairs which is shared by many lesser lay patrons, and which antedates by many centuries the century of the reformation.

# 7

## *The Rise of Puritanism*

IN THE PREVIOUS two chapters we have followed the modern tendency to play down the importance of the purely religious factor in the English reformation, and have discussed it largely in terms of politics and economics. Were we to leave it at that we should scarcely be giving an adequate account of a movement which was after all primarily religious. Without the support of the considerable number of people who were in one degree or another dissatisfied with the structure, practices and beliefs of the existing church, none of the changes in its organisation, or of the acts of confiscation which we have described, could have been carried out. The religious movement may have been influenced and directed towards certain ends by men who had little of religion in them, but to admit that is not to deny that there was any religious movement at all.

### *The Survival of Lollardy*

The religious side of the English reformation is most easily traced in the early history of puritanism, that movement in belief, thought and practice which was the spiritual ancestor of later non-conformity, and was to have such a profound influence upon so many aspects of English life. Whence did puritanism take its origin? This is the first question which must be faced. Was it a growth native to England, or was it a seed planted by an alien hand?

Both these questions have been answered at various times in the affirmative. Some have seen in early Tudor England a nation so devout and orthodox that "protestantism" or "puritanism" could hardly have been a native growth, but must have been imported ready-made from the university towns and ports of Germany. Others have reminded us that a century and a half earlier England had produced, in John Wycliffe, a very notable heretic and forerunner of the reformation whose followers, the Lollards, though driven underground by persecution, lived on in hope of a better day which came at last when Henry VIII broke with Rome.

As so often is the case each view has a lot to recommend it, but the truth lies somewhere between. Recent local studies have demonstrated the existence, in the earlier years of the sixteenth century, of a small but important element of religious dissent of the Lollard kind at a time when the name, let alone the message, of Martin Luther could not yet have been heard in England. This same kind of heresy continues to be found right through the 1520s and into the '30s. By then, of course, the name and the writings of Luther were well known in England and no one can say how much of this dissent was now due to his influence, and how much was simply the survival of the Lollard tradition, for the Lutherans and Lollards shared many points in common, notably a dislike of indulgences, relics and pilgrimages.

Lollard belief about the sacrament was, however, more akin to the more extreme protestantism of Zwingli or Calvin than to the more moderate views of Luther. And so, where we find a denial of the Real Presence on the lips of an English heretic in the 1520s we can be fairly sure that he is more of a Lollard than a Lutheran. Lollardy also bred in its adherents a lack of respect for both the person and the authority of the priest, a sturdy individualist self-reliance, and a love for, and wide knowledge of, the text of Holy Scripture. These factors were of course common to many varieties of protestantism, but when we find convincing evidence of their presence in England in the first two decades of the sixteenth century, before any known alien influence could have been at work, it is hard to deny Wycliffe the credit.

And yet there are no signs that this type of heresy was on the increase, nor yet any indication that it was widespread. Of itself it could hardly have given rise to the potent movement that was puritanism in the reign of Elizabeth I, for it lacked leadership, and seemed to flourish mainly among the humbler and less influential levels of society.

## The Influence of Erasmus and Luther

What was lacking in native Lollardy was to be supplied from abroad. There came to England in the reign of Henry VII the first real taste of that re-awakening intellectual curiosity which we call the Renaissance. Scholars, such as Thomas Linacre and John Colet, returning to England after long periods of study in Italy, brought with them new ideas, new ways of teaching and learning, a revived interest in the classical languages and a new enthusiasm for the Latin style of the best of the ancient writers.

The Latin of the Vulgate, the generally accepted version of the Scriptures, no longer satisfied the fastidious. The discovery and critical comparison of ancient manuscripts revealed defects and corruptions in its text. A new version was clearly desirable, and when this was supplied by one of the greatest of the scholars of the day, Desiderius Erasmus of Rotterdam, the effect was widespread. Many men, such as the Protestant preacher Thomas Bilney, first turned to Erasmus' New Testament when it appeared in 1516, because of the reputation of the translator as a master of the best Latin style, and because they wished to improve their own command of that language, but continued to read it for the sake of its contents when they encountered in it so many significant departures from the familiar wording of the Vulgate. They found themselves compelled, as a consequence, to question not only the accepted text, but much of the interpretation and doctrine which rested upon it. The foundations of the structure of their theology were disturbed, and many found it necessary to erect the building afresh.

The influence of Erasmus in this direction was not, of course, confined to England, though his following in this country was considerable. Through the agency of Lord Mountjoy and others he had been encouraged to visit England from time to time, had made many friends among English scholars such as Colet and More, and had also lectured at Cambridge. Though he did not stay at that university for very long, his reputation remained, his writings were eagerly read and his New Testament acclaimed.

And then, just when the young scholars at Cambridge were, thanks to the influence of Erasmus and others, at their most receptive to new ideas, Luther sprang into the limelight with his rejection of accepted doctrine and his challenge to the papal authority which had condemned him. It is small wonder that Lutheranism soon gained quite a foothold in Cambridge. A number of the men who were at Cambridge in the early 1520s were later to become prominent as leaders of protestantism, whether as bishops such as Cranmer, Ridley and Coverdale, or as preachers like Latimer, Barnes, Bilney and Frith, and many of them were to end their days as martyrs for the reformed faith. These men supplied the intellectual leadership which English protestantism had so far lacked.

When popular preachers and respected bishops took to uttering Lollard-like sentiments, the Lollards themselves need no longer hide in corners but could emerge to take their proper place in the ranks of the English Protestant movement. Popular and intellectual heresy, native and alien influences, Lollardy and Lutheranism joined hands in the 1520s, and English protestantism became a living force.

But at this point a note of caution must be sounded. The connection between the "new learning" of the Renaissance and the first beginnings of a Protestant movement are so often stressed that we are inclined to forget that the one did not necessarily or always lead on to the other. There were many Renaissance scholars of the highest reputation, including some of the most famous like Erasmus and More, who, though they were most earnest advocates of the "new learning", and were highly critical of much that they saw in the church of their day, were never "Protestants", for they never turned against or rejected the authority of the church in which they had been brought up. Similarly, there were notable contemporaries and near contemporaries of the Protestant scholars at Cambridge who, while they drank deeply from the wells of the new learning, never tasted the waters of Lutheranism. Among the older generation there was Cuthbert Tunstall, a scholar of international repute, but, throughout his long life, a conservative in religion. Among the contemporaries of Cranmer and Latimer we find Stephen Gardiner, Nicholas Heath and George Day, who, though subjected to the same intellectual influences in their youth, were, in later years, to resist most stoutly all that the reformers stood for. The "new learning" might lead a man to Lutheranism, it did not oblige him to take that road.

## Protestant Influence in the Reign of Henry VIII

It must not be thought that the promotion of so many of the Cambridge Lutherans to positions of responsibility was entirely a matter of chance. Here the King's matrimonial difficulties had their part to play. The great virtue of the Lutherans, in the King's eyes in the 1530s, was that they did not accept, and produced convincing arguments against accepting, the primacy of the Pope. They and their views were very favourably received by Henry VIII during the decade of the 1530s when he broke with Rome, and anti-papal preachers and theologians were needed to help to consolidate the new régime. Cranmer came to the King's notice in 1529 through his suggestion that Henry might well appeal to the authority of the university faculties of theology and Canon Law throughout Europe for support in his contention that no pope could license a man to marry his brother's widow. A little over two years later Cranmer was raised to the archbishopric of Canterbury when Henry lost patience with the papacy and decided that the authority of his own archbishop was sufficient to bring his case to a final conclusion. During the 1530s the English Lutherans also had a valuable patron and friend in Thomas Cromwell who had gained the royal favour through his invaluable services in drafting and guiding through Parliament the statutes which had secured for the King the fulfilment of his desires. While Cromwell was in virtual command of the government there was a remarkable number of promotions of Protestants like Latimer, Shaxton and Barlow to the episcopal bench. The promotion of these men undoubtedly gave great encouragement to their following.

During the same decade of the '30s English protestantism received further and important encouragement by the official acceptance and widespread distribution of the English version of the Bible. The Word of God could now be read and studied by all without the assistance of a Latin-trained clergy. The individualism and independence of thought which we have already noted as features of Lollardy had now further scope for development with the Bible in every man's hand. English protestantism began to spread. How rapidly it spread may be gauged by the fact that less than five years after the publication of the Great Bible the government thought it necessary to impose restrictions upon the formerly free possession of, and access to, Holy Scripture.

The opponents of the vernacular Bible had always feared that it would encourage an undesirable "variety of opinions" or even downright heresy. Within a very few years their fears were justified. Despite repeated warnings that the Great Bible set up in every church was there to be read, and not to be expounded by every unlearned layman, the habit of arguing over its meaning was spreading, and such popular debates too often degenerated into unseemly brawls. Consequently restrictions had to be imposed in 1543.

But these restrictions came too late. Amateur theological speculation could not be suppressed by edict, and the Protestant pressure continued to build up despite the reactionary efforts of the government in the closing years of Henry's reign. Protestantism could by now claim converts in high places. Those rising stars of the younger generation at Court, Edward Seymour and John Dudley, better known by their later dukedoms of Somerset* and Northumberland,* were professedly of the reform party, as was the last of Henry's queens, Catherine Parr, and also the tutors appointed to supervise the education of his son and heir, Prince Edward. A Protestant wind was certainly blowing.

## Protestantism Triumphant under Edward VI

When Henry VIII died in 1547 and Somerset and Cranmer took over control of state and church in the name of the boy King, the English Protestants had their real chance. It was during Edward VI's brief reign that the English church became most thoroughly protestantised, and that English protestantism put down roots so strong that no subsequent reaction was ever able to uproot it.

We have already noticed elsewhere the Protestant character of the 1552 prayer book, and the sweeping nature of the attack upon ornaments and ritual. These were the main achievements of a movement for reform which had passed beyond the moderate stage of merely wishing to purge the church of a few "popish abuses" and now wanted to break completely with the immediate past and to re-create the church in what it thought of as its primitive simplicity and purity. No longer did the radical reformers speak sadly of the errors of the church of Rome, they were beginning to denounce it in savage terms as a vast conspiracy to delude the faithful, and to equate the Pope with antichrist. The battle was truly joined. Reformer and conservative no longer understood or attempted to understand the attitude of the other but entered into competition in the extremity of the abuse they interchanged.

It was an unhappy period for both parties, and its importance to the story of English protestantism is in the militant spirit it engendered. The enthusiastic Protestants were still only a minority (otherwise the accession of Mary, of well-known Catholic sympathy, would not have been marked with so widespread expressions of pleasure), but they were a forceful minority spurred on by an intense conviction that they were the "chosen people" whose task and privilege it was to spread the gospel light to every corner of their land, and to wage continuous and unrelenting warfare against the "powers of darkness", by which they meant the church of Rome. This zealous sense of mission, this unshakable belief in the ultimate triumph of their cause, the Edwardian Protestants were to pass on in full measure to the Elizabethan puritans, and through them to their successors in the following centuries.

England was, of course, only one of the many fronts upon which this great religious war was being waged. The English Protestants had from their earliest days maintained close links with their spiritual brethren, the Protestants of other lands, aiding and encouraging each other in what they regarded as a common struggle. These ties of sympathy with continental protestantism were further strengthened by the activities of Cranmer in Edward's reign. Anxious always to create some sort of unity out of the different varieties of European protestantism, he kept in close communication with reformers abroad, and encouraged some of the more noteworthy, such as Martin Bucer, Peter Martyr and John à Lasco, to come on protracted visits to England.

## Protestantism in Peril under Mary

With Protestants thinking and acting thus internationally, it was quite natural that, when the death of Edward and the accession of Mary promised to undo all that the English

Protestants had done, many of them should seek refuge abroad among their Protestant brethren in such cities as Frankfort, Strassburg, Basle and Geneva. In the time of their distress their fellow Protestants could be relied upon to offer them shelter. In their cities of refuge abroad they could keep their faith untarnished and work and pray for the day when they could return to England to resume their interrupted labours.

Not all the English Protestants went abroad, but the exiles did number sufficient (nearly 800 according to one estimate) to create and maintain several exile congregations which kept their English identity, lived according to their own lights with little interference from the local authorities in the places where they settled, and developed strong bonds of fellowship and an intense sense of mission which were to make them potent beyond their numbers when the accession of Elizabeth permitted them to return to their homeland. It was in these exiled communities that English puritanism took shape. After their return to England the former companions in exile kept in close and constant touch with one another, and continued to work together with a real sense of common purpose towards the common goal of an England "purified" according to their lights. They formed the active core of Elizabethan puritanism.

The Protestants who remained in England throughout Mary's reign had also their contribution to make to the common cause. By the steadfast refusal of many to accept the undoing of the Edwardian reforms, and by the death at the stake of nearly three hundred of them, they drew public sympathy to their side, and showed that their faith was no idle frenzy but something for which men and women were prepared to die.

## Protestantism Disappointed under Elizabeth

When Elizabeth succeeded her half-sister in 1558, the re-action against the burnings of Mary's reign was quite marked and greatly assisted the campaign of the returning exiles and their sympathisers for a restoration of Edwardian protestant-ism. We have already seen how near they came to getting the 1552 prayer book restored without amendment even though the Queen herself was not in favour of it. But despite this considerable success, there were many who were to be disappointed with the Elizabethan church from the very first because it was not sufficiently purged or "purified" of popish practices and observances.

There were by now all sorts and degrees of Protestants or "puritans", as those who thought the established church was insufficiently Protestant were coming to be called. For the really extreme, anything in the way of ceremonial or ritual which was in any way reminiscent of the old ways was immediately suspect. Only a complete break with the past would have satisfied these men. If the clergy of the reformed church were to continue to wear the vestments of the unreformed (and this was what the ornaments rubric which the Queen insisted upon inserting into the prayer book seemed to require), then it would be impossible for simple people to appreciate that anything had changed and that the new ministers performed a very different function from that of the "massing priests" which the reformers now so heartily despised. Even the plain white surplice which the Archbishop, Matthew Parker,* tried to enforce when he realised that full vestments were out of the question, had Roman associations which made it unacceptable to the thorough-going puritan. Furthermore all symbols and signs were suspect as tending to superstition. The giving of a ring in the marriage service, the making of the sign of the cross in baptism, kneeling to receive the Holy Communion, these and many other practices which the prayer book still required were unacceptable to the extremer puritans.

But, fortunately for the success of the Elizabethan church, there were many other less radical puritans who, although if left to themselves they would have liked to dispense with such practices, nevertheless saw less positive harm in them, and believed that, for the sake of good order and the peace of the church, they should accept them when required to do so by properly constituted authority. Those who thus regarded symbols, dress and ceremonies as "things indifferent", to be regulated and standardised as authority saw fit, were probably always in the majority, but many of them had every sympathy with the conscientious scruples of the more rigid of their brethren, and it would have been difficult to have disciplined the recalcitrant too severely in the earlier years of the reign when the new establishment had many critics to face, and before it had acquired acceptance by the growing up of a generation which had known no other kind of church. In the end the extremists were disciplined, but not before they had carried their campaign for a further reformation into both convocation and Parliament, and come close to meeting success.

## Puritanism not Schismatic

It is important to a proper understanding of Elizabethan puritanism to remember that, with a very few exceptions, these early puritans did not form separate organisations or congregations, but remained within the church. The unity of the international church had been irreparably broken by the time of Elizabeth's accession, but the unity of the national church had not. It was axiomatic to most of Elizabeth's subjects that, as there was but one Christian faith, so there could be only one church professing that faith. The question in Elizabeth's day was what form should the national church take, not what church should be the national one. The word "anglican" had as yet no meaning, for whether the Elizabethan church ended up thoroughly calvinistic or all-but Catholic it would still be the only English church and the adjective anglican would be used to describe it.

Both the Elizabethan puritan and his opponent accepted the necessity of church unity, but each wanted that unity to be cast in his own particular mould. The puritans thus worked to purify the church from within, and did not ask for freedom to go their own ways outside it.

The early campaigns of the puritans were directed in the main against vestments and ceremonies, but when their reluctance to conform to the requirements of the prayer book brought down upon them the disciplinary authority of the bishops, they began to have doubts about the validity of that authority. Clearly it could not rest upon divinely ordered foundations, for if it did, it could hardly be used against them, the godly. And so, under the influence of Thomas Cartwright* and Walter Travers a substantial section of the puritans began to assert that a disciplinary episcopate had no warrant in Holy Scripture, and that all ministers of the church should be equal in authority.

Attempts were made in some parts of the country to translate these egalitarian ideas into practice by setting up secret presbyteries, or committees of clergy, called "classes", which undermined or by-passed the authority of the bishop. This was too much for Elizabeth who had no love for presbyteries or liking for popular government. A challenge to the authority of the bishops was a challenge to her own, and so she encouraged her bishops to be energetic in hunting out and dealing with this presbyterian or "classical" movement. Archbishop Grindal, who declined to act as the Queen wished, was suspended from his functions. In John Whitgift who succeeded him in 1583, the Queen found an archbishop more to her liking, but the real work of repression fell in the end to the ecclesiastical high commission under the influence of Richard Bancroft. By 1593 the work was done and the presbyteries were no more.

It is a remarkable testimony to the fundamental loyalty to the church of most of the puritans, that the majority of those who had been involved in the presbyterian movement quietly abandoned their assemblies when authority made its disapproval plain. Only a few, the Brownists, the first "congregationalists", preferred expulsion from their livings to abandoning the principle of self-government and the equality of ministers.

Puritanism in Elizabeth's day was, therefore, not so much a party as an attitude. Most Elizabethan puritans were loyal sons of the church they were trying to reform who accepted the need to submit private judgment to the dictates of authority in the interests of unity and good order. In the earlier years, as we have pointed out already, authority itself had to proceed with caution lest it break the delicate fabric of the newly established church. But, as the reign advanced and the church took root and found its strength, the reins of discipline were held with a firmer hand, and a more consistent effort was made to make the puritans conform. The disciplinary campaign began with the promotion of John Whitgift to the see of Canterbury in 1583, and gathered momentum with the appointment of Richard Bancroft to the high commission in 1587. By the end of the century it was clear that puritanism alone, unless aided by other forces, would never mould the church of England to its liking. It was also clear, however, that puritanism was far from dead. It was still a very potent force in English church life. The achievements of Whitgift and Bancroft had been at the expense of no more than the fringes of the movement. Their successors would have trouble in abundance with puritanism before many years were out.

# 8

## Catholic Recusancy

THE PURITANS, to whom we devoted the last chapter, were not, of course, the only people who found the Elizabethan church settlement unsatisfactory. Indeed, their dissatisfaction, being focused initially upon such comparatively minor matters as dress and observance, was far less fundamental than that of another group to whom the very basis of the settlement, let alone the finer points, was quite unacceptable. These were the men and women who were later to be known, because of their consistent refusal to participate in, or even to attend, the services of the state church, as recusants.

To these recusants the chief fault of the Elizabethan church was that it rested upon a national basis which entailed a second rejection of the authority and supremacy of the Pope. They were unable to accept the Queen as supreme governor of the church in England, for to do so meant for them severing the unity of the Catholic or universal church of which the Pope, as Christ's vicar on earth, was the supreme head and central focus. The recusants therefore presented the government in Elizabeth's reign with a problem fundamentally more serious than that created by the puritans. The latter were, for the most part, as we have seen, content to work within the framework of the church settlement, and to accept it as the basis from which to work for further change. The recusants, on the other hand, refused to have anything to do with the official church, and did not accept the relationship of church to state upon which it was based.

### The Origins of Recusancy

The problem of recusancy was not something which grew up gradually, it was a difficulty which Elizabeth and her councillors had to face at the very outset of her reign. When Mary died and Elizabeth was proclaimed queen, England was a Roman Catholic country, fully integrated into the papal system. When Elizabeth's first Parliament passed the Act of Supremacy and severed the links with Rome, those who refused to accept what had been done became the first recusants.

The contrast between what happened in 1559 when Elizabeth assumed the supreme governorship of the church in England, and in the 1530s when her father, Henry VIII, had made himself supreme head, is quite remarkable. In Henry's reign only a handful of his subjects refused to acknowledge his new title. Only one of his bishops, John Fisher of Rochester, continued to uphold the Roman supremacy. But in 1559 when Elizabeth reasserted the substance of her father's claims, even though she was careful to take the less objectionable title of supreme governor, a much more substantial number of her subjects declined to approve of her action.

It is particularly noticeable that on this second occasion the bishops did not conform. Only one, Anthony Kitchen of Llandaff, who almost alone had survived all the changes since Henry's reign, was now prepared to take the oath prescribed by the new Act of Supremacy. The rest preferred to suffer the penalty of deprivation. Among the bishops deprived were at least three (Nicholas Heath of York, Edmund Bonner of London and Cuthbert Tunstall of Durham), who had in their earlier years accepted Henry VIII's supreme headship, though they now refused to follow Elizabeth into this second rejection of the papacy.

The other Henrician bishops, had they outlived Mary, would in all probability have taken the same stand against the new Queen. Certainly Stephen Gardiner would have done so, and yet he had been, in 1535, the author of one of the first and most cogently argued tracts in defence of the royal headship, his *De Vera Obedientia*.

There was no appreciable recusancy under Henry VIII. Sir Thomas More, Bishop Fisher, the Carthusian priors and the few others who dared to stand up for the papacy and who suffered execution for their temerity, were the exceptions in their generation. They created no party and left no following. Though rightfully claimed by the Roman Catholic church as martyrs for the faith, they were not the founding fathers of English recusancy which must look rather to those, such as

Gardiner, Tunstall, Bonner and the rest, who initially accepted and approved of Henry's royal headship, but later had second thoughts, welcomed the restoration of the papal supremacy in Mary's reign, and thereafter refused to abandon it a second time. This refusal to accept the governorship of Elizabeth was not, as some have unkindly hinted, a mere act of stubbornness on the part of men who had by their earlier changes of front already earned an unenviable notoriety as trimmers, and could not now risk further damage to their reputations. (Gardiner, the staunch papalist under Mary, had, during her reign, been unkindly reminded of his Henrician past by the appearance in print of an unauthorised English translation of his *De Vera Obedientia*.) No, this refusal was the deliberate act of men of conscience who had, for very adequate and weighty reasons, come to see in the papal supremacy merits, and in the royal headship dangers, which they had not seen in Henry's day.

## The Disillusionment of the Henricians

In the 1530s the acceptance or rejection of the papal claim to supreme ecclesiastical jurisdiction had been virtually the only point at issue, and for most churchmen of the day it had been a point of no great consequence. It had certainly not been held to be a matter of faith. To most of the English clergy in Henry's day the papal supremacy had meant little more than a power to over-ride or supplement the work of local ecclesiastical courts, and a right to impose taxation. Few of Henry's subjects had appreciated the importance of the papacy as the symbol, and indeed the instrument, of contemporary Christian unity. Rejecting the papal claims had not necessarily meant going into schism or forming a break-away church. The King already possessed, and exercised in a fairly responsible manner, extensive powers of patronage and control over the church in England. To acknowledge an anointed monarch as head of the church had presented no great difficulty to the majority of churchmen who had viewed the matter in this way. It had taken the mind of a More or a Fisher to see the momentous implications of what had been to many of their contemporaries a matter of no great consequence.

It was the short reign of Edward VI which opened the eyes of the Henricians to the full implications of what had been done. Henry VIII had always done his best to keep the movement for the reform of the church under control. The few changes that he had permitted after the establishment of his supremacy had been of no great substance, and such as even the most conservative among his bishops could, and did, approve. Having a royal head as conservative as Henry was had naturally concealed the full potentialities of that office.

But Edward VI, or, more correctly, the government which acted in his name, was far from being conservative, and soon it seemed to men like Gardiner and Bonner that the whole English church was in danger of overthrow by the actions being taken in the name of its anointed head. Prayers were no longer offered in that international language of the church, Latin. The ancient mass was abandoned in favour of the new-fangled communion service. Altars were overthrown, images pulled down, vestments destroyed and heretical doctrine taught through the compulsory reading of ready-made sermons (the homilies). Ceremonies and observances with a very respectable length of tradition behind them were being held up to ridicule. Truly the church seemed upside down.

How had all this come to pass? Mainly because the seats of power had been seized by a radical minority who were using the royal headship to impose their own views upon the church and country. Had the church in England still been part of that international body whose head was in Rome it would have possessed the strength to resist such radical innovations. But the breakaway from Rome and the subjection of the English church to the power of the Crown had left it too weak to resist when that power was exercised to its detriment.

Their former acknowledgement of the royal headship was now seen by many of the Henricians to have been the first step in the process which had led to the virtual overthrow of all that they valued in the old church order. Without that first step the subsequent disasters could not have occurred.

But it was not only the church that seemed to be in danger. The social upheavals of Edward's reign, culminating in Kett's rebellion in 1549, seemed to the conservative churchmen to be intimately linked with the religious revolution. The repeated emphasis which some of the more extreme reformers placed upon equality and the "brotherhood of men" seemed to be undermining the stability of the existing society in which rich and poor each had his appointed place with which he should learn to be content.

Society as well as the church seemed to be in danger from the radical minority in power. Only a return to the old ways, including a re-acceptance of the papal supremacy, could hope to save England from social and religious chaos. There might be drawbacks to the papal headship, but they were as nothing when compared with the chaotic consequences of England's experiment in ecclesiastical independence.

Thus it was that their experiences in Edward's reign made papalists of so many of the Henricians. And thus it was that they were not prepared to take the risk of a second departure from Rome when Mary died. And so, even though Mary at the time of her death was at war with the papacy, and her Archbishop of Canterbury, the Cardinal Reginald Pole,* had lain under threat of papal excommunication, yet her bishops, almost to a man, stood up for the papacy against Elizabeth, because the papacy was now to them the rock upon which all else stood. And so Mary's bishops became the first recusants.

## The Numbers of the "Catholics" in 1559

The lead of the bishops in declining to accept the restored royal supremacy was not extensively followed by the lesser clergy. No very significant number of deprivations followed upon the proffering of the supremacy oath to the clergy throughout the country. But then the parochial clergy did not have to live so fully in the public eye as did the bishops, and many of them may have found it possible to lie low and hope for the best.

The estimates that are given of the number of Catholics in England in 1559 vary very widely, and depend very much upon what particular meaning the investigator cares to attach to the word "Catholic". If among the Catholics at this time are counted all those who were generally conservative in their religious views, those who had been happy to conform under Mary, and who had no particular desire to see the old forms of worship abandoned once again, but who were not, on the other hand, actively concerned about the papal issue, nor yet likely to object to worshipping as they were told by those in authority, then it is probably true to say that the vast majority of Englishmen were Catholic.

If, however, this word is given a slightly more precise meaning, and its use confined to describing those who privately would have preferred the church in England to have remained in association with that of Rome, but who felt it to be their duty for the time being to accept the ecclesiastical arrangements imposed upon the country by the government, the number to be counted as Catholic would be much smaller, though still quite considerable. But if the name of Catholic is to be reserved strictly for those whose loyalty to the papacy was stronger than their sense of duty to the Crown, and who, as a consequence, refused to have anything to do with the Elizabethan church, that is to say if only active recusants are to be counted as Catholics, then their number initially would not be greater than a few thousand.

This need not surprise us when we bear in mind the strength of the tradition of conformity which the recusant had to overcome before he made his decision to disobey the law as set forth in the Act of Uniformity. We who are accustomed to a variety of Christian traditions in a country where active churchgoers are in a minority, must make a considerable effort of the imagination if we are to carry ourselves back into an age in which the only church was the parish church and everybody went to it as a matter of course. Those who absented themselves from church, whether through sloth or disbelief, received little sympathy either from the authorities or from their neighbours. They were shunned as social outcasts. Churchgoing was as regular a part of life as eating and sleeping.

The Catholic who ceased to attend his parish church when the new prayer book came into force in 1559 was putting himself voluntarily in much the same position as the medieval heretic. He was making himself socially unacceptable, and deliberately cutting himself off from his neighbours. It was a big decision for any man to take, and few took it unless encouraged by the example of some local landowner or other natural leader of society, so that recusancy tended to be found in local "cells" centered upon some local family of standing which had given the lead.

Another factor which made the decision to refrain from church-going more difficult, and tended to keep down the number of active recusants, was the fact that in the first fifteen years of Elizabeth's reign no other spiritual comfort was available save that dispensed in the parish churches. Was it not better, many potential recusants may have thought, to continue to worship, albeit in a schismatical manner, than deliberately to cut oneself off from public worship altogether? After all, it was a Christian duty to submit to those in authority. If the church in England was now schismatical, or even heretical, surely the blame must lie at the doors of those who had made it so, and not of those who merely continued to worship in the only way open to them?

Furthermore it was to be some years after the accession of Elizabeth before the papacy finally turned its face against her. At first, for political as well as religious reasons, considerable efforts were made to persuade the Queen to return to the Roman fold. For reasons of her own Elizabeth chose to encourage these papal hopes while making no concessions. During these early years of uncertainty many who were Catholic in sympathy may well have conformed to the state church in the expectation that its deviation into schism would be shortlived. When at last the Pope lost patience and excommunicated Elizabeth, it would have been hard for those who had conformed to break the habit of so many years.

## The Clarification of the Catholics' Position, 1559–74

For a variety of reasons then, the position of the English Catholics in the first decade of Elizabeth's reign was unsettled and obscure. Some were recusants, some conformed for the time being in the absence of other ministrations, some out of duty, yet others out of habit. But as time went on the position was gradually clarified. In the first place the long-sitting council of Trent at last wound itself up and published its decrees in 1564. These contained a closer definition of the Catholic faith than had ever previously been attempted, and re-emphasised the primacy of the Pope by requiring all to give obedience to him. Catholics were from henceforth of necessity papalists. It was no longer possible to argue that one could reject the papacy and still be a Catholic as Henry VIII had claimed to be. Consequently any Englishman who accepted and approved of Elizabeth's supreme governorship could no longer be reckoned a Catholic. This made it more difficult now to conform to the established church and yet remain a Catholic in sympathy. The dividing line between Catholic and anglican was becoming clearer.

The process of clarification was carried a stage further by the papal excommunication of Elizabeth in 1570. By this act English Catholics were declared released from their obligation to obey their sovereign, and released therefore from any moral obligation to comply with the acts of supremacy and uniformity. The hesitant Catholic could no longer plead a conscientious duty to obey the law of the land as an excuse for continued churchgoing.

The sole remaining argument of the conforming Catholic, namely that nowhere save in his parish church could he find spiritual comfort, was rendered inoperative after 1574 with the arrival in England of the first of the continental-trained Catholic missionary priests. Now half measures were no longer possible. Either one abandoned the parish church and accepted the ministrations of the secret missionary priesthood, or one continued to conform and ceased to be a Catholic. Recusancy had come to maturity.

## The Elizabethan Persecution

The swiftness and severity of the reaction of the government to the arrival in England of the Catholic missionary priests shows how seriously they took the question of recusancy. From the point of view of the authorities this was no mere matter of religious nonconformity, or civil disobedience, but of a dangerous subversive element threatening the very security, and even the independence, of England. After all the bull of excommunication of 1570 had made it clear that in Catholic eyes Elizabeth was no longer Queen. The next in succession, indeed the one the Catholics had always been bound to regard as having a better title to the English throne than Elizabeth herself, was Mary, the Queen of Scotland. It is true that Mary was throughout the 1570s a prisoner in England, but she was at the same time the focus of an endless series of plots against Elizabeth's life. And Mary's claim was backed by England's enemies abroad, first France, and later Spain. Catholics were thus, so the government believed, bound to regard Mary as rightful Queen, and to work for her release and the overthrow of Elizabeth, and were almost certain to invoke the aid of Spain in so doing. Catholicism was therefore a disloyal element which must be crushed before it could grow dangerous. Hence the severity of the fines imposed for recusancy (raised in 1581 to £20 a month with confiscation of the offender's property if he defaulted), and the savage nature of the sentences imposed upon priests who fell into government hands (from 1585 their very presence in England was deemed treasonable). Measured by the number of recusants and priests who suffered execution or died as a consequence of the rigours of imprisonment, the Elizabethan persecution of the Catholics was every bit as harsh as the Marian persecution of the Protestants. However, it lasted over a longer period and therefore did not make so deep an impression upon the public mind.

The element of tragedy in the story of the Elizabethan recusants lies in the fact that to a great extent the government's suspicions about the political intentions of the missionary priests, and their doubts about the loyalty of the people they ministered to, were quite unjustified. There were of course some who set out to stir up sedition, and others who hatched conspiracies against the Queen, but the instructions given to the first Jesuit missionaries, who were sent to England in 1580, expressly forbade them to dabble in politics, and the great majority of the recusants remained loyal Englishmen and did good service against Spain when the testing time came in 1588. But the public pronouncements of the papacy, the sending of a papal army into Ireland in 1579 and the activities of English Catholic exiles seeking foreign aid for their cause, were not calculated to reassure an anxious privy council.

In the closing years of the sixteenth century, however, more moderate counsels prevailed, and serious efforts were made in private discussions between Richard Bancroft for the establishment and Father Bluet for the recusants, to find a formula by which the latter could express their loyalty to the Queen in temporal matters while reserving their spiritual allegiance to the Pope. That these discussions took place at all is evidence of the earnest desire of many of the recusants to prove themselves both Englishmen and Catholics. That the negotiations came to nothing was not the fault of the English Catholics but of the Pope who vetoed the agreed formula, and of the ageing Queen who refused to countenance any bargaining with recusants.

And so recusancy remained into the seventeenth century an offence to which severe penalties were attached, but it ceased to be a major problem since the Spanish threat had been faced and beaten off, and England no longer went in such fear of her enemies as to see them in her midst where none existed. English Catholics still had to tread warily, and the Gunpowder Plot did them no good, but there were no more priest-hunts, and no more intensive persecution.

Popular mistrust of and uneasiness about Catholics was another matter and was to live on for centuries yet. The picture of catholicism painted by the pen of John Foxe* whose *Acts and Monuments* (popularly known as the *Book of Martyrs*) first appeared in Elizabeth's reign and chronicled in detail the fate of every Protestant martyr of the previous reigns, had a lot to do with the creation and maintenance of this popular fear and mistrust. Next to the Bible Foxe's book was the most widely read in England, and had a profound and lasting effect.

# 9

## The Unification of the British Isles

### ENGLAND AND SCOTLAND

FOR MORE THAN two centuries before the accession of the Tudors, England and Scotland had been at enmity. The claim of the kings of England to be overlords over their northern neighbours, which had been asserted as early as the reign of Edward I, was renewed from time to time, but the Scots consistently refused to acknowledge it, and kept alive the independent spirit of Wallace and Bruce.

### The Ancient Enmity of the Neighbouring Kingdoms

It was almost inevitable that two kingdoms which had to share the comparatively narrow confines of a single island should have found it almost impossible to live at peace. The common land frontier provided frequent occasions for dispute, and the hardy, but unruly, breed of men who were to be found in the border lands of both kingdoms, could only with the greatest of difficulty have been restrained from raiding and plundering each other, and creating inflammatory situations.

From the time of Edward III, however, the main military effort of England had been directed against France in the long contest known as the Hundred Years' War, and the Scottish front had of necessity taken second place. Yet this war between England and France had its own important consequences for Anglo-Scottish relations, since, in their common enmity towards England, France and Scotland drew closer together in a firm alliance, and every English king who sailed to attack France had to take the risk that the Scots would invade England in his absence.

Relations between England and Scotland were hardly altered at all by the victory of Henry VII at Bosworth. Though in his invasion of England he had received some help from

France and even a little from Scotland, it was soon very clear that this assistance was not going to have much influence upon the new King's foreign policies. Henry VII, and James IV who succeeded to the Scottish throne in 1488, were soon engaged in intrigues against each other, and by 1496 were openly at war when James chose to support the pretensions of Perkin Warbeck to Henry's throne. There was war again in the following reign; the war which culminated at Flodden Field in 1513, the minor war of invasions and counter-invasions in 1522–3 and the full-scale conflict which began in 1542 and continued into the reign of Edward VI.

The only years in the earlier part of the Tudor period which saw anything like a stable peace between the two kingdoms were those between the signature of the truce of Ayton in 1497 and the outbreak of naval hostilities in 1511. This truce, which was later converted into a formal peace, was the product, in the main, of Henry VII's pacific nature. The subjection or conquest of Scotland was never a necessary part of that monarch's policy. It was peace upon the northern borders of his kingdom that he wanted, freedom from the threat of invasion by the Scots, and guarantees against Scottish support for claimants to his throne. If these ends could be obtained by negotiation and without war, so much the better.

## Union by Marriage

It was during the negotiations which led to the signing of the truce of Ayton that it was first proposed that the young Scottish King should marry the English King's elder daughter. Such royal marriages were very commonly written into international treaties in that generation when diplomacy was so much a matter of the personal relationships of kings and princes, and it is very unlikely that this particular marriage was designed to do more than any other similar agreement, that is simply to bind the two royal houses by a personal tie which should help to keep the peace between them. It is true, of course, that it was from this particular marriage between James IV and Margaret Tudor that the Stuart claim to the English throne was to arise,[1] and that almost exactly a century after its consummation the great-grandson of this royal

[1] See genealogical table No. 2 in Appendix B, p. 233.

couple would unite in his person the two neighbouring thrones.

This dynastic union was, however, something of an accidental by-product of the match, and could not have been envisaged as more than a very remote possibility when the marriage was first suggested before the truce was signed at Ayton. At that time Henry VII had two sons, Arthur and Henry, who, with all their descendants, would always take precedence over Margaret and her Scottish husband in the matter of succession to the English throne. In 1499, while the negotiations for the marriage were still in train, a third son, Edmund, was born to Henry, and Margaret's chances of succeeding became even slighter. And though by 1503, when the marriage at last took place, both Arthur and Edmund were dead, the surviving son, Henry, was so robust and vigorous that it would have needed a very gifted prophet to have foretold that he would never be a grandfather, and that his sister's family would inherit the English throne. When this Scottish marriage was first negotiated the possibility of its leading to a union of the two crowns, though it did undoubtedly occur to some minds, was too remote to have entered the realm of practical politics. It would be giving Henry VII credit which he does not deserve to suppose that he deliberately planned the match as a step towards a dynastic union of the two kingdoms and the ultimate settlement of the age-old Scottish problem.

It was not Henry VII, but his son and successor Henry VIII, who, in the closing years of his reign, deliberately planned a dynastic union of England and Scotland. The opportunity to do so was provided by the birth of a daughter to James V just six days before the monarch died. Being the sole surviving child of her father, this infant, best known as Mary Queen of Scots, was heir to her father's kingdom, and Queen of it almost from birth. Henry's own heir, the Prince Edward, was at this time but five years old, but it was never too early in those days to plan the marriage of royal children. And so Henry imposed upon the Scots, who had just met defeat in battle at Solway Moss, the treaty of Greenwich by which the two royal infants were pledged to wed each other when they came of age. Such a marriage would have meant, of course, the almost immediate union of the two kingdoms.

But the Scots, arguing that it had been dictated to them

under duress, repudiated this treaty as soon as they could and the infant Mary was sent for safety to France. The most vigorous efforts of the affronted Henry, and of the Duke of Somerset in the following reign, were expended in vain. The marriage could not be brought about.

Henry VIII's interest in Scotland in the 1540s was considerable. It was just at this period that he entertained his most ambitious dreams of uniting the several parts of the British Isles in a single British kingdom under his own authority.

But it was not only Henry's imperialistic fancy that drove him to attack Scotland. It was also highly advisable for the security of his new anti-papal régime that he should take measures to protect himself against the possibility of a papal counter-attack being launched against him through Catholic Scotland. All his efforts to persuade his nephew James V to follow his example and cast off the yoke of Rome having failed, it was necessary to take more active measures.

To attain his ends, both imperialistic and defensive, Henry was prepared to use whatever instrument lay most conveniently to his hand, and whatever method seemed most likely to succeed. In earlier years, when James V had been a minor under the tutelage of regents, Henry had tried to keep Scotland as a client kingdom in submission to him through his influence over the powerful Earl of Angus, second husband of the Scottish Queen-Mother, Margaret, and therefore brother-in-law to the English King. Now, nearly twenty years later, Henry tried his marriage scheme, and when that failed unleashed his forces in a vain attempt to force the Scots to submit. But the Scottish nut was too tough to crack, and all that Henry achieved was a re-awakening of that bitter Anglo-Scottish hostility which his father's diplomacy had tried to overcome.

Down to the middle of the sixteenth century, then, hostility continued to be the normal state of affairs between the neighbouring kingdoms, and there were no obvious signs that Anglo-Scottish relations were ever likely to be anything but bad. Indeed the exile of the young Scottish Queen at the French Court, and her eventual marriage to the heir to the French throne, seemed only to confirm, for the next generation at least, the "auld alliance" of Scotland and France against England.

## A Revolution in Anglo-Scottish Relations

In the decade of the 1550s, however, events occurred both north and south of the Anglo-Scottish border which were, in the space of little more than a single generation, to bring to an end the centuries of animosity and to prepare the way for the peaceful succession of a Scottish king to the English throne.

The new factor in the situation was religion. In its early stages the Scottish reformation lagged far behind the English. In 1528 Scotland found her first Protestant martyr in Patrick Hamilton, and the activities of George Wishart and a few others in the 1530s foreshadowed what was to come. But the Scottish King remained a loyal papalist. Even his uncle Henry's suggestion that a rejection of the papacy could be followed by a profitable seizure of monastic property did not tempt James V to revolt. And just because the Scottish Protestant movement received in these early days support and encouragement from across the border, it was suspect to Scottish patriots who saw the shadow of English domination behind every gospel preacher. After all even John Knox* himself at one time enjoyed official patronage in England.

But the death of Edward VI in 1553, and the accession of Mary Tudor to the English throne, began to change the picture. Now there could be no more official English support for Scottish protestantism, for the English Protestant leaders were themselves all either in prison or exile. Their Scottish counterparts no longer, therefore, suffered from the suspicion that they were the undercover agents of English ambition. On the contrary, indeed, they were able, in a very short time, to pose as the true Scottish patriots.

## The "Monstrous Regiment of Women"

During the minority of the infant Mary Stuart her mother, Mary of Guise, a member of a powerful French and Catholic noble house, ruled Scotland as Regent, and supported her authority with the aid of French troops. This French interest in Scottish affairs was all part of the great design of the French King, Henry II, who planned to marry his eldest son to the

Scottish Queen and thus unite the two kingdoms in the next generation. In the meantime, while he waited for the royal couple to be old enough to wed, and to be sure of the ultimate success of his plans, he sought to gain control over Scotland by planting French garrisons at strategic points and by exerting his influence upon the Queen-Regent. Thus the regency of Mary of Guise in Scotland began to assume the appearance of a French-dominated government seeking to undermine Scottish independence. In the eyes of Scottish patriots the greatest danger to the independence of the nation seemed now to come no longer from England but from France and from the French and Catholic government of the Regent.

At the same time the Queen-Regent was engaged upon an energetic campaign against the Scottish Protestants. As a consequence her political and her religious opponents drew closer together. The persecuted Protestants, as the bitterest and most consistent enemies of the French-dominated government of the Regent, found sympathetic allies among those whose chief concern was to preserve the political independence of Scotland, and, freed from the taint of association with England, rapidly became the real heart of the patriot party.

Meanwhile, south of the border, the marriage of the English Mary to the Spanish King, Philip II, was producing a parallel result. Catholicism and Spanish domination seemed now of necessity to go together. In England, as in Scotland, the persecuted Protestants became the patriot party, and in their common plight the patriots and Protestants of both kingdoms turned to each other, and Anglo-Scottish amity was born.

The similarity of the fates of England and Scotland under the government of the two Marys, the Regent, Mary of Guise, and the Queen, Mary Tudor, inspired John Knox to write one of his better known pamphlets, his *First Blast of the Trumpet against the Monstrous Regiment of Women*. It was a pity that Knox should have chosen to be quite so sweeping in his condemnation of female rulers. Queen Elizabeth never forgave him, and her goodwill would have been invaluable to him and to his cause.

## The Scottish Reformation

The long-delayed Scottish reformation broke out in violence in 1559, as much a political movement against the alien Regent as a religious movement against the Roman church. In the same year the English Protestant exiles returned to their homeland, and England re-severed her links with Rome. It seemed natural then that the Scottish rebels should look to England for support, and almost inevitable from then onwards that England should from time to time lend encouragement and assistance to the Scottish Protestants in their long struggle to gain the upper hand.

And yet the struggle in Scotland lasted longer than perhaps it might have done because of the reluctance of the English Queen to interfere in the domestic affairs of her cousin's kingdom. Elizabeth was no universal champion of protestantism. It took more than the cause of religion to prevail upon her to help the Scottish rebel Lords of the Congregation in 1559–60. It was the presence of French troops in Scotland and the fact that Mary, at that time both Queen of Scots and Queen-Consort of France, claimed also to be Queen of England (for in Catholic eyes Elizabeth was the offspring of a bigamous marriage and therefore illegitimate), and seemed ready to press her claim, that decided Elizabeth to act. It was primarily in defence of her own throne that she joined with the Scottish lords to drive out the French.

Thereafter Elizabeth's ardour for the Protestant cause cooled. When Mary, now a widow, and no longer of any account in France, returned to her native Scotland in August 1561, and tried to hold the Scottish reformation in check, Elizabeth was quite prepared to be friendly, provided no mention was made of Mary's claim to England. Even after Mary's disgrace and deposition in 1567 as a consequence of her alleged connivance in the murder of her second husband, Darnley, Elizabeth was reluctant to use her influence against a fellow queen, but tried unavailingly to secure her restoration. What Elizabeth really wanted was security on her northern frontier, and to obtain that she would rather negotiate with a Catholic queen than with Protestant rebels.

It was not until Mary's cause became inextricably linked with the ambitions of Spain, and the coming of age of Mary's son James meant that there was available in him an alternative, Protestant and acceptable monarch for Scotland, that Elizabeth at last came to terms with her northern neighbour in the treaty of Berwick of 1586. The seeds of that treaty had been sown, as we have seen, in the time of the two Marys, but the plant had been a long time in coming to fruit.

From 1586 onwards the neighbouring island kingdoms were closely bound in a defensive treaty, the Scottish King was in receipt of an English pension, and, though never expressly acknowledged by Elizabeth as her heir, was cultivating the approbation of the English Queen and her ministers in order to smooth the way for his own inheritance of the crown of England.

The only ripple to disturb the peaceful waters of Anglo-Scottish amity after 1586 was the consequence of the execution of the imprisoned Scottish Queen in the following year. This act, which was virtually forced upon Elizabeth by her anxious subjects, was made the occasion for a hostile demonstration from the Scottish capital. But it was only a token demonstration. James VI had not set eyes upon his mother since his early infancy, and had been brought up to regard her as the incarnation of evil. Her execution can hardly have touched him personally at all, but some protest was surely expected of him as a dutiful son, and so protest there was, but not such a one as would upset for long the new-found friendship with England to which James looked for the eventual fulfilment of his dearest hope, to be the first to rule both kingdoms.

## ENGLAND AND IRELAND

The problem which the Tudors faced in Ireland was one of security, and so was in some ways similar to that posed by Scotland, though the basic relationship between England and Ireland was very different from that between England and Scotland. The latter two were separate and independent countries, and so their interrelationship expressed itself in terms of diplomacy or war. Ireland was also a separate country with its own institutions, council, law courts, Parliament and administrative offices, but it was firmly tied to England in that the kings of England were, and had been for nearly three hundred years, also lords of Ireland. This should have meant that England and Ireland were as closely bound together as England and Scotland were to be after the dynastic union of 1603. The authority of the English king, expressed in Ireland through the person of his Lord Deputy, should have been an adequate safeguard for English interests there, and averted any danger that Ireland would open her shores to the enemies of England or take any action that was not to the liking of the English king.

## The Weakness of the English Hold on Ireland

In practice, however, at the time of Henry VII's accession, the power of the king of England as lord of Ireland was almost nil. There were two reasons for this. In the first place the Anglo-Norman conquest of Ireland in the twelfth century had never been complete, and had not been followed by a very effective occupation. Many Anglo-Norman families had carved out estates for themselves and settled in Ireland, but not enough to make a permanent impression, especially as the kings of England from John onwards had tended, with a very few exceptions, to ignore Ireland and to leave the settlers there to fend for themselves. Consequently, from the second half of the thirteenth century onwards, the Anglo-Norman colony shrank steadily in extent and influence. The gaelic chieftains of the north and west regained their former power over their own peoples, and pressed back the frontiers of Anglo-Norman influence. At the same time many of the descendants of the Anglo-Norman conquerors steadily lost their separate identity and, adopting the language and customs of the subject population (as, of course, their cousins did in England too), became as Irish as the native peoples over whom they ruled, and as little amenable to control by the king's Lord Deputy.

By the middle of the fifteenth century, by this double process of shrinkage and absorption, the area of Ireland in which the English law and the authority of the English king were treated with any real respect was reduced to the lowland coastal strip between Dublin and Dundalk together with a narrow hinterland which included parts of the counties of Louth, Meath, Dublin and Kildare. This was the English Pale in which all that was left of the Norman lordship of Ireland stood on the defensive against the still flowing tide of gaelic resurgence.

Beyond the Pale the authority of the English king was not entirely extinguished and some showing of it was made from time to time. Despite these occasional gestures, however, it

1 The presentation of the Speaker in the Parliament of 1584

From Glover, R., *Nobilitas politica vel civilis*, 1608

a Weaving

b Dyeing

c A Shearman

d Tailors

2 Sixteenth-century tradesmen at work

From Schopperus, H., *Panoplia Omnium Illiberalium Mechanicarum aut Sedentariarum Artium genera continens . . .* 1568

3 The submission of Shane O'Neil to Sir Henry Sidney

From Derricke, J., *Image of Ireland*, 1581

4 Queen Elizabeth I

Frontispiece to *Pacata Hibernia*. 1633

5  Henry VIII embarking at Dover

6  The Field of the Cloth of Gold

From the paintings at Windsor Castle and Hampton Court.
By gracious permission of Her Majesty the Queen.

7 Cardinal Wolsey

8 Thomas Cranmer

9 Sir Thomas More

10 Thomas Cromwell

11 William Cecil, Lord Burghley

12 Sir Francis Walsingham

13  Mary, Queen of Scots

From facsimile in Maxwell, Sir William, *Examples of Engraved Portraiture in the Sixteenth Century*, 1872

was clear to contemporary observers that most of Ireland was for most of the time beyond effective control and wide open to the enemies of England. This was the first reason for the weakness of Henry VII's position.

This lack of internal discipline was, however, only one half of the Irish problem which the first Tudor inherited. Not only was the authority of the government in Dublin virtually limited to the area of the Pale, but that very government was itself firmly in the hands of men who had little respect for the wishes of their nominal master, the English king.

## The Kildare Supremacy

The Lord Deputy in 1485 was Gerald Fitzgerald, eighth Earl of Kildare,* who had held that office since 1477 when he had virtually inherited it from his father, and who was in turn to pass it on at his own death, in 1513, to his son, the ninth Earl. For three successive generations the Earls of Kildare ruled Ireland like independent princes. The real foundations of their power were their own extensive estates, and their network of alliances and intermarriages with some of the more important Anglo-Norman and gaelic families. Their possession of the deputyship merely gave formal acknowledgement to the power they already possessed. So strong was their position that, as Henry VII himself said, "all Ireland could not rule" them. Consequently the Yorkist kings of England, who were too busy defending their own throne against their Lancastrian rivals to have much time to spare for Ireland, had found it easier to give way to the Kildares' determination to possess the deputyship than to try to oppose their ambition. Even Henry VII, so famed for his putting down of the "overmighty subject" in England, found the cost of any alternative to the Kildare supremacy in Ireland too great to bear, and had in the end to leave that overmightiest of subjects in power.

The real danger to England of this "all-but kingship" of Kildare was demonstrated very clearly early in Henry's reign when, in 1487, Lambert Simnel was not only warmly welcomed in Ireland by the Lord Deputy, but was actually crowned as King Edward VI of England in Christ Church cathedral in Dublin, with Kildare in attendance at the ceremony.

This particular Yorkist threat was defeated at the battle of Stoke a few months later, but Henry could not afford to let Ireland remain a recruiting ground for his enemies and would-be supplanters. And so, when a few years later Perkin Warbeck threatened to repeat the exploits of Simnel, Kildare was summoned to England and removed from the deputyship. In his place was sent over a modest English knight, Sir Edward Poynings, who would be sure to act in every matter as the King wished, and would have no pretensions to independent rule.

The gesture was sufficient. Warbeck was driven off. Kildare was given a taste of the power of the English King. But the cost of supplying Poynings with the military support he needed to make his authority respected proved in the end too great, and Kildare was restored to Ireland and to office in 1496. Thereafter, however, the Earl treated Henry with much more respect.

Thus, from the point of view of the Tudors, the problem of Ireland was twofold. They had to reassert effective control over the government which acted in their name in Dublin, and they had to make the authority of that government respected throughout an island which, for the most part, was in the habit of ignoring it. They had to restore to Ireland both internal discipline and external control.

## The Breaking of the Kildare Supremacy

The second of these two tasks was to prove the easier to perform. The Poynings' interlude had shown that the position of the Kildares was not impregnable, but it had also shown that it would take a more sustained effort than Henry VII was prepared to make to provide a really adequate alternative to the "Anglo-Irish home rule" of the great Earl and his partisans. That sustained effort was not made until the following reign, and then only when a dangerous rebellion forced Henry VIII to act decisively in 1534.

In the earlier years of his reign Henry VIII had, like his father, made occasional rather half-hearted attempts to assert his authority over the Irish government. Twice, in 1520 and in 1526, he had replaced the ninth Earl of Kildare by an English-born governor, but each time had found the cost too great, and, after a comparatively short interval, had restored the Earl to power.

In 1534 Henry tried again. This time the Earl's son, "Silken" Thomas, fearing for his father's safety, broke into rebellion, and, because King Henry had now fallen out with the papacy, sought to widen the appeal of his revolt in deeply conservative Ireland by adding the cause of the Pope and the old religion to that of his father and family.

This appeal to religion awoke Henry to the extent of the danger to his position in England created by an undisciplined Ireland open to papal counter-attack. Ireland had now to be taken seriously. It was clearly unwise to continue the old practice of entrusting the governmental power there to an Irish-born nobleman. There could be no more Anglo-Irish deputies. For the rest of the Tudor period the power of the English Crown in Ireland was to be wielded by English-born Lords Deputy who were closely bound by their instructions from England and were in a very real sense responsible to the English government for all their actions.

The Kildare supremacy was broken when the Earl died in the Tower, and Silken Thomas and five of his uncles were hanged at Tyburn. The reformation statutes were forced through the Irish Parliament, which had already been seriously weakened by the enactments of Poynings' time, and the problem of external control was largely solved.

## The Problem of Internal Discipline

The other problem, that of internal discipline, was not so easily disposed of. It was if anything the more urgent for there was little advantage to be gained from establishing a firm control over the Irish government if that government had itself no control over large parts of the island.

All the earlier Tudor attempts to create an effective government in Ireland were, however, wrecked upon the rock of finance. It was almost a point of principle, and certainly one of policy, with both Henry VII and Henry VIII, that their Irish government should pay for itself out of the Irish revenues, and that the resources of the English monarchy should not be called upon to subsidise those of the Irish lordship.

In fact the Irish revenues, if taken at their book value, should have been sufficient not only to meet the cost of governing Ireland but also to provide the English king with a surplus for his own use. But there was a world of difference between the book and the actual values of the Irish revenues, and that was the lesson which the Tudors were so slow to learn. The monarchs of England might be, by inheritance, titular Earls of Ulster and Lords of Meath and Connacht and other lands, but until they could make good these titles by force of arms not one half-penny could they expect to draw from the extensive estates that were nominally attached to their various titles, but had in fact reverted to the unencumbered ownership of the native inhabitants. And yet, to raise and maintain a force sufficient to make good these titles would cost far more than the actual Irish revenue could provide. This was the repeated dilemma of the Tudors which delayed the solution of the Irish problem until Elizabeth at last saw that the subjection of Ireland was so essential to England's security that the English exchequer must be called upon to contribute substantially to its cost.

## Various Solutions

Though in nature the Irish problem remained unchanged throughout the Tudor period, the solutions suggested and attempted varied quite distinctly from time to time.

The policy of repression and outright conquest was seldom without its advocates and was occasionally adopted. Notable among the would-be conquerors were Thomas Howard, Earl of Surrey, Henry VIII's Lord Lieutenant in 1520–1, and Sir Edward Bellingham and Sir James Croft, Lords Deputy to Edward VI in the years 1548–50 and 1551–3 respectively.

The story of Surrey's lieutenancy is typical of the fortune of such military men. Confident that he could reduce Ireland to order with 6,000 men, he was given a force of only 1,100, and the submissions which he managed to exact from so many Irish chieftains were effective only as long as he and his army were in the vicinity. Once the Lord Lieutenant and his men disappeared over the horizon, the local chiefs resumed their lawless ways, and no permanent result was obtained. Whether, had Surrey got the 6,000 men he asked for, the result would have been much different we have no means of knowing, but 1,100 was all that the Irish establishment could afford, and proved quite inadequate for the task expected of it. Neither Bellingham nor Croft was any more successful.

One alternative to direct rule by the sword was some form of indirect rule through native authorities. The restored deputyship of Kildare after the recall of Poynings in 1496 came closest to this pattern. Henry VII had demonstrated his power in deposing the great Earl, and so, for the rest of the reign, the latter enjoyed the deputyship only on trust. If he displeased the King he would soon lose his place again, but as long as he kept Ireland in a reasonable state of order (and only a man of Kildare's great personal power could hope to do so) Henry would not interfere with his government.

On the whole Kildare seems to have lived up to Henry's expectations, but the crisis of the reformation in the following reign made it highly dangerous any longer to leave the government of Ireland in the hands of one who might very easily join the ranks of the King's enemies.

A more promising effort to produce a long-term solution to the Irish problem can be seen in the various attempts made from the reign of Henry VIII onwards to assimilate Ireland to England and to make loyal Englishmen out of disloyal Irish. One of the most able exponents of this kind of policy was Sir Anthony St Leger who first became acquainted with Irish affairs as a member of a royal commission sent over to survey the whole state of the country and its government in 1537.

The root of the Irish problem, thought St Leger, was the presence in the one island of two peoples, two laws and two modes of living. The native Irish had always been kept apart from the Anglo-Norman settlers and their descendants by the refusal of the Dublin administration to admit them to the benefit of English law, and by those acts of the Irish Parliament which condemned deeply rooted Irish social customs. Instead of continuing to drive wedges between the two peoples which only forced the native Irish into disloyalty, St Leger suggested that every effort should be made to over-ride the distinctions between the races and to merge the two populations into one.

## "Surrender and Regrant"

As a first step St Leger proposed that the Irish system of

landholding by the clan and succession to an elected chief, should be transformed into the English system of personal holdings and succession by primogeniture. This could best be done by persuading the Irish chiefs to surrender the lands of their people to the Crown so that they might be re-granted to them as feudal holdings after the English pattern. The bribe to secure that co-operation of the chiefs upon which the whole scheme depended was to be the offer of English-style titles of nobility and the promotion of Ireland from a mere lordship to the dignity of a kingdom in which the new title-holders would form the peerage.

This policy of "Surrender and regrant" with which St Leger's name is so closely associated was pursued persistently during his three terms of office as Lord Deputy (1540–7, 1550–1 and 1553–6). It was a well-conceived and well-intentioned plan, but it foundered upon the twin rocks of the English authorities' reluctance to admit the new gaelic aristocracy to any real share in the government of the new Irish kingdom, and the refusal of the Irish clans to abandon their former practice of electing their leaders or to acknowledge the validity of the surrenders executed in their name by their chiefs.

And so, before very long, there arose a whole series of family disputes between those who were the heirs, according to the English law, of the new Irish peers, and those who were their successors according to the still persisting Irish custom. There also developed a succession of rebellious outbursts by discontented chiefs who soon found that in their new guise as English earls they were fast losing their former authority over their own people, and being ordered about by petty government officials.

Thomas Radcliffe, Earl of Sussex, and Lord Deputy at the time of Elizabeth's accession, suggested that, to avoid disputes over inheritances, it would be best for the future to recognise, and to give legal validity to, the Irish system, but his suggestion did not meet with the approval of the common lawyers and was not adopted.

Elizabeth herself did try on at least two occasions to come to terms with the gaelic world. Early in her reign she recognised Shane O'Neil as "Captain" of his people though the English law still recognised his nephew Hugh as heir to his father's earldom of Tyrone.[2] At the same time she had the young Hugh brought to England, partly for his own safety, and partly so that he might be brought up to English ways.

Later, when the ambitious Shane had betrayed her trust and died a rebel, Elizabeth sent Hugh back to Ireland to govern the O'Neils, in the hope that his English upbringing had made a loyal subject of him. But she was again to be disappointed, and Hugh's great rebellion in 1595 was to be the most serious of her whole reign.

Neither of these two expedients adopted by Elizabeth could conceal the fact that the ultimate object of the English government was to turn Irishmen into Englishmen, and this touched the pride of the native, even the pride of Hugh, the English-educated, where it hurt. Besides, both Shane and Hugh had inherited the independent spirit of their ancestors, and could not stand idle while their liberty of action was progressively curtailed.

The only attempt to mould a part of Ireland to the English pattern without resort to the confiscation of lands which met with any success was the series of agreements collectively known as the Composition of Connacht. In that far western province in 1585, during the deputyship of Sir John Perrot, a commission was appointed which worked patiently and steadily to persuade the native lords one by one to accept the English law and to hold their lands for the future according to its terms. Careful provision was made in each of the individual agreements negotiated for the compensation of all those whose rights were in any way affected, and the operation was on the whole very successful.

## Plantation

Elsewhere in Ireland, with the failure of the "surrender and regrant" policy, another solution had to be found. This was generally that of "plantation", in the long run the most successful of all. It was first tried in Mary's reign on the borders of the Pale, in the territories of Leix and Offaly which were redesignated Queen's county and King's county in honour of the reigning sovereigns.

In these lands the rebellions of the O'Mores and O'Connors in Edward's reign provided an opportunity for declaring all

[2] See genealogical table No. 5 in Appendix B, p. 236.

their lands forfeit to the Crown. The territories thus seized were then to be secured for the future from rebellion by planting in them a loyalist population brought over from England. To make the proposition attractive to the immigrants the rents asked were kept low, but, on the other hand, it was made clear to the planters that once they were put in possession of their holdings they were expected to provide for their own defence.

Thus there was profit in plantation for both the Crown and the planter. The former gained not only new revenue from the rents paid by the planters, but also the advantage of having a self-defending "buffer state" to protect the western frontier of the Pale. The latter obtained abundant and fertile land at a price well below that current in England. The only dissatisfied parties were the native peoples who were to be confined to the western third of their former territories, and who made their natural resentment felt in a fierce and stubborn guerrilla resistance to the process of settlement. The Leix-Offaly plantation was not therefore an immediate success, but the settlers fought back, and held their own, and by the 1570s it seemed an experiment promising enough to be repeated elsewhere.

By that date the lure of cheap land was strong enough to make men offer to undertake plantation with the minimum of governmental assistance. The ill-fated attempts of Thomas Smith in the Ards in 1572–3, and of the Earl of Essex in adjacent Clandeboye in 1573–5, were virtually private undertakings whose legality rested on a grant by the Crown of lands held to have been forfeited by the rebellion of Shane O'Neil in 1566–7. These were plantations on the cheap, and did not succeed against the determined resistance of the local population.

The later plantation of Munster, again the sequel to the suppression of a rebellion, was more carefully supervised from London, and seemed set for success when the last great Irish rising of the Tudor period, the Tyrone rebellion, swept south and drove the settlers headlong to the shelter of the ports.

## The Tyrone Rebellion

The Earl of Tyrone who led this last uprising was that same Hugh O'Neil whom Elizabeth had in earlier years brought to England to save him from the enmity of his uncle Shane.

But neither his English upbringing, nor the trust reposed in him by the Queen when she sent him back to Ireland to take up his inheritance as Earl of Tyrone, could make Hugh O'Neil forget his proud descent from the ancient High Kings of Ireland, nor yet, more recently, the way his grandfather, the first earl, had lorded it freely over his vassals and his people in the hilly heart of northern Ireland, with hardly ever a thought for the opinions or policies of the English king's government in distant Dublin. Now, in his own day, Hugh found things very different. His own freedom of action was hampered at every turn, and his hold over his own people was seriously weakened by the constant flow of directions and emissaries from Dublin. The authority of the Queen's Lord Deputy was at all times very much in evidence.

Hugh was not a nationalist. He was proud, rather than ashamed, to be the great Queen's vassal, but he was not prepared to accept what that vassalage now seemed to mean in the undermining of his own authority.

To his own discontents Hugh found a sympathetic echo in those of many of his fellow chieftains, and when a clash between the Maguire and Sir Richard Bingham, Lord President of Connacht, touched off rebellion, O'Neil had no great difficulty in bringing together a really formidable league of gaelic peoples, including in his confederacy even those hereditary enemies and near neighbours of his, the O'Donnels. There was no longer room in Ireland for inter-tribal disputes. The gaelic world had to stand or fall as one body.

In the end the Tyrone rebellion was suppressed, but only after a long and very bitter struggle (which, incidentally, ruined the reputation and led to the downfall of the young Earl of Essex), which was aided at one stage by an expeditionary force from Spain, and which was only brought to an end by the dogged military genius of Lord Deputy Mountjoy, and the brutal thoroughness of Sir Arthur Chichester, his lieutenant in the north.

The reign of Elizabeth and the Tyrone rebellion ended within days of each other. At long last all Ireland was subjected to the authority of the English Crown. The Munster plantation could be restored and the process of colonisation proceed apace in the new century and the new reign. The close of the Tudor period saw the English conquest of Ireland at last complete.

# 10

## England and Europe

SO FAR, in the course of this book, we have concerned ourselves almost entirely with English affairs in isolation from the rest of Europe and the world beyond. The only foreign country to enter our field of vision has been Scotland, with whose relations with England we dealt in the last chapter. Our purpose in this chapter, therefore, will be to look beyond the coasts of the British Isles, and to see how England stood in relation to the rest of Europe in the sixteenth century.

### The Comparative Weakness of England

The first point to be made, and one that those of us who have grown up accustomed to considering the United Kingdom as one of the "great powers" of the world are sometimes reluctant to concede, is that England in the Tudor period was not a first-class power. By the closing years of Elizabeth's reign she was, perhaps, showing signs of being on the way to becoming one, but, earlier in the century, particularly in the reigns of Henry VII and Henry VIII, despite the magnificent pretensions of the latter monarch, it would be closing our eyes to realities to allow ourselves to believe that England could count as anything more than a second-class power.

It is true of course that a century earlier (at the time of the great victories of Henry V in the war against France) England had no fear of any rival in Europe and almost alone among her neighbours was worthy of the name of a great power. It is also probably true that the strength and resources of the England of Henry VII, despite the intervening years of civil strife, were as great as those of the England of Henry V, but in the years between the European scene had changed. New powers had emerged whose potential strength in terms of men and resources was far greater than that which England, with her comparatively small population, could ever hope to muster.

England, who in earlier centuries had led the rest of Europe along the road to national unity, was now being left behind in terms of power. Though probably as strong in absolute terms as ever she had been, England, compared with her new neighbours, was now in the ranks of the second-class powers because the qualifications for membership of the first rank had been raised to a level she could not attain.

Chief among the new powers was the kingdom of Spain, formed by the personal union of the Crowns of Aragon and Castile which had resulted from the marriage of Ferdinand and Isabella, and by their subsequent joint conquest of Granada, the last of the Moorish kingdoms in the Iberian peninsula. Isabella was also the patron of Columbus, and the Spanish conquerors who followed up his discoveries soon added the resources of a great central and South American empire to the power of their homeland.

France, meanwhile, had recovered from her earlier defeats at the hands of England, had driven the invaders out of all France save the town and district of Calais, and, since the re-conquest of her lost territories, had gained a stronger sense of national unity and a better discipline under the energetic Louis XI.

On the eastern borders of France, and in the Netherlands, the dukes of Burgundy had acquired, by various means, a complex of provinces which they had tried their best to weld into a new and sovereign kingdom. But in 1477 their house had become extinct in the male line, and their territories had passed, by the marriage of the heiress, into the possession of the house of Habsburg. This latter family, from their base in Austria and the Tyrol, had already acquired virtually hereditary possession of the nominally elective Imperial crown, and were well embarked upon that remarkable series of marriages and inheritances which was to make them the foremost power in Europe.

The addition to the Habsburg territories of Franche-Comté and the Netherlands, which resulted from the marriage of Maximilian of Habsburg to Mary, the daughter of the last Burgundian duke, was a big step forward, but the son of that marriage, the Archduke Philip, was, by his own union with Joanna, the eldest daughter and heiress of Ferdinand and Isabella of Spain,[1] to raise the fortunes of his family to even greater heights. Though this Philip was to die before both his father Maximilian and his father-in-law Ferdinand, his son Charles of Ghent, better known as the Emperor Charles V, was in due time to enter into the vast inheritance prepared for him by the marriage of his parents, and to unite under his personal authority the Habsburg and Burgundian lands, the Imperial title and the kingdoms and overseas empire of Spain.

Thus, when the first of the Tudors ascended the English throne, there were three major powers in Western Europe, France, Spain and the Habsburgs. Early in the reign of Henry VIII, these three powers were to be reduced to two when the deaths of Ferdinand in 1516 and of Maximilian in 1519 led to the union of their territories and titles in the person of their grandson Charles V. *opposed marriage*

England could scarcely hope to compete unaided against these new great powers which dominated the European scene. Yet she was not to be entirely without influence in European affairs, for the bitter rivalry which grew up between France and the Habsburgs was to create a situation of virtual balance in which the adherence of England to either side might well prove critical.

## Franco-Habsburg Rivalry and the Balance of Power

With the causes of the almost continuous wars which occupied the energies and resources of the major monarchies of Europe for most of the first half of the sixteenth century we need not here be concerned in any detail. Suffice it to say that French ambitions in Italy led first to a rivalry with Spain, and then with the Habsburgs, and that this became the major conflict which dominated the international scene throughout the period.

It is against this background of wars interspersed with periods of active diplomatic rivalry that we must examine the relations of England with the other countries of Europe, or, more accurately (for in those days international affairs were still primarily a matter of the personal relations of the crowned

---

[1] See genealogical table No. 4 in Appendix B, p. 235.

heads of states), the relationship of the monarchs of England with their fellow sovereigns abroad.

In the Franco-Habsburg struggle the honours were fairly evenly divided. The greater size of the dominions of Charles V had its disadvantages as well as its advantages. Though his potential resources in terms of men and money might well be greater than those of his great rival, Francis I of France, Charles had as many problems as he had territories (the constant pressure of the Turks upon his eastern flank, the insubordination of the Lutheran princes in Germany, the reluctance of the Spaniards to submit to the authority of a man they regarded as a foreigner, to name only a few) and was seldom able for long to concentrate all his energies against France. In this state of near balance between the principal parties to the dispute, the addition to either side of the resources of even a minor ally might well prove critical. And so, around the main contestants, there gathered a wide and often changing collection of subordinate allies, many of them unashamedly switching their allegiance freely from one side to the other in the hope of gaining some advantage. England, as one of the more important of the secondary powers, could of course be a most valuable ally, and there were times, like those years of Wolsey's glory 1519–22, when he and his royal master Henry VIII were assiduously courted by both Francis and Charles, and met and negotiated with these great princes on terms of equality.

It is with these particular years in mind that so many people have tended to give to Cardinal Wolsey the credit for having originated the English policy of seeking to maintain "the balance of power" in Europe. This policy, which, when consistently applied, meant always supporting the weaker party in any European conflict lest any one power should become dangerously strong, was certainly much talked about, and even acted upon, by later generations of English statesmen, but any close examination of Wolsey's actual diplomacy soon reveals how little he cared for this principle of balance.

For example, when Francis was soundly defeated by Charles at the battle of Pavia in 1525, and made prisoner, Wolsey did not at once try to restore the balance by siding with the defeated French. Instead his first reaction was to propose to Charles that he and Henry VIII should partition France between them. It was only when the Pope changed sides and sought to revive the fortunes of France as a counterbalance to the dominant influence of Charles that Wolsey followed suit, severed relations with the Emperor, and entered into alliance with France.

An alternative interpretation of Wolsey's policy which is more acceptable than the "balance of power" thesis, is that which makes him the consistent follower of the papal lead in order to further his own ambitions in the church. Certainly the Popes, for their part, were endeavouring to maintain a local balance of power in Italy in order to protect their own temporal influence there, and Wolsey was seldom out of step with the papacy for long.

And yet there is no need to postulate even this degree of consistency in Wolsey's actions in order to make them understandable. Like most of the statesmen of his day he probably seldom looked beyond the immediate situation and the immediate advantage to be gained from it. It is a mistake to probe too deeply in search of "principles" underlying the diplomatic manoeuvres of a generation to which diplomacy and war were still the sport of kings.

## The Burgundian Alliance Netherlands.

There were, however, certain aspects of the international scene which could not for long be ignored by any English monarch or statesman, and can therefore be said to have shaped the mould in which English diplomacy had to be cast.

In the first place there was the very long-established and very valuable two-way traffic across the narrow seas between England and the Netherlands. The nature of this trade might change from time to time (as, for instance, when the export of raw wool from England tended to yield pride of place to that of cloth), but the value of it, not only to merchants on both sides of the sea, but also to their princes who derived a very considerable revenue from tolls and duties imposed upon it, continued steadily to increase. Now this commercial and economic link made a political alliance between England and the Netherlands almost inevitable. Neither side could afford for long the interruption of trade that any war between the two countries would entail.

And so we find that the Burgundian dukes who ruled the

Netherlands in the fifteenth century were fairly consistently in alliance with the kings of England, whether Lancastrian or Yorkist. And we find this Burgundian alliance, despite the Yorkist origins and loyalties of the dowager duchess in Brussels, re-established and confirmed by Henry VII, though he was the heir of Lancaster. Right through the first half of the sixteenth century this Burgundian alliance, transformed progressively into a Habsburg, and then a Spanish alliance, remained the foundation stone of English diplomacy. The departures from it were few, and, with one exception, not prolonged.

The natural complement of the Burgundian alliance was the ingrained and almost natural tendency of England to be at enmity with France. The roots of this animosity were many; the English kings' claim to the French throne, maintained with varying degrees of earnestness since the reign of Edward III; the memories of victories, and of defeats, in the Hundred Years' War; a widespread feeling that large areas of France belonged by ancient right to England; the close friendship between France and England's other ancient enemy Scotland; all these helped to strengthen the general preference of most Englishmen for an alliance with the enemies of France.

Henry VII's foreign policy was supplementary to his domestic. He sought, in his negotiations with other monarchs, first their recognition of his right to the English throne, and their rejection of the pretensions of all rival claimants, and secondly to establish his own government upon a firm foundation by avoiding where possible the strains of war. And so he supplemented the Burgundian alliance by treaties with Spain, with France and with Scotland. His only aggressive action, his campaign against France in 1492, secured its objective (the abandonment by France of Perkin Warbeck) with the minimum of bloodshed.

Wolsey, for all his reputation as an advocate of the balance of power, only once broke away from the Burgundian-Imperial alliance and actually committed England to war against the ruler of the Netherlands. This was in 1527, and was not a happy occasion. Though for a few months in 1528 a state of war existed, there was no actual fighting, and so great was the popular outcry at the possibility of the Netherlands' trade being interrupted that the Cardinal had to make special arrangements to keep it flowing despite the official state of hostilities.

## The Burgundian Alliance Broken

This ineffective little "war" of 1528 was the sole active consequence of the Anglo-French alliance which Wolsey had signed in the previous year, which was to last until 1533, and which was to constitute the only serious break in the long history of the Anglo-Burgundian alliance before the events of the latter half of the sixteenth century were to bring about a complete reversal of England's traditional position. This temporary switch of alliances had less to do with the "balance of power" than with King Henry's matrimonial troubles, though it is possible to explain it also in terms of Wolsey's personal desire to stand well with the Pope.

Henry's first marriage, which by 1527 he wished to have declared null, was to Catherine of Aragon, an aunt of the Emperor Charles V.[2] For personal as well as diplomatic reasons the latter, when he learned of Henry's intention, brought pressure to bear at Rome to prevent the Pope from meeting Henry's wishes. Only the French King could hope to bring sufficient counter-pressure of the same sort to bear. Indeed it was only when a French army temporarily gained control of Italy in the spring of 1528 that the Pope felt able to issue his commission to the cardinals Wolsey and Campeggio to hear the King's case in England. Though that French success was shortlived, its consequences had shown that it was only with the assistance of Francis that Henry could hope to get his way at Rome.

That there was very little other foundation for the French alliance is clear from the rapidity with which it disintegrated when Henry, in 1533, at last lost patience, turned his back on the papacy, and dealt with his own affairs in his own way. The anxiety of the English King to get back to the safe haven of the Imperial alliance was also made plain upon the occasion of Queen Catherine's death in January 1536. Now that death had removed the chief cause of their dispute Henry was quite unable to conceal his earnest hope that the good

---

[2] See genealogical table No. 4 in Appendix B, p. 235.

relations which had formerly existed between him and the Emperor would be quite rapidly restored.

But Charles was in no hurry to make up the quarrel, and between 1533, when Henry fell out with Francis, and 1541–2, when the position of 1520 was repeated and Francis and Charles, about to renew their interminable conflict, both sued for Henry's help, the King of England endured a potentially very dangerous isolation. His rejection of the papacy had brought down upon him the threat of papal excommunication, and there was, at times, a real risk that Francis and Charles would sink their differences in a joint crusade against their schismatic brother-sovereign.

It was during these years of danger that Henry, probably at the instigation of Thomas Cromwell, explored the possibility of entering into an alliance with the Protestant princes of Germany. But these negotiations with the Lutherans were seldom more than half-hearted on Henry's part, and were dropped without any ceremony immediately there was any prospect of a renewed understanding with the Emperor. In 1543 this was at last achieved, and for the rest of the reign England's foreign relations settled down into their old familiar channels.

There was to be one other, and much less important, diplomatic breach between England and the Habsburgs, in the reign of Edward VI. This occurred during the period of the ascendancy of Northumberland, and was occasioned by the attempts made to oblige the Princess Mary to abandon the Latin mass and to accept the English prayer book in her private chapel. Once again Charles V came to the defence of a relative, this time of his first cousin, and Anglo-Imperial relations became so strained that a not very satisfactory peace had to be made with France in 1550. But with the death of Edward, the fall of Northumberland and the accession of Mary, the old Imperial alliance was resumed, and made yet firmer by the marriage of Charles' son and heir Philip to the English Queen. When the war against France began again in 1555 England was, by virtue of this marriage, once more engaged upon the Habsburg side.

*The Diplomatic Revolution*

And so, in 1558, when Elizabeth succeeded her half-sister,

England and Spain were partners in war against France, and had been allies, save for the two interruptions we have noted above, for at least seventy years, to take the connection back no further than the treaty of Medina del Campo in 1489, though of course the Burgundian connection out of which the Spanish alliance had in part grown, went very much further back than that. This being so, we have next to ask ourselves why England and Spain should, during the first two decades of the new reign, have become such bitter enemies that the conflict between them should dominate the rest of the century? And why should the diplomatic turn-about have been so complete that in the fight against Spain, England should seek to co-operate with one of her ancient enemies, France, and to live on the best of terms with the other, Scotland?

The abruptness of this "diplomatic revolution" in Elizabeth's reign is made the clearer when we recall that her very accession was itself a cause of further friction between England and France. The French King, now Henry II, chose to regard Elizabeth, the daughter of Anne Boleyn, as the offspring of a bigamous match and therefore illegitimate and incapable of succeeding to the throne of England. At the same time he championed, in the most threatening manner, the claims of his own daughter-in-law, Mary Stuart, who was not only already Queen of Scotland in her own right, but was also married to the heir to the throne of France, and stood next in line of succession to the English throne through her descent from Henry VIII's elder sister.[3] If Elizabeth was illegitimate, and had as a consequence no title to the English throne, then it was Mary of Scotland who was rightfully Queen of England.

The best defence that Elizabeth had against this strong challenge to her title was the sure knowledge that Philip of Spain, who had brought England firmly into the Habsburg orbit by his marriage to Mary Tudor, would never allow that country now to fall into French hands to form, with France and Scotland, a solid bar across his line of communication between the two main centres of his power, the Netherlands and Spain. Henry II of France knew this too, and it was this knowledge that helped to restrain him. In 1558 he and Philip were negotiating to bring to an end a mutually exhausting

[3] See genealogical table No. 2 in Appendix B, p. 234.

war in which, on the whole, the Spaniards had fared the better. The French King was in no position to risk a renewal of hostilities by pressing his daughter-in-law's claims to the English throne too vigorously. Thus the threat that Spain would intervene on her behalf was one of Elizabeth's greatest assets in the perilous early days of her reign.

And yet, only eleven years later, in 1570, it was Spain's turn to be the enemy to be feared in England. Spanish ships sailing up the English channel in that year created widespread fears of invasion. It was now Spain who supported most actively the claims of the deposed and imprisoned Queen Mary of Scotland. The hand of Spain was now to be seen in nearly all the many plots against the English Queen's life. France was now, on the other hand, the friend to be courted, and negotiations were on foot for the marriage of Elizabeth to a French prince.

The diplomatic revolution was not yet complete. English relations with both France and Spain had yet to pass through many vicissitudes before they settled down into what was to be the pattern for the last decades of the century, but already in 1570 the alignment of the future, with England and France in alliance against Spain, could be seen by the discerning eye to be taking shape.

## The Religious Factor

There are several good reasons why this fundamental change in England's alignment with the other powers of Western Europe should have taken place at this time, and it is difficult to give any one of them priority. We have already seen in the last chapter how religion and national pride combined had helped to bring England and Scotland together in a new-found friendship after centuries of hostility, and there can be little doubt that religion also played a part in embittering Anglo-Spanish relations once they had started to deteriorate. The constant emphasis, from the English side, upon the need to defend the reformed religion from the counter-attack of Rome, and, from the Spanish side, upon the need to put heretics in their place, was not all insincere propaganda.

Of course the English buccaneers who sailed to plunder Spanish ships and bases were mainly inspired by hopes that had little to do with religion, but that is not to say that they did not derive additional satisfaction from the knowledge that they would also be striking a blow against the Catholic enemy. Religion still permeated the life of the whole nation, and even the hardiest son of the sea was in his own way a devout man who felt himself personally involved in the world-wide conflict of religions. Likewise the English soldier of fortune who fought against the Spaniards in the Netherlands, though his chief objective may have been the indulgence of his taste for adventure and the improving of his personal fortune, also derived considerable satisfaction from the knowledge that he was fighting against the enemies of his religion as well as of his country. Those who, in reaction against the older notion that the Anglo-Spanish war of Elizabeth's reign was solely and simply a war of religion, have attempted to dispense with the religious motive entirely, and have left us with nothing more than a façade of religion deliberately erected to cover the less attractive realities of economic nationalism, have gone too far.

On the other hand we must concede that religion was clearly not the only factor in the conflict, and that it is very unlikely that religious differences alone would have led to war. The Elizabethan church, sheltered behind the physical barrier of the English channel, soon developed sufficient strength to resist the counter-attack of the Catholic missionaries. Spanish assistance to and encouragement of this religious campaign was not sufficiently serious to warrant more than a diplomatic protest. But once England and Spain began to fall out over other matters, with which we have yet to deal, then the fact that the Spanish King was the self-appointed champion of the counter-reformation, and that the causes of catholicism and Spain were still as closely linked as they had been in Mary's day, added another and urgent reason for keeping the pretensions of the enemy in check.

Of course the degree to which men let the religious question colour their loyalties and direct their actions varied considerably in individual cases. The Queen herself probably felt the pull of religion least of all. The main objective of her diplomacy at all times was to safeguard her own tenure of the English throne. To do so she had on occasion to lend active support to the Protestants of Scotland and the Netherlands, but she was just as ready on other occasions to try the alternative course of negotiating with the Catholic King of Spain or Queen of Scotland when it suited her to do so.

Indeed the half-hearted nature of Elizabeth's support for the Netherlands' rebels, and her search for a negotiated settlement with Spain right up to the moment that the Armada was sighted, exasperated those of her councillors and subjects who viewed the European scene through more positively Protestant eyes and could see no profit in trying to come to terms with papists. Burleigh,* so long Elizabeth's right-hand man, was inclined to share her nonreligious approach to diplomatic problems, but Leicester and Walsingham,* more closely in touch with the aggressive heart of the puritan movement, had little patience with any suggestion of negotiating with the arch-enemy of "true religion".

The fact that France continued to be governed by Catholic kings until the assassination of Henry III in 1588 complicated matters for those who let religion colour their outlook, and the widespread massacre of the Huguenots on St Bartholomew's day in 1572 made it harder than ever for them to accept the fact that England on her own could not risk the hostility of both France and Spain together.

And yet in some ways France was the ally to be preferred. There was, even after the massacre, a substantial Protestant community in France which managed from time to time to win official recognition for itself, and from 1588 to 1593 the King of France was himself a Huguenot. Moreover, France, whether under Catholic or Huguenot kings, had shown herself on more than one occasion to be sufficiently the enemy of Spain to consider supporting the Protestant rebels in the Netherlands. France was therefore not so uncompromisingly Catholic as Spain. French protestantism was making an important contribution to the general cause of the reformed religion. In Spain there was no protestantism at all.

## Commercial Rivalry with Spain

Religion then undoubtedly had a part to play in deepening and widening the split between England and Spain once the first cracks had appeared in the long-established Anglo-Burgundian alliance, but it did not of itself cause the initial breakdown. As the real foundation stone of the Burgundian, and later Imperial and Spanish, alliances, had been the mutual commercial advantage, so it was an increasingly bitter commercial rivalry which brought Anglo-Spanish friendship to an end.

This rivalry expressed itself in contests on both sides of the Atlantic ocean. In the Americas John Hawkins* and his successors refused to accept the Spanish claim to monopolise the trade and resources of the New World, and when their attempts to gain a share of these for themselves met with spirited resistance from the Spanish authorities it was not long before a state of undeclared war prevailed around the shores of the Caribbean sea.

The opening engagement in this conflict took place in the Mexican port of San Juan de Ulloa in 1568. There Hawkins' little fleet, having put in for repairs, was attacked and almost destroyed by a Spanish squadron. The Spaniards justified their action as necessary to defend their imperial monopoly against an alien "pirate" who had used force to infringe it. But to Francis Drake,* who commanded one of Hawkins' ships, the Spanish attack was an unprovoked and treacherous assault upon a merchant fleet, and merited retribution in kind.

Revenge for the humiliation of San Juan and hatred of all Spaniards were to be the mainsprings of Drake's later career which he devoted to attacking Spanish ships and harbours in many parts of the globe. Even his famous circumnavigation of the world in 1577–80 was little more than an extended piratical raid upon the Pacific coast of Spanish America, from where the safest way back to England clearly lay westwards across the open Pacific, rather than eastwards through the narrow confines of the straits of Magellan.

Nearer home the government of Elizabeth, not content to maintain the trading agreements which Henry VII had made to regulate the lucrative traffic between England and the Netherlands, began to try to gain further advantages for English merchants by restricting the activities and reducing the privileges of their Flemish competitors in England. Naturally this economic nationalism produced in reaction a similar attempt on the part of the Netherlands' government to advance the interests of its own nationals at the expense of their English rivals. The consequence was what neither side really wanted, a series of counter-strokes culminating in a complete stoppage of trade between England and the Spanish Netherlands which led many English merchants to develop alternative links with their continental markets through north German ports such as Emden and Hamburg.

The trade links which had held the Anglo-Burgundian alliance together were thus loosened by mutual embargoes in 1563–4. When, a decade later, the Netherlanders rose in open revolt against their Spanish overlords, and the ports in Spanish hands were very effectively blockaded by the sea forces of the insurgents, these links were finally snapped. Now, increasingly, it was to the ports of Holland and Zealand, under independent Dutch control, that the commerce of England was directed, and it was with the struggling young Dutch republic that the sympathy of English merchants lay. War with Spain no longer of necessity meant hardship for the English trader, indeed war with Spain might well seem necessary if the Dutch republic was to be kept alive and its ports kept open to English traffic. England and Spain, from having been commercial partners, were well on the way to becoming commercial rivals.

## English Intervention in the Netherlands' Revolt

A further, and very important, contribution to Anglo-Spanish hostility was also made by the outbreak of the Dutch revolt. From the earliest days of her reign Elizabeth had encouraged Netherlands' discontents and supported the growing movement for independence. This underground activity against the King of Spain upon whose goodwill she was initially so very dependent clearly demonstrates that Elizabeth had no wish to be the client of Philip II or to have to rely for her own security upon his charitable benevolence. Though, for the time being, Philip must be her friend in opposing the ambitious schemes of the King of France, Elizabeth probably saw clearly enough, even at the very beginning of her reign, that English and Spanish interests were bound to clash at some time in the fairly near future, and was already preparing for that day by stirring up trouble for Spain in the Low Countries.

And yet, in the long run, it was English interference in the Netherlands which did more than anything else to bring England and Spain to actual war. Time and time again, when the Spanish forces in the Netherlands seemed about to succeed in their task of reducing the provinces to obedience, English intervention would keep the revolt alive. Elizabeth's seizure of the Spanish gold in 1568, her expulsion of the Sea Beggars from Dover in 1572, her sending of an expeditionary force under Leicester in 1585, are all cases in point. It eventually became clear to Philip, with whom the suppression of the Netherlands always took priority over other ambitions, that he had little hope of succeeding in this his main task until he had put a stop to English intervention. The attempted invasion of England in 1588 which began the Anglo-Spanish war was, in a way, a reply to the landing of Leicester's force in the Netherlands some three years before.

Undeclared war in the Caribbean, piracy on the high seas, English assistance to the Dutch rebels and, on the Spanish side, support for the Catholic missionaries to England, intrigues with Irish rebels and plots against the Queen's life, brought the crisis between England and Spain to a head in 1588. Thereafter, to the end of Elizabeth's reign, a state of war existed between the allies of former days.

Two years before the Armada sailed England and Scotland had come to terms. In the Armada year itself the accession of the Huguenot Henry IV to the French throne helped to complete the diplomatic revolution. The French Catholic League, which refused to accept a Huguenot as king, sought the aid of Spain in pressing the claims of their own candidate for the French throne, and in these circumstances it was only natural that Henry IV and Elizabeth, both now at war with Philip II, should enter into an active alliance. Even the politically inspired conversion of the French King to catholicism in 1593 did not break this Anglo-French accord which was maintained as long as the Spanish war lasted.

## The Growth of English Naval Power

This switch of alliances during the latter part of the Tudor period is not the only point to notice about England's position internationally during the sixteenth century. We must also observe the signs of England's re-emergence as a major power. This was a re-emergence as a naval rather than a military power, for English armies remained small and of little account compared with the forces which the Spanish General Parma or the Dutch leader Maurice of Nassau could lead into battle. This new-found naval strength of England was first made plain to the rest of Europe in 1588 in the fighting against the Armada. It is true of course that by far the greater proportion of the losses suffered by the Spanish fleet on that occasion were inflicted by the weather and the rocks of the Scottish and Irish coasts, and not by English gunfire. It is also true that the English fleet did not prevent the Armada from attaining its first objective by sailing through the channel. But it had been no part of the English defence plan to try to block the channel. As long as the invasion force from the Netherlands, which the Armada was to convoy across the narrow seas, could be kept at bay, then England would be safe and her fleet would have done what was expected of it. And so, because their presence and that of their Dutch allies had made impossible a peaceful junction between the Armada and the force it was to convoy, the English ships had gained an important defensive victory. They had denied to Spain that command of the channel crossing without which no invasion could be attempted.

More important still, the English ships had given such a good account of themselves during the passage up the channel that the Spanish commanders preferred to risk the hazards of the weather on the long north-about passage home rather than run the gauntlet of English guns in the channel a second time. England was clearly now a naval power to be respected, and even though Spanish seapower made a rapid recovery and the naval honours were about even for most of the rest of the war, the memory of 1588 lived on.

This emergence of England as a naval power rested upon two foundations, both Tudor. First there was the care bestowed upon the navy by Henry VIII. Though considerations of prestige may have played their part in the building of some of his larger ships, such as the *Henry Grâce à Dieu,* it was Henry who saw the need not only to build a nucleus of royal ships designed primarily as fighting vessels, round which the merchant auxiliaries could gather in time of war, but also the equally vital need to provide an effective behind-the-scenes organisation to keep his ships in fighting trim in peace as well as war. Consequently it is to Henry VIII that we owe the creation of royal dockyards and the re-organisation of the Admiralty.

The other founder of the Elizabethan navy was John Hawkins, who during his years at the Admiralty supervised an extensive reconstruction programme whose object was to create a fleet of ships of improved design and heavier armament, more suited to the newer tactics of the long-range cannonade than to the older of grappling and boarding. Of course, the Spanish Armada was also largely composed of ships of this improved pattern so that Hawkins' efforts only resulted in England keeping pace with her rival, and did not give her any advantage. Yet it remains true that without Hawkins to keep things moving at the Admiralty the fleet that put to sea to meet the Spanish threat in 1588 might have been very sadly inferior in manoeuvrability and armament.

For the future England's strength would rest with the navy, and would vary directly with the degree of care and attention devoted to that service. When the navy was in good hands England's name would be respected abroad, when it was neglected England would be of little account. It was natural that an island power should concentrate its strength at sea, and yet England was slow to grasp the logic of her position. As long as her monarchs dreamed of making good their ancient claim to France, as long as the continental foothold in Calais was there to tempt them and as long as a hostile Scotland threatened them from the rear, so long would the navy play a minor rôle merely as guardian of the army's supply lines across the channel. The loss of Calais in 1558 and the agreement with Scotland in 1586 thus had their part to play in shaping England's naval future, as important in its own way as the victory over the Spanish fleet in 1588.

# 11

## Economic Developments

PROBABLY THE MOST widely known feature of the economic history of Western Europe in the sixteenth century is the inflationary movement variously termed "the price rise" or "the price revolution". That it was a very important movement, affecting in various ways every part of the economy, is scarcely to be denied, but how and why the movement began, and to what extent it was a cause or a consequence of other developments, are questions which cannot be answered with the same degree of certainty.

### The Causes of the Price Revolution

The once generally accepted idea was that the price rise was mainly due to monetary causes such as the greatly increased supply of the precious metals, particularly of silver, coming both from the exploitation of new sources in the Americas and from the increased production of the established European mines. The greater abundance of these metals, relative to the quantity of goods and services produced, resulted in a fall in their value, and in the value of the various European currencies which were coined from them, and this general fall in the comparative value of money expressed itself in the form of a general rise in the level of all prices.

The rate at which prices rose was at the same time greatly accelerated in some countries by another monetary cause, debasement, which resulted from the action of governments in deliberately reducing the gold and silver content of the coinage in circulation.

In England, for instance, there was a series of recoinages in the reigns of Henry VIII and Edward VI. The first of these, designed to make a profit for a hard-pressed treasury, took place in 1526. A new silver currency was issued which was reduced in size though it still bore the same face value as the old. The new gold coinage, issued at the same time, retained its former size, but was increased in nominal value. The gold and silver saved by this operation would, it was hoped, help to finance Wolsey's war plans. But the chief result of this tampering with the coinage was to reduce the purchasing power of the new issue so that the actual profit reaped by the government was scarcely sufficient to compensate for the damage done to the good name of sterling, or for the difficulties created by the consequent acceleration of the price rise.

And yet, less than twenty years later, in 1544, the coinage was interfered with once again in the same vain hope that a profit could be made. This time there were several recoinages in succession, which resulted, by 1551, in an all-round reduction in the proportion of good metal to alloy while an attempt was made to maintain the original face value of the coins concerned. Worst affected were the smaller coins, the groat, half-groat and penny, whose silver content was eventually reduced to about one-third of what it had been in 1520. The final state of the English coinage was deplorable. Its reputation was not to be fully restored until all the base coins were finally called in in the reign of Elizabeth. We shall have more to say about the further consequences of these debasements at a later stage.

However, were we to rest content with this kind of explanation of the price revolution which accounts for it primarily in terms of such monetary factors as the influx of silver and debasement of the coinage, we should be accepting as adequate what is now generally held to be rather too simple an explanation of a movement that was rather more complex in its operation and had other causes which would have tended to set it in motion even without the assistance of Mexican silver and Henry VIII's coin-clipping. We must not, for instance, overlook the importance of population pressure.

## The Increase in Population

England, in Tudor times, was experiencing a steady and quite remarkable growth in population which had in all probability a more important contribution to make to the general rise in prices than either of the purely monetary factors we have so far mentioned.

Statistics of population in the centuries before the initiation of regular censuses can at best, of course, be only very approximate, and we must be prepared to find very considerable variations in the figures supplied by different authorities. And yet, making all allowances for these differences, it is apparent that between the reigns of Henry VII and James I the population of England increased by nearly fifty per cent., from about 3½ millions to about 5 millions. The causes of this increase have yet to be satisfactorily explained, but the consequences are plain enough.

Although England today supports about ten times as many people as it did in the reign of Elizabeth I, we must not therefore conclude that the maintenance of a mere 5 millions should have presented no difficulties to that earlier age. It was not the actual size of the population that caused the trouble, but the rate at which it had expanded to that figure. The English economy, geared for a long time to the maintenance of a population of about 3½ millions, predominantly rural and agricultural, and supplying their own food from their own village fields, with few towns large enough to need to look very far afield for their supplies, now found itself required, in the space of a couple of generations, to provide for half as many people again, with an increasing proportion of them gathered in rapidly expanding urban centres, in London, in the West Riding of Yorkshire, in the Black Country and on Tyneside.

The population of England was growing and at the same time becoming more urbanised. Both these developments produced pressure upon the land, pressure for more foodstuffs and for more land upon which to grow them. At the same time, for other reasons which we shall discuss later (see below, p. 165), the demand for land for wool production was increasing, and every enclosure of arable acres for sheep pasture aggravated the food situation still further.

Land itself was not yet a scarce commodity, for the forests and wastes still surrounded and separated the villages and their fields like the waters of the ocean flowing through the channels of an archipelago. But improved, reclaimed or cultivated land was in short supply and rose in price, as did the foodstuffs and other materials which it could produce.

The pressure of increasing population thus set on foot not only a rise in the price of food, but a movement to bring new lands under cultivation, and gradually the forests and waste lands contracted as "new intakes" made inroads upon them, and forest timber, once so plentiful as to be virtually without value, now began to become a scarce and much-prized commodity. But all this took time, and while agriculture was taking some steps to meet the new demand for supplies, the population increase itself continued to keep ahead of the expansion of output, and prices rose relentlessly.

The growth in population, the debasements of the coinage and the influx of gold and silver thus all worked in the same direction, and kept prices rising throughout most of the sixteenth century, with a great acceleration in the 1530s and 1540s.

## The Effects of the Price Revolution

This inflationary movement was not, however, without its beneficial as well as its harmful consequences. The price revolution was selective in its victims, some it hit hard, some it touched hardly at all, and there were yet others who derived considerable benefits from it.

The least affected by the fall in the value of money were those who had least occasion to use it in their daily lives, such as the smaller farmers who normally supplied most of their own needs from the produce of their own holdings, and who could reap a considerable profit from the sale of their surplus foodstuffs which were increasingly in demand. Those whose land was a freehold were of course the best off, for the terms on which they held their property could not be altered. However, many copy-holders and other tenants were equally well protected against the possibility of a rise in rent by the force of ancient custom. It was chiefly leaseholders and tenants-at-will who were liable to suffer from the attentions of a rent-raising landlord, yet even a leaseholder might have little to fear if his lease had sufficiently long to run.

Hardest hit by the general price rise were those, whether in town or countryside, who had nothing to live on but their wages (the artisans and landless labourers), for, as nearly always in a time of inflation, and almost certainly in those days when the wage labourers had no unions to protect their interests, wages tended to lag behind prices, and the wage-earner was perennially hard-up.

Yet, almost as hard hit as the labourers were those landowners whose tenants' rents were fixed by immutable custom, or whose lands were let out on long leases which had many years to run. Only those who farmed their lands themselves, or whose tenants were not protected by custom, or whose leases were falling in, could hope to adjust their income, by rent increases or by reorganisation of their estates, to meet their new level of expenditure. Those whose incomes were not open to expansion in any of these ways had to take drastic action to keep themselves solvent, and many did not succeed.

The price rise put a premium upon efficient estate management. Those who would not, or could not, reorganise their properties to meet the new conditions soon had to sell out to those who could, or thought they could.

Some landlords were fortunate in that they possessed supplementary sources of income from mineral deposits upon their estates. Coal, iron ore, lead and other minerals kept many a landowner out of bankruptcy, and it was fortunate for those who possessed such assets that the need to develop them came at a time when, as we shall see, the demand for such raw materials of industry was on the increase.

Other landowners, not so blessed by nature, tried to salve their fortunes by engaging, or at least investing, in trade, privateering or perhaps piracy. The initial financial backing for many an Elizabethan overseas adventure came as much from the landed gentry as from the city merchants, though as successful merchants still liked to buy land and to set themselves up as country gentlemen, and as the younger sons of the gentry quite frequently sought to carve out careers for themselves in the world of commerce, it is not always easy to keep merchant and landowner in separate categories, so easily was the borderline between them crossed in either direction.

Yet other landowners were persuaded to diversify their investments and augment their income by putting some of their capital into schemes to develop new products or new trades. Many of these "projects" were rather more fanciful than sound, and the race of "projectors" which grew up in Elizabeth's reign was quite a plague to the landowners upon whose resources they attempted to grow fat.

Other landowners sought refuge in government office, or in the favour of the Court. The adaptable and enterprising throve, the rest suffered, and in many cases were forced to sell out to others who knew better how to make their estates pay.

## The Reorganisation of Agriculture

The price rise thus gave the landed interest in England a thorough shaking-up, and accelerated the movement towards commercialised agriculture and away from mere subsistence farming. No longer was the pattern of agriculture on the great estates determined mainly by the immediate needs of the landowner's own household. Instead, the demands of an increasingly wide market made their influence felt upon the choice of crops and the distribution of acreage. This was especially true in those districts which felt the pull of the growing urban centres, as for example the Thames valley, Kent and Suffolk, which increasingly catered for the London market. In regions such as these the presence of a large neighbouring population provided opportunities for agricultural specialisation and growing for the market rather than for the house became the rule.

Reorganisation of agriculture along these lines was, of course, more easily carried out where the enterprising farmer, whatever the size of his holding, had sole control of the management of his estates. This he could only have where the open field system with its co-operative husbandry had been replaced by separate holdings and individual ownership. And so the movement towards enclosure, which had a long history behind it before the Tudor period, was given a further stimulus by the economic pressures of the sixteenth-century price rise.

## Industrial Expansion

The steady rise in prices also stimulated industrial growth. The increasing demand which helped to push up prices could best be satisfied either by an increase in the production of existing industries, or by the establishment of new manufactures. In either case the manufacturer could expect to make a good profit, as wages tended to lag behind prices and to make labour a comparatively cheap commodity, while at the same time there was little difficulty in getting a good price for the completed product.

The peaceful state of the country had, of course, its contribution to make as well to the expansion of industry. In an ordered society, where rebellion and civil strife need no longer be daily expected, men felt freer to indulge their taste for comfort and luxury. The man who filled the windows of his house with glass, adorned its walls with tapestries, set his table with a silver service and draped his bed with expensive hangings, was no longer in immediate danger of despoiling by an avaricious neighbour. He could reasonably expect to enjoy his purchases for many years. Furthermore, fashions were changing, and it was no longer enough that the great house should supply food and shelter without stint, but these now should be dispensed in an atmosphere of elegance and distinction.

All the expenditure which was necessary to create and maintain these new standards of living called into being industries to supply its needs. Glass, copper, brass and luxury fabrics were among the new manufactures to be developed in England in Tudor times. At the same time the old industries were expanding. Coal production in particular took a big step forward as timber supplies began to run low and domestic hearths were converted to use the alternative fuel.

The principal manufacturing interest of England, however, remained in textiles. The spinning of yarn and the weaving of cloth, mostly woollen, still occupied more people than any other industry, and the expansion of the export trade in cloth in the earlier half of the sixteenth century ensured that the clothing industry remained on top.

All this industrial expansion, it should be noted, was accompanied by comparatively little industrial reorganisation. This sixteenth-century expansion was not in that sense the beginning of an industrial revolution. It is true that attempts were made by such celebrated figures as William Stumpe and Jack of Newbury, to bring the weavers out of their cottages and to gather them and their looms together under one large roof in a manner foreshadowing that of a modern factory, but these experiments were not in the long run successful, and were not followed up. For the most part the cloth industry remained organised on a domestic basis, with the weaver working at his own loom in his own cottage.

Where a certain degree of reorganisation did come in was in

the increasing tendency for the weavers to work for a wage on materials supplied to them by the clothiers, instead of purchasing their own raw materials and selling their own product in the open market as hitherto. The beginnings of modern industrial capitalism are to be seen more clearly in this sort of development (which was not, however, altogether new in the sixteenth century) than in the "factories" established for a few years in the cloisters of some suppressed monastery. The day of the large factory had to wait until the application of power to spinning, weaving and other machinery, made it economically advantageous to drive a number of machines from a common source of power. The day of the small master did not suddenly end in the Tudor period, though his position was being undermined.

## Boom and Slump in the Cloth Trade

The expansion of the export trade in cloth, to which we have already referred, was the dominant feature in the commercial scene in the earlier part of the Tudor period. Its influence upon the life of England was widespread. It was not merely those engaged in the manufacture and marketing of cloth who felt its effects.

This expansion began about 1460, and continued steadily through to the reign of Henry VIII, by which time the number of cloths exported annually had more than doubled, and, in terms of value, the trade in cloth had outstripped the trade in wool. Then, in the 1540s, the fate of the pound sterling on the international exchanges created a situation so favourable to this particular trade that the rate of expansion reached the proportions of a boom.

This was largely a consequence of the progressive debasements of the English coinage to which we have already referred. The reduction in the metal content of English money cheapened it in terms of other currencies, and this reduced the price of English cloth to the foreign buyer. The stimulus that this gave to English exports and English manufacturers was so great as to be unhealthy. Everybody in the business, and many newcomers too who knew little about it, wished to make a profit from the boom.

The almost inevitable result of this stimulus to manufacture was overproduction and a flooding of the market, which in its turn produced a sudden slump in 1551 when buyers had taken all they could hope to dispose of and the exporters were left with large unsaleable stocks on their hands.

The effect of the slump was heightened by the otherwise admirable efforts made by the Edwardian government from 1551 onwards to restore the English currency to its former standards. Their efforts, though only partially successful, did mean that English cloth no longer enjoyed to quite the same degree the advantage of comparative cheapness which had helped to set the boom in motion.

Meanwhile the slump in cloth exports was creating widespread unemployment in the various branches of the trade, and bankruptcies among the merchants, and appeals were being made to the government to prevent, by the exercise of a closer control over industry and commerce, any repetition of the great disaster.

The cause of the breakdown seemed, to most of those who gave it any serious thought, to have been the undisciplined rushing-in of inexperienced newcomers anxious to have a share in the steadily rising profits of cloth manufacture or trade, and who, through their ignorance of the business, grossly overestimated the capacity of the market. Exclusivism seemed to be the answer. Let those already in the business continue to follow it, but let them be properly qualified, and protected from the speculative outsider.

We can trace this exclusivism in the regulative statutes of the 1550s which culminated in the Statute of Artificers (5 Eliz. cap. 4) in 1563. This last attempted to make more rigid the system of apprenticeship which was the usual method of entry to a trade, and to protect industry from the harmful effects of a sudden expansion by imposing strict limits upon the number of apprentices any one master could employ.

The same principle of exclusivism can also be seen applied to commerce by the charters of the various companies of merchants (the Muscovy Company, the Levant Company, the East India Company, etc.) which were established during the second half of the century. The regulated company of merchants was a device designed, among other things, to make more difficult any sudden influx of newcomers into any particular trade. The keynote of Elizabethan economic legislation was therefore "regulation", and the desire for regulation had its roots in the collapse of 1551.

## The "Decay of Tillage"

The great boom of the 1540s also had its effects upon agriculture. It added to the other pressures towards enclosure, and in particular towards enclosure for pasture, by putting a premium upon wool. The conversion of land from tillage to pasture, the enclosure of common land, the throwing down of villages to make sheep-runs, all these well-known features of the "enclosure movement" so familiar to us through the complaints of sixteenth-century writers, can be found in train long before that particular century dawned. Indeed it seems highly probable that the bulk of this sort of enclosure (which was so very different in intention and consequence from the enclosure of former wastes to bring them under the plough, or from the consolidation and enclosure of strips in the open fields in order to introduce more efficient methods of farming) was done before the reign of Henry VII began. Its consequences were a commonplace to the men of Sir Thomas More's day. It was no novelty of which they wrote, nor was it a newly arisen evil with which Cardinal Wolsey attempted to deal with his "Act concerning the pulling down of towns" (6 Henry VIII cap. 6) in 1515.

And yet the continually rising demand for wool as cloth exports went on expanding provided a constant temptation to go over to sheep. The boom of the 1540s must have had some effect, and may perhaps be given some credit for the agricultural discontent which broke in open rebellion in Norfolk in 1549.

Of course the concurrent increase in population (see above, p. 158) also helped to exaggerate the consequences of any conversion to pasture. With ever more people to feed and find employment for, a movement which tended to reduce the acreage available for crops was bound to cause hardship and discontent.

## The "Decay of Hospitality"

The rural discontent created by the change from subsistence

to commercial agriculture, and by the continuing switch from crops to pasture, was further aggravated in the middle years of the sixteenth century by the breakdown of the medieval system of relief.

Though the amount of charity dispensed in pre-dissolution days by the monastic orders is a matter of some debate, and must remain so since only the obligatory charities imposed by the will of a benefactor are on record, we must, at the very least, credit the monks with the same measure of generosity as their lay neighbours displayed.

"Hospitality" is a word in frequent use in the sixteenth century, and it is generally employed to cover not only the selective entertaining of one's own friends and family, but the indiscriminate entertaining of all travellers and others who might need food and shelter for the night. The "decay of hospitality" is lamented in the same terms as the decay of tillage, but for hospitality to be capable of decay it must first have flourished.

Just when hospitality began to decay it would be difficult to say. The Act for the Dissolution of the Lesser Monasteries (27 Henry VIII cap. 28), passed in 1536, specifically requires that all new holders of former monastic properties shall maintain "an honest continual house and household" after the fashion of their predecessors. It is also clear from other references that this clause was designed to maintain not only local employment (in the household) but also local hospitality (in the house) at its former level. This in turn suggests that the habit of hospitality was already in decline at the time the Act was passed, and that some fears had been expressed that the dissolution of the monasteries would accelerate the process.

Such legislative provisions were, however, quite inadequate to halt a movement which was impelled by strong economic forces. The lay successor to the monks might fully intend to keep up the accustomed level of hospitality, for the keeping of a hospitable house was one of the marks of the true gentleman, but if his income was fixed and his costs were rising he might well be forced to economise by being more selective about his guests. His friends and social equals he would still entertain as lavishly as he could, for it would be a matter of pride not to let himself down in their eyes, but the casual vagrant, or the paupers from the neighbouring village, might well find themselves less welcome than before.

At the same time the pressures created by the increasing population, the continuing enclosures and evictions, and by the cutting down of the size of noble households, were increasing the number of able-bodied persons who were unable to find work and were forced into beggary and vagabondage. All these movements were taking place independently of the dissolution of the monasteries, and had more to do with the creation of the problem of the sturdy beggar than had the eviction of the monks and nuns.

Of course, in some cases, the transfer of the monastic estates to lay hands did result in a reorganisation which led to unemployment, and, in other instances, the new owner, though he continued to work the estates in the old way, might well have no need for as large a domestic staff as the monks had retained. But in what was probably the majority of cases the dissolution produced little more than a change of ownership, and the monks' former employees retained their posts. The monks and nuns themselves were provided with government pensions, which were in some cases very meagre, and were often in arrears, but there is no evidence to suggest that any substantial number of them was forced to take to begging.

And so, although the increase in vagabondage coincided in time with the dissolution of the monasteries, we must not be tempted to see in these two movements a case of cause and effect. The most that we may say is that the dissolution may have accelerated a process that was in the main due to other causes.

## The Poor Law

The decay in hospitality and the increase in vagrancy created for the Tudors a social problem of the first magnitude which was considerably aggravated by the unemployment among cloth-workers caused by the collapse of the export trade in the 1550s. Though individual philanthropy did make some attempts to deal with this problem, the most satisfactory solution was eventually found to lie in imposing upon the parish, on a compulsory basis, the responsibility for the welfare of the unfortunate.

This solution, which was given its fullest expression in the codification of the Elizabethan Poor Law in 1601, was only arrived at by slow degrees. The first important step was the recognition, in a statute of 1531 (22 Henry VIII cap. 12), of the distinction between those who could not and those who would not work. The former were to be licensed to beg in their own localities. The latter were to be severely punished if they did not turn to some honest work.

Recognition of the fact that many who wanted to work, and were fit for it, could nevertheless not find work through no fault of their own, was the next step in the evolution of the Poor Law. Some towns, notably London, began, from about the 1540s onwards, to make some attempt to find work for their able unemployed, but the adoption of their methods on a national scale had to wait until 1576 (18 Eliz. cap. 3) when all municipal authorities were required to provide materials and work for those who could not otherwise find it.

Four years earlier (14 Eliz. cap. 5), a compulsory poor rate had for the first time been imposed to raise funds for the relief of those who were too old or too ill to work, and whose maintenance had hitherto been left to the consciences of their more fortunate fellows. The adoption, at the same time, of the practice of apprenticing pauper children completed the main structure of a system of poor relief which was to last for two and a half centuries.

Pauperism provides the dark tones in the picture of Elizabethan England, but at the same time as the system of relief was being developed the population pressure which had helped to create the problem was also working to bring it under control. The steadily increasing demand for foodstuffs, and the slump in the cloth trade, worked together to slow down the swing from tillage to pasture. By the end of the sixteenth century the growing of wool was no longer so profitable, and food production, which required a larger labour force, had outstripped it in importance. Enclosure continued, but enclosure for pasture became rarer. Rural depopulation was checked, and the problem of vagabondage eased. At the same time the new and expanding industries provided employment for idle hands. England, by 1603, had surmounted the worst of the domestic crisis of the sixteenth century, and was on the threshold of a great expansion overseas. The beginnings of that expansion we shall endeavour to trace in the following chapter.

# 12

## Expansion Overseas

THE IMPORTANCE IN the history of Europe, and indeed of the world, of the progressive expansion into every part of the inhabited earth of European men, European commerce and European influences, need hardly be stressed. This movement, which began in the closing years of the fifteenth century and became increasingly important in the following one, was to continue right down to the early years of our own century when the rising forces of Asian and African influence began to stem the tide. It is one of the great movements of modern times which have helped to make the world what it is today. The reasons for this expansion, though partly intellectual, were mainly commercial.

### Europe and the East

Europeans, though for the most part content in earlier centuries to confine their activities to their own continent, had for long enjoyed important trading links with the Far East, in particular with China and the Indonesian archipelago. It was from the former country that there came the silks and other luxury goods which the wealthier levels of European society delighted in, and from the latter area that Europe drew its supplies of those flavouring and preserving spices which were so important to a society which had not yet developed the ability to maintain its own supplies of fresh meat throughout the winter months.

European trade with the East had a long history before the sixteenth century, but Europeans themselves, with the exception of the Venetians, the Genoese and some other Italians, took little share in that traffic. Asian and Arab merchants brought their Eastern wares to the ports of the Levant and

Egypt, and from there the Italians distributed them throughout Europe.

As European society began to grow more prosperous and the demand for Eastern luxury goods and spices began to rise, so the potential profits to be made by traffic in such goods increased, and merchants of other nationalities began to cast around for ways to circumvent the Italian and Arab monopoly of the established trade routes. It was difficult for an outsider to enter into direct competition with the established traders, partly for fear of reprisals, and partly because those who had been in the trade for many years had the great competitive advantage of expert knowledge of the routes and hazards involved, and enjoyed established commercial contacts. It was therefore in the newcomer's interest to try to open up a new route to the East for himself.

The established trade routes included a considerable amount of overland traffic along the caravan trails of central Asia which added considerably to the costs of transportation, for it took a very substantial number of pack animals to carry even as much as would fit in the hold of one of the little ships of those days. Furthermore, slow as they were, because of their ability to keep sailing night and day when men and animals had to rest, ships could cover a much greater daily mileage than any overland caravan. Thus ships had the advantage both in carrying more and carrying it faster, and so an all-sea route to the East, if one could be found, would, even if it was longer in terms of miles, almost certainly prove shorter in terms of time, and would in any case be cheaper.

Improvements in ship design, and in the techniques of navigation, and the more widespread use of an improved type of magnetic compass made long voyages far from land less hazardous, so that what the merchants dreamed of the mariners were now prepared to try. By the middle years of the fifteenth century it needed only the patronage of some influential person to set the great expansion in motion.

This patronage came initially from Prince Henry of Portugal, known to subsequent generations as "the navigator", who encouraged his countrymen to undertake a series of increasingly ambitious voyages down the western coast of the African continent. By 1486 Bartholomew Diaz had rounded the Cape of Good Hope, and eleven years later Vasco da Gama had found the way to India.

Spain was not far behind Portugal, and it was Isabella of Castile whose patronage made possible Columbus' bold venture to reach the Indies by sailing west-about. By then the imagination and enthusiasm of the bolder mariners of Europe were thoroughly aroused, and many were ready to venture their ships and their lives in search of a new swift route to the riches of the East.

## John Cabot and Newfoundland

At this stage England was not far behind the leaders. Only five years separate the first voyage of Columbus from that of John Cabot, and the outlines of the North American continent were still largely unknown when the latter sailed from Bristol with the backing of Henry VII. But after the initial voyages of Cabot and his imitators which led to the discovery of Newfoundland and provided the basis for all subsequent English claims to North American territory, England dropped far behind in the race, and did not begin to catch up again until nearly half a century later.

Why was there no follow-up in the reign of Henry VIII of the discoveries made by Cabot and others in the reign of Henry VII? Why did no English conquerors and colonists sail to imitate the exploits of Cortez in Mexico or Pizarro in Peru? There are several reasons which may be alleged in explanation of this lapse of England into inactivity.

In the first place, the initiative for the earlier voyages had come from outside England; from John Cabot himself, who, although he may have been English born, had gained his experience of the sea and his zest for exploration during his long years in the service of Venice; and from certain men from the Azores who, in the early 1500s, came to England to continue the work which Cabot had begun. Whatever claims the men of Bristol were in the habit of making in later days to the effect that some of them had reached the New Found Land several years before Cabot, it is difficult to escape the conclusion that, but for this injection of foreign enterprise, there would have been no English participation in the early discoveries. Strength is lent to this supposition by the fact that after the withdrawal from England of the younger Cabot,

Sebastian, who had led the last of the exploratory voyages of Henry VII's reign, there were no similar undertakings until after his return in 1548.

In the second place, such voyages of exploration required not only leaders, but backers, and backers looked for profit. When the explorations of Henry VII's reign failed to open up the expected trade with the wealthy lands of the East (for John Cabot, like Columbus, had set out to find a way to China and Japan), and brought back nothing but the promise of good fishing off a barren shore, there was little to encourage anyone to subscribe to further voyages. Even Henry VII, who might have had the vision to see the potential value of Cabot's discoveries, lost interest when the expected profits were not made. And after his death the interests of his son and successor were too closely concentrated upon the winning of martial fame in Europe for him to have much enthusiasm to spare for the exploration of distant and apparently not very profitable shores.

But even if Newfoundland had fallen short of expectations, why did English mariners not turn in some other direction? Why were no attempts made to follow the Portuguese to India or the Spaniards to the Caribbean?

Here we must remember the strength of the navies of Spain and Portugal, and the agreement which had been made between these two Iberian kingdoms with papal approval at Tordesillas in 1494. In this treaty they had divided the waters and coasts of the world beyond Europe between them. They had recognised each other's "spheres of influence", and, by implication, had denied to any other nation the right to trespass in them. The other maritime nations of Europe might not like this, and might even argue, as did Henry VII, that such a paper partition had no validity unless followed up by an effective occupation of the lands in question, but no other European power, England included, could yet risk incurring the enmity of either Spain or Portugal by officially sponsoring expeditions in defiance of the Tordesillas agreement.

And so, although individual Englishmen did from time to time in the 1530s and 1540s ignore the treaty, they did so entirely at their own risk and could not count upon the support of their government if they encountered trouble. It was to be a long time, not until the last quarter of the sixteenth century, before English sailors in any numbers felt bold enough regularly to defy the Spanish and Portuguese claims to monopoly.

Thus English mariners in these earlier years had to keep away from the Spaniards in tropical America, and from the Portuguese on the sea route to India, and so there was little left for them to do but to attempt to find a passage round the north of what was now proving to be a new continent, and to pioneer their own route through that passage to the coveted markets of the East. But the experience of the Cabots in this direction had not been very encouraging. The North-west passage had not been found and promised to be difficult to find, if indeed it existed at all. Nor did Newfoundland and Nova Scotia seem likely to provide the trader with easy riches.

Quite naturally, with such a limited and unprofitable region alone open to their exploitation, with the English King no longer interested in overseas ventures, and with the enthusiast Sebastian Cabot gone abroad, English merchants in the reign of Henry VIII were for the most part content to ply the well-tried routes to the Netherlands and the Bay of Biscay. Before English overseas expansion could really get under way some new stimulus to adventure was required.

## Sebastian Cabot and the North-east Passage

In 1548, just over a year after the death of Henry VIII, Sebastian Cabot left the Spanish service and returned to England at the invitation of some of Edward's privy council who showed themselves readier to take an active interest in his projects than had been the late king.

Though Cabot was now an old man by the standards of his age, he still retained the full measure of his former enthusiasm for discovery, and had added to this in his years abroad an invaluable fund of knowledge and experience acquired during his tenure of office as Pilot-Major in the Spanish mercantile marine. The geographical knowledge of the Spanish navigators, which was not generally available to outsiders, had been his to command, and his information about Spanish discoveries and exploits was right up to date.

To this treasury of experience and enthusiasm was added the skill and imagination of English geographers such as the versatile John Dee, and the mixture soon resulted in the production of ambitious plans for a new attack upon the problem of pioneering a trouble-free route from England to the East. The North-west passage was no longer the chief attraction. Now that it was known that a whole new continent barred the western route to China, and that beyond that continent lay another vast ocean, it seemed that, even if the North-west passage could be found, the voyage through it to the East would still be too long to be profitable. The longer the western route appeared to be, so much the shorter, by comparison, seemed the eastern alternative. And so Dee and Cabot turned their backs upon the North-west passage, and studied instead the possibility of sailing in the other direction, and reaching China round the north of Asia.

A certain optimism coloured their geographical speculation. They believed that the Asiatic mainland was rather smaller than in fact it is. They imagined that the population of Siberia was both substantial, and badly in need of English cloth, and they expected the coastline to tend towards the south from a point not far beyond the Kara strait, so that an easy passage in temperate waters would await the voyagers on the second half of their journey. They also had little idea of the coldness of the Arctic ocean once the benign influence of the north Atlantic currents has been left behind, nor did they fully appreciate the shortness of the Siberian summer, or the difficulties of the ice barrier which was to defeat all the early attempts upon this North-eastern passage.

But plans alone were not enough. The project needed backers, and why should English merchants who had found no profit in the North-west passage be prepared now to attempt the North-eastern alternative just because the geographers thought it feasible?

The answer to this question is to be found in that collapse of the export market in cloth in 1551 with which we dealt more fully in the last chapter. With the stoppage of the normal channels of trade not only was there a glut of English cloth for which an alternative outlet had to be found, there was also a pressing need to find some new route for the import of those Eastern luxury goods and spices which could no longer be transhipped from the Netherlands since there were no outgoing cargoes of cloth to pay for them. The lure of the East for English merchants was not merely the lure of new markets.

There was also always the hope of cutting out the Portuguese and Netherlands middlemen as they had cut out the Arab and the Italian, and of bringing Eastern goods directly to England in English ships.

And so, when shipments to the Netherlands fell off, the more enterprising among the English mercantile community were ready to give a fair trial to such visionary schemes as those of Dee and Cabot. The result was the sailing of Chancellor and Willoughby to the White sea in 1553, a voyage which was prepared in the reign of Edward VI under the patronage of Northumberland, though it took place in the reign of Mary.

The immediate results of this voyage were not very encouraging, but the men involved remained confident, and the Muscovy Company which they formed eventually achieved a partial success. They did not of course attain their original objective, the finding of a sea route to China, but they did at least, thanks to the overland travels of Anthony Jenkinson, pioneer an English-monopolised route to the markets of Persia, whence Eastern wares were diverted northwards along the rivers of Russia to the White sea port of Archangel. They also worked up quite a profitable trade with Russia itself, finding a good market for English cloth and a valuable source of furs, hides and timber products. This was not quite what Cabot and Dee had envisaged, but it was a very good second best.

## Sir Humphrey Gilbert: the North-west Passage Again

The lure of the Far East remained strong, and dominated the thinking of English merchants and explorers throughout the rest of the sixteenth century. The North-east passage having proved impossibly difficult, interest was once again, in the 1570s, switched back to the North-west, and a more thorough search was made for it under the leadership of Martin Frobisher in 1576-8.

This revival of interest in the older project which Sebastian Cabot himself had attempted in the reign of Henry VII, was in very great measure due to the enthusiasm and activities of Sir Humphrey Gilbert,* whose treatise *A Discourse for a Discovery for a New Passage to Cataia*, though it was not published until 1576, had been widely circulated in manuscript before publication. Having studied Cabot's own writings and maps and a mass of other relevant literature, Gilbert was convinced that the North-west passage not only existed but would be easy to find (if in fact Cabot had not himself "discovered" it on his last voyage), and when found would provide an easy and profitable route to the East.

The same geographical optimism which had coloured Dee's thinking about Siberia affected Gilbert's ideas of America. Contemporary mapmakers, when filling in the outlines of the yet unknown regions of the new continent, tended to make the northern extremity of it narrow to a point to match the southern, and to show a comparatively short passage leading to the Pacific ocean in the region of 50° north latitude. The strait was there, the passage was short, it was only necessary to find its eastern end and the way to China would be open. So argued Gilbert; and Dee, and Michael Lock who raised the money for Frobisher's voyages, were ready to agree with him, as were many other mariners and merchants throughout the rest of the country.

Right down to the end of Elizabeth's reign, and beyond, the myth of the North-west passage continued to lure English mariners into unprofitable northern seas. John Davis, who in three successive voyages in the years 1585–7 pressed ever farther up the strait which bears his name, reached 73° north on his last voyage without proving either the existence or non-existence of the passage. He himself remained convinced that an easy passage did exist, but for the remainder of Elizabeth's reign the war with Spain so occupied England's maritime energy that neither ships nor men nor money could be found for any further northern exploration.

## The Challenge to Established Trades

The early concentration of English explorers upon the northern regions of the world was in part due, as we noted earlier, to a desire to avoid trouble by keeping clear of the waters and coasts already monopolised by the ships of other nations. But at the same time as new routes were being sought these very monopolies were being progressively challenged by increasing numbers of English merchants and captains who could see no profit in lengthy voyages to the icy waters of the Arctic, and preferred to take the risks involved in breaking in upon established trades.

The first foreign traders to feel the force of this English challenge were the Germans (the Hanseatic League) in the Baltic, and the Italians in the Mediterranean. In the reign of Henry VII, with the encouragement of that King, a regular, though limited, trade with both these regions was established. With the progressive decline of Hanseatic power, English interests in the Baltic and Scandinavia steadily expanded, and the chartering of the Eastland Company in 1579 to control and profit from this traffic was a sign that English merchants no longer feared their German rivals in this area.

English merchants in the Mediterranean had a hard struggle before their trade was put on a firm footing. The increase in piracy which accompanied the rise of Turkish power in the eastern Mediterranean in the sixteenth century led to a decline, and eventually, by mid-century, to a virtual cessation of English trade on that sea. The revival of Mediterranean commerce in the 1580s had to await the establishment of diplomatic relations between England and Turkey and the building of a strong fleet of armed merchantmen by the members of the Levant Company which was chartered in 1581. Thereafter the merchants of this company, and their fellows in the Venetian Company, founded two years later, were so successful in developing an import trade in Eastern goods loaded in Levantine ports that the Muscovy Company's roundabout route to the White sea became uneconomic and had to be abandoned.

This success of the Levantine merchants is significant. For the first time those who were prepared to challenge an established trading monopoly had fared better than those who thought it best to try to circumvent it.

It was one thing, however, to challenge the failing Hanse or the declining power of Venice and Genoa. It was quite another to invite a clash with the rising strength of Spain or Portugal. And yet, even as early as the 1530s, William Hawkins, the father of the redoubtable John, was already making voyages to West Africa, technically a Portuguese preserve. Others followed his example, and by the reign of Edward VI a regular traffic to the Gold Coast and the Bight of Benin had been established. This continued throughout the reign of Mary despite the efforts of her husband Philip to have it suppressed.

In the following reign John Hawkins carried matters a stage further by attempting to trade in the American colonies of Spain with slaves purchased in West Africa. But his voyages, in the 1560s, led first to trouble with the Spanish authorities, and then to disaster, and contributed substantially to the deterioration in Anglo-Spanish relations. They can hardly be considered a successful challenge to the Spanish monopoly of America.

It was, in the end, the outbreak of open war with Spain which helped English commerce to find its most profitable field for expansion. Once the naval threat from the combined forces of Spain and Portugal (for the former had absorbed the latter in 1580) had been faced and checked in the Armada year, English captains shed what little was left of their reluctance to trespass upon the Spanish and Portuguese monopolies, and commercial interests in London began to make plans for entering into direct competition with the latter power in the trade with India and the Spice Islands.

The long overland wanderings of Ralph Fitch and the exploratory voyages of James Lancaster provided invaluable and encouraging information about the possibilities of trade in the Indian ocean, and led to the foundation, at the turn of the century, of what was soon to become the greatest of English overseas commercial enterprises, the East India Company. At long last, after much pioneering but fruitless search for a new and exclusively English route to the East, English commerce had found the courage to enter into direct competition with the Portuguese along the route which the latter had opened up more than a century earlier, and in doing so had opened the door to that great overseas expansion which was, in the space of little more than another century, to make of England one of the foremost commercial and colonial powers in the world.

## Early Attempts at Colonisation

The opening up to English ships of the sea route to the East around the Cape of Good Hope did not put an end to English interest in America. While Frobisher and Davis had concentrated their energies upon finding a way round this inconvenient continent to the wealth of the East beyond, other Englishmen had already begun to think that America itself might be made to yield almost as much profit as the elusive China trade.

It was by then widely known, despite Spanish reluctance to let such information circulate, that Spanish expeditions had discovered and over-run rich native Empires in Mexico and Peru, and had redirected the wealth of the gold and silver mines in those regions into the coffers of their King. What had been found in Central and South America, it was argued, should also exist in the north. America thus became for some no longer of interest merely as a possible halfway station on the route to the East, but as a land worth exploring for its own sake, in the hope of finding gold and silver, or at least rich native cities with which a profitable trade could be developed.

Great interest was at one point aroused by some promising-looking ores which Frobisher brought home from one of his voyages, and for a time the North-west passage took second place in interest to the possibility of developing rich mines in Baffin Land or Labrador. Even when Frobisher's "gold" proved to be worthless, the hope that profitable mines or wealthy cities still awaited discovery in regions as yet unvisited by Spanish explorers remained alive and played its part, not only in later schemes for colonies in the region Raleigh* named Virginia, but also in setting on foot Raleigh's other enterprises in Guiana and on the Orinoco.

To these hopes of quick profits Sir Humphrey Gilbert, and others who like him gave the matter of colonisation some considerable thought, added a long list of other advantages to be derived from the establishment of an English settlement in North America in imitation of the Spanish colonies farther south.

Such a settlement, even if it did not develop a profitable trade with the hoped-for rich cities of the interior, could provide a useful provisioning point for English ships bound for China by the North-west passage which must surely be discovered soon. It would also be a haven of refuge from Atlantic storms, a convenient port from which to fish the Newfoundland banks, and, if war should come, a base from which to attack Spanish ships and settlements in the New World.

The constant traffic to and fro across the Atlantic which the establishment and maintenance of such a settlement would require would encourage the building of ocean-worthy ships and breed a hardy race of seamen who, with their ships, would make an invaluable contribution to the defence of England in time of danger. Finally, such a settlement would draw off from England some of the surplus population which was unable to find employment at home. Gilbert even suggested that the problem of the Catholic recusants might be solved by offering them the chance to emigrate.

Surprisingly little is made, in colonial promotion literature of the time, of the great opportunities for investment and development presented by the vast acreage of almost virgin land in North America. It was, in the end, land in virtually unlimited quantities, which was to prove the great attraction to emigrants and investors, but the earlier promoters seem to have underestimated its value.

Perhaps it was because they had got their list of priorities in the wrong order that Gilbert's, and after him Raleigh's, colonists failed. Had they limited themselves at first to the planting of a self-sufficient agricultural community, and made their preparations accordingly, they might have had a better success. As it was, the lure of gold, the hopes of trade and the search for the elusive North-west passage distracted the attention of the settlers from what should have been their prime task.

Elizabethan colonial promoters were too ambitious, and tended to underestimate the difficulties of the task they had set themselves, but out of the experience gathered from their failures was in large measure to come the success of their imitators in the following reign. The continuous history of English imperialism does not go back beyond the reign of James I, but the ultimate success of the Jacobean ventures cannot be satisfactorily accounted for without some acknowledgement of the work of the Elizabethan pioneers.

# 13

## The Arts and Sciences

WE HAVE ALREADY traced in an earlier chapter (chapter 2) the remarkable change in the attitude of the laity towards education and book learning which took place in England during the sixteenth century. One consequence of this intellectual revolution which should hardly need emphasis was the creation of a wider reading public and a greater demand for books. At the same time the production of books to satisfy this demand was being made easier by the development of printing which, though introduced into England by William Caxton in 1477, was only really beginning to make its influence widely felt in the reign of Henry VIII.

### Book Production Expanded

The increasing literacy of the laity and the expanding output of printed books went hand in hand, and it is difficult to say which was cause and which was effect. Certainly each development stimulated the other. When books, thanks to printing, became more plentiful and cheaper they were the more likely to fall into the hands of wider numbers of people and to stimulate their interest in the written word. On the other hand the increasing interest of the laity in books assured the printers of an expanding market which they were only too pleased to supply.

However, the awakening literary interest of the laity, and especially of the gentry and the nobility, not only increased the reading public, it also facilitated the production of new books to meet the new demand. When an active interest in literature came to be expected of the gentleman and courtier, those who were unable themselves to write with distinction (as many in fact were) were eager to offer their patronage and encouragement to those who could. And so the ground was prepared for a literary "boom". Even without the flowering of the native English genius which it was to experience, the reign of Elizabeth would probably have seen a very considerable increase in the volume of literature produced.

The Tudor peace also had its contribution to make to this English literary renaissance. By the 1580s the worst of the internal disorders were over. The last great rebellion was that of the northern earls in 1569; the last really serious conspiracy (with the exception of the Gunpowder Plot in the next century) was the Throckmorton Plot of 1583. By the 1590s the external threat from Spain had been met and defeated. Life for everybody in England was a good deal more secure. No longer need the defence of life and property occupy the forefront of every man's attention. There was time to live graciously and to cultivate the arts of peace as well as those of war.

At the same time men's minds were being stimulated by the expanding horizons of geography, their wits sharpened by the heat of theological and political controversy and their appetite for enquiry whetted by the breaking down of old standards of value and habits of thought. Intellectually the Tudor period, especially the latter half of it, was a stimulating time.

In the light of all this the Elizabethan literary renaissance seems natural and hardly needs explaining. The ground was prepared, the seed had only to germinate and the plant to grow to maturity. And yet the seed had to be there first. Although it is clear for many reasons that the circumstances of the reign of Elizabeth were such as to favour and encourage the growth of literary activity, we should be doing Shakespeare and his generation less than justice if we attributed their achievements solely to the influence of their environment and left no room for genius.

## Early Tudor Literature; the Accent Upon Instruction

In the earlier part of the sixteenth century the share of creative writing in the total output of the still very elementary printing presses was very limited. It was as though this new medium of communication, the printed word, was still too precious a novelty to be wasted upon mere entertainment. It is true, of course, that Caxton's most popular productions did include a fair proportion of imaginative writing, such as tales

from Greek mythology, or the Arthurian cycle, but even
these were regarded by his contemporaries as of considerable
practical value in encouraging the reader to heroic effort and
noble sentiment; that is to say they had a decidedly didactic
aspect. The writings of Chaucer and Gower also remained
popular and went through many editions, but nevertheless
the purely literary output of the early Tudor presses was of
minor importance.

Far more typical of the literature of the early sixteenth century were the many books of instruction: handbooks of
hawking and hunting; guides to courtly behaviour and good
manners; devotional literature such as primers and books of
hours; and avowedly educational works such as Sir Thomas
Elyot's *Boke named the Governour* (1531), or Robert
Ascham's *Toxophilus* (1545). Another important category of
publications was the historical, generally in chronicle form,
all designed to inform, and some to point a lesson too, such
as Edward Hall's *Union of the two Noble and Illustre Fame-
lies of Lancastre and Yorke* . . . which was concerned to make
abundantly clear the many blessings which England enjoyed
under that noble scion of both houses, King Henry VIII. Even
Edmund Dudley's *Tree of Commonwealth* (1509) and Sir
Thomas More's *Utopia* (1516) were in a sense didactic,
exposing to criticism the evils of contemporary society and
pointing to ways in which such ills could be avoided. Indeed
one might almost add to the list of didactic writings the
poems of Alexander Barclay and John Skelton, so much of
whose work was devoted to social criticism.

And yet at the same time there are signs foreshadowing in
the earlier Tudor period the great flowering of imaginative
literature which was to come in the last decades of Elizabeth's
reign. The sonnets of Sir Thomas Wyatt, some of the earliest
in the English language, set the fashion for many an Elizabethan imitator, and the blank verse of Henry Howard, Earl
of Surrey, provided the Elizabethan dramatists with a model
of which they made good use.

But both Surrey and Wyatt were dead before the end of the
reign of Henry VIII, and they had no immediate disciples or
successors. They had indeed been exceptional in their own day
in that they had kept their writings so free from the bitter
controversies which were already in the 1530s coming to

dominate the attention of writers and publishers to the almost total exclusion of all else. It is in controversial pamphlets, scurrilous broadsheets and partisan literature that the middle years of the sixteenth century abound. There was little room in this period of intense controversy, when the energies of some of England's most able writers were engaged in arguing one case or the other, for non-partisan writing of a more purely literary kind. About the only work with decidedly literary merits which has come down to us from this period is Thomas Cranmer's *Book of Common Prayer*.

Thus the storm of controversy delayed the arrival of the English literary renaissance. It was not until Elizabeth had been on the throne for nearly twenty years, and the old arguments, though far from dead, were losing some of their former virulence, that a new generation of creative writers was able to follow where the pioneers like Surrey and Wyatt had tried to lead.

## Elizabethan Literature; Creative Writing Comes Into its Own

The great period of what we call Elizabethan literature begins about 1579 with the publication of Edmund Spenser's *Shepheards Calender* and John Lyly's *Euphues*, and runs on into the reign of James I. It is of course dominated by the poets and the dramatists, and presided over, from the 1590s onwards, by the genius of William Shakespeare. Of the great names, of Shakespeare, Marlowe, Spenser and Sidney, it would be impossible to write anything worth while in a short account of this nature, but it is perhaps worth emphasising that they were not alone in their generation. They were simply the greatest of a multitude of writers.

The list of Elizabethan dramatists worthy of note is very long, and their output was prodigious. But then it had to be. There were not many theatres in Elizabethan England, perhaps six in London in the latter years of the reign, and the theatre-going public was quite limited, but plays then had, by modern standards, very short runs of only a few days at the most. There was therefore a constant and very pressing demand for new material if the theatres were to be kept open and the actors employed.

Not only was there a multitude of dramatists, but likewise

a multitude of lyricists and sonneteers. Indeed every gentleman worthy of the name was expected now to be able to turn a tidy sonnet with the same ease and grace which he displayed in dancing or fencing. Imaginative writing, pure literature, literature for its own sake, had certainly come into its own.

Literary style, which to the Elizabethans meant the filling of their pages with appropriate allusions (mainly classical), sustained similes, wittily contrived conceits and every sort of exuberant ornament, after the manner of some of their architecture, was now something to be prized, praised or criticised, something worthy of study equally with the content of what was written. Creative writing began to attract round it a subordinate literature concerned with language and its uses.

Although the enormous output of imaginative literature is the dominant feature which attracts our attention when we survey the Elizabethan literary scene, we must not forget that the current of didactic writing was still flowing strongly. Indeed it was probably, in absolute terms, flowing even more strongly than it had been in the earlier Tudor period, though we are less inclined to notice it when there is so much more writing of other kinds more attractive to the eye. The Englishmen of the generation which spanned the turn of the sixteenth and seventeenth centuries were avid for knowledge and information of all kinds.

## The Advance of Knowledge

We have seen earlier (chapter 12) how the search for geographical knowledge was given practical expression in the voyages and travels of English explorers right through Elizabeth's reign. But these adventurous journeyings would scarcely have been possible but for the "back-room" work of English geographers, astronomers and cartographers who, though they did not attain the international fame of a Mercator or a Galileo, kept themselves well informed about the latest developments in their particular fields of study, and supplied the mariners with up-to-date information which was invaluable to them on their long voyages.

The Copernican heliocentric theory of the universe was well known to these men (though it made surprisingly little impact upon contemporary literary works), and they worked assiduously at charting the motions of the planets and improving the navigational apparatus of the deep-sea voyager. The properties of the magnetic compass also attracted their attention, and it was an Englishman, William Gilbert, who produced a pioneering work on magnetism in 1600.

Meanwhile the appetite of the geographical non-specialist who could not get to sea himself could be satisfied through the pages of Richard Hakluyt's *Voyages and Discoveries* (1589), and those whose curiosity turned rather towards the land in which they lived could find plenty to interest them in the works of quite a number of their contemporaries; William Harrison's *Description of Britain,* John Speed's *Theatre of the Empire of Great Britain,* John Norden's *Speculum Britanniae* or Christopher Saxton's maps. Those whose interest lay rather in national history were well catered for by the chronicles of John Stow and Raphael Holinshed, the frankly partisan pages of John Foxe's *Acts and Monuments,* the more scholarly writings of the great antiquary William Camden or John Speed's pioneer attempt to write a complete *History of Great Britain.*

But history and geography were only two of the many branches of learning to which men were turning at that time. There was also an increasing interest in such subjects as botany, zoology and medicine. The first two of these were only in their infancy. The unexciting but essential work of collecting and naming specimens, and of purging older accounts of their mythological element fell to the pioneers of the sixteenth century, such as the "father" of English botany, William Turner.

Medicine made rather less progress in England, and, despite the influence of the Paduan school of Vesalius, and the introduction, in the early years of Elizabeth's reign, of dissection as a regular part of medical training, the "four humours" (the phlegmatic, the choleric, the sanguine and the melancholic) retained a firm place in medical parlance, and the treatment of disease remained rather more haphazard than methodical. Chemistry made even less progress, being still in the hands of the alchemists and retarded by the persistence of their efforts to transmute base metals into gold.

Only the faintest glimmer of light yet heralded the approaching dawn of the scientific age. Some few, especially those whose interest was focused upon the "navigational" sciences (astronomy, geography, magnetism), were already well advanced along the road to new ways of thinking. They no longer accepted without question the authority of the ancient Greeks, but were learning how to feel their way by hypothesis and observation, checked where possible by experiment, towards a new vision of the world and its place in the universe.

They no longer assumed that the earth, as the home of man who was created in God's image, must needs be at the centre of the whole of creation. They could see, as Copernicus had pointed out, that the apparent motions of the sun and the planets could be accounted for as readily by supposing the sun to be the focus round which the earth and the planets revolved, and they were ready to accept this hypothesis if it could be confirmed by observation.

Because such confirmation had to await the invention of the telescope in the early years of the seventeenth century, we must leave our Elizabethan astronomers speculating but not fully convinced. The full impact of the new cosmology was not to be felt in England until the Stuart period, but at least the speculations of the Elizabethans had prepared the minds of their fellow countrymen to accept, without too great an intellectual shock, the confirmation by the observations of Galileo of the much discussed theories of Copernicus.

## Tudor Music

It is not, of course, only for its literary brilliance and the speculations of some of its pioneering scientists that the reign of Elizabeth is justly famous, but also for its music. Musicians as well as writers benefited from the increasingly generous patronage of the laity in the sixteenth century, and most of all from the patronage of the house of Tudor itself.

Henry VII inherited a chapel royal which had been founded by the Lancastrian kings in imitation of the famed *capella* of the Burgundian dukes, and lavished much care upon it. Henry VIII patronised secular as well as sacred music, and was himself, even allowing for the flattery of courtiers, no mean performer both as a singer and as a player upon the lute and clavichord. He also kept a substantial establishment of players and instruments, and all the many festive occasions of his reign were graced by music. His children kept up this tradition of royal patronage, so that conditions were extremely favourable for the development of musical talent.

Despite the reformation sacred music continued to flourish. It had, of course, to adapt itself to the new and more restricted forms of worship prescribed by the English prayer book. One consequence of this was the increase in the popularity of anthems, for in them the composer could find more freedom to express his talent.

The reputation of English church music had long stood high. The great John Dunstable had been an international figure in the early part of the fifteenth century and had given a strong lead both to the composers and to the performers who came after him, but the English tradition really reached its climax in the reign of Elizabeth. The anthems and services of William Byrd, Thomas Tallis, Thomas Weelkes, Orlando Gibbons and others, which still appear so regularly in the repertoire of many cathedral and minster choirs today, have made an ineradicable mark upon English church music. Written primarily for unaccompanied choral singing, or for choir and organ, much of the attraction of their work lies in its smoothness and lack of ostentation. Kept within the limits of the ordinary performer's abilities, and not written for *virtuosi*, this late Tudor music is pleasantly free from ornate passages, flourishes, excessive intervals and other showy devices, and is none the worse for that.

Secular music also flourished in Tudor times. Indeed the increasing importance of secular music is one of the notable features of the sixteenth century. To a certain extent this was but part of the general secularisation of society, and a consequence of the increase in lay patronage, but it is likely that the more restricted limits of the new liturgy also encouraged composers to turn from church music to other forms, and the same composers are to be found writing both sacred and secular pieces.

Vocal music dominated the secular scene as well as the ecclesiastical. Unaccompanied part-songs, or pieces for solo voice with simple accompaniment on lute or spinet, were the forms most commonly adopted. There was little as yet in the way of purely instrumental music, save for dancing. Chamber groups were in their infancy, and concert orchestras were unheard of. The compass of the human voice set strict limits which the composer could seldom exceed.

The writers of part-songs and madrigals had, perhaps even

more than the writers of anthems and services, to remember the limits of the capabilities of the performers for whom they wrote. Playing and singing were, in Elizabeth's reign, extremely popular forms of recreation. Furthermore it was expected of the accomplished gentleman that he should be able to join in part singing at sight or to perform competently upon some instrument. Consequently there were many performers and an assured market for any composer who kept his work within the capabilities of the ordinary amateur.

The day of the professional musical performer, with the majority reduced to passive participation in the rôle of audience, had not yet come. In Elizabeth's reign the "musical" man was the one who played and sang, not the one who sat back and listened. And yet, despite, or perhaps because of, these limitations within which the composer had to work, Elizabethan music at its best has a simplicity of form and a delicacy of touch which has seldom been equalled in vocal music since.

## Architecture

It is strange that an age which had such a good ear for music should have had such a bad eye for architecture. Perhaps the explanation of this apparent inconsistency lies in the rather different history of the two art forms. Elizabethan music came as the natural climax of a long period of steady development reaching back over at least two centuries. Elizabethan architecture was produced by the impact upon the native and traditional style of three revolutionary influences at almost one and the same time. It is little wonder that the result should at times be rather chaotic and artistically unsatisfying.

The full flowering of the native English tradition in architecture is to be seen in some of the great buildings erected in the early years of the sixteenth century: Henry VII's chapel at Westminster; King's College, Cambridge; Christ Church, Oxford; Bath Abbey church; Abbot Bradley's tower at Fountains; Wolsey's work at Hampton Court; to name but a few examples. These all stood in the direct line of descent from the early work of the Norman builders through centuries of gradual adaptation and progressive improvements in building techniques and skills.

These inherited ways of building were not suddenly rejected, and many structures, particularly churches and smaller houses and cottages, continued to be erected in the accustomed manner for more than another century. And yet, in the reign of Henry VIII, new influences began to be felt which were to direct the energies of the builder and architect into new and untried channels.

In the first place the secular interest began to prevail over the ecclesiastical. This did not mean that there was an immediate end to all church building. A lot of care and attention was still lavished upon the chapels of the new schools and colleges and of the new houses of the gentry, but far fewer parish churches were enlarged or rebuilt. The men who made money in the sixteenth century and wanted to build monuments for posterity no longer put their money into parish churches or chantry chapels. They built instead either houses for themselves as individuals, or guild and town halls for themselves in their corporate capacity as merchants or burghers.

This switching of building interest from the ecclesiastical to the secular made it easier for the builders and architects to adopt new styles and methods. It was easier to experiment when you were called upon to build a large country house, a type of building for which there was no set form required by tradition, than when your appointed task was the creation of a church, a type of building in which certain conventions were so rigidly established as to be almost unbreakable.

In the second place, the effect of the Tudor peace was being felt in English architecture as much as in English literature and music. Greater domestic security meant greater liberty for the designer of gentlemen's country residences. The castle-like and fortified manor house, with stout outer walls, slit windows, battlements and defensive towers, was still being built in early Tudor times. A very good example may be seen in Compton Castle, the home of the Gilbert family, near Torquay. But from the reign of Henry VIII onwards the domestic architecture of the nobility and gentry, being freed from the need to concentrate upon defence, was ready to expand and experiment, to try new plans and to take on a radically new appearance.

It was just at this point that the third of the new influences began to take effect. The English gentleman, anxious to build a fine house for himself, and now free to get away from the cramping discomforts of the older semi-fortified manor, was wide open to the reception of suggestions from abroad. Foreign influences, particularly Italian, began to make their mark on English buildings.

It was in Italy, which had always been less affected by Gothic influences than northern Europe, that the classical Renaissance had taken its origin, and this reawakened admiration for the civilisation of the ancients had had its influence upon architecture as well as the other arts. Italy, in the late fifteenth and early sixteenth centuries, was enjoying something of a building boom, in which classical motifs, classical ornament, classical proportions and classical styles were becoming predominant, and it was to Italy that the educated Englishman was turning increasingly for his example, not only in building, but in every aspect of life.

And so from Italy the Italian and classical fashions began to creep in, and the combined result of all the three influences we have mentioned was to produce a marked departure from the traditional English manner of building which is most readily seen in the plans and external appearance of the new houses of the gentry.

## The Houses of the Gentry

The old domestic plan for the larger house had been quadrilateral, a building round an enclosed courtyard. This plan was dictated partly by defensive needs, and partly by convenience, for in the days before window glass was cheap enough to be commonly adopted only a courtyard plan with the main windows on the inner-facing walls could provide good light with a modicum of protection from the weather. The courtyard plan also owed a good deal to the example of the monastic cloister.

However, the quadrangular plan was not thought to be so necessary when defence no longer rated a high priority, and window glass was no longer so expensive. It was even held by some to be unhealthy because it impeded the free circulation of air about the house. Besides, it was now more important to have an extensive prospect from one's windows than to have them protected from the weather and other enemies. And so the courtyard plan became less popular. It was still used for some really big houses, and by those who converted monastic cloisters into private residences, but by the end of Elizabeth's reign it was becoming exceptional, and a plain rectangle, with only vestigial wings, or an E shape with a centre extension as well, had replaced it in popularity. But whatever ground plan was now adopted the prime consideration was the achievement of a pleasing symmetry. This, rather than functional necessity, tended now to determine the external appearance of a house.

The effect of the Tudor peace is seen not only in the abandonment of the defensive courtyard, but even more strikingly in the exuberant proliferation of windows. Earlier houses had perhaps boasted a single fine oriel window protruding safely over the courtyard from an inner wall. With glass now, thanks to improvement in the process of manufacture, more plentiful and cheaper, windows blossomed forth, and were even knocked through the thick defensive walls of ancient habitations. The general rule in new-built Elizabethan houses seems to have been to have as many and as large windows as could possibly be managed. Individual lights were of course still small, and the light that shone through these later Tudor windows was much diffracted by the multitude of tiny panes. But from the outside the transformation was truly remarkable. To appreciate it fully one has only to compare the sombre bristling defensiveness of a place like Compton Castle with the frank openness of somewhere like Hardwick Hall which, as the old rhyme says, contains "more glass than wall".

At the same time as they were devoting more attention to windows the architects and house builders of the reign of Elizabeth were also trying their best to capture something of the Italian fashion, and to incorporate classical features into their buildings. But for the most part they failed and produced a hotch-potch which is neither gothic nor yet renaissance. Square-headed doors and windows made some concession to classical taste, but the subtlety of true classical proportion was not understood, and Hardwick, with its windows larger in the upper stories, looks ready to fall over, so top-heavy does it seem.

Chimneys, uncatered for in the classical style which evolved in warmer lands, presented a very great problem which was seldom very happily solved. Pilasters, wreaths, urns, garlands and statuary were tacked on here and there with little appreciation of the over-all effect. One feature of classicism alone was satisfactorily achieved, and that was symmetry of elevation. But symmetry alone is not a virtue, save where it is coupled with good proportion, and that the Elizabethans seldom achieved.

## Furnishings and Interior Decoration

The interiors of these new mansions which were rising in such numbers in all parts of the country received every bit as much care and attention as was lavished on the outsides. In decorating and furnishing their houses in the style now approved, the nobility and gentry provided employment for, and gave encouragement to, a wide range of artists and craftsmen whose work on the whole benefited from the increasing demand. Joiners, cabinet makers, silversmiths, plasterers and others filled the great houses with their handiwork, and provided those carpets, carved chairs and tables, elaborate beds with testers, tapestry hangings, carved wooden panelling, ornate plasterwork on ceilings and friezes and other embellishments which were called for by the new standards of elegance and comfort now held to be as necessary in a gentleman's house as a sound roof and stout walls.

Among the list of craftsmen catering for the comfort of the gentle householder we might almost have included the portrait painter, for it was as a craftsman rather than as an artist that he tended to be regarded by his patrons. Family portraits were needed to adorn the walls of the great man's house, and to record his image, and those of his relatives, for posterity. These the painter would supply to order with as little hope of being remembered for his work as had the maker of the household linen-chest. Most Tudor portraits are by unknown artists, unknown because it was the purpose of the portrait to bring the sitter, not the painter, immortality. However, this anonymity of so many Tudor portrait painters is no very great loss because so much of their work is dull and uninspiring.

There was little native English talent for painting in the sixteenth century. The one great name is that of Hans Holbein, a German employed to fill the post of Court painter to Henry VIII which no contemporary Englishman was capable of filling so well, and Holbein was far from being the only foreign painter to find employment in Tudor England. Where the names of artists are known it is those of Netherlanders and Italians which predominate.

Only in one branch of the painter's art did native Englishmen acquire outstanding skill, and that was in the painting of miniatures. Yet even this art was not entirely native, for it was introduced into England by Holbein, but from his time onwards there was a flourishing school of English miniaturists of whom one of the greatest, with an international reputation, was the Elizabethan Nicholas Hilliard.

Of landscape painting there was practically none. The Tudor Englishman was not interested in the natural scene save as a background to a hunting picture in which the individual portraits were all-important. It is only rarely that we catch a glimpse of a contemporary landscape, and even then it is more often in needlework or tapestry than in paint.

The scarcity of religious painting is also noteworthy, and is just another reflection of the secularism of the age. The layman, in freeing himself from clerical predominance, had laid his hands firmly upon the arts as upon government, wealth and education. In that it was the period in which, as we have seen during the course of this book, the lay interest superseded the clerical in so many different departments of life, the age of the Tudors has still a strong claim to be considered the first of the modern period in the history of England.

# The Elizabethan Age

THE REIGN OF Elizabeth I, in which the English monarchy reached the peak of its power and popularity, is rightly one of the most famous in our annals. There has hardly been a generation since the passing of the great Queen which has not looked back upon her day with a sense of pride in its achievements and regret for its passing. Indeed the "Elizabethan Age" has probably crossed over the border from history into popular mythology, so that it is extremely difficult for us even today to shake ourselves free from our predisposition to think favourably of it, and to subject it to an unprejudiced examination.

Clearly there is much to praise in the activities of that generation which grew up under the benign governance of the Virgin Queen. It would be hard, for instance, to deny the claims to immortality of the principal writers and musicians. The chief men of action are also worthy of our admiration for their courage, their hardihood and their enterprise. But here we must begin to make our reservations. Selfless devotion to the national cause was less frequently the mainspring of their actions than a self-centred desire to secure personal advancement or to heap up riches. Courage was often paired with cruelty, hardihood with indifference to the sufferings of others. Philanthropists and saints were rare. Ambitious, flattering, intriguing courtiers abounded.

The exploits of the men of action must also be kept in perspective. Certainly they sailed farther abroad and engaged in more perilous enterprises than ever their fathers did, yet their activities were no more remarkable than many that men of other nations had engaged in in earlier years.

Why then has the reputation of the Elizabethans stood so high in subsequent generations? Probably mainly because of the admitted genius of the writers of that age. Their pens have preserved for us their view of their own generation, setting down for us in their own words their hopes, their enthusiasms, their ambitions, their achievements. And there were very few adverse critics among them. The doleful complaints of a Dudley or a More, seeing and exposing the evils of the society in which they lived, have few echoes in the writings of their Elizabethan successors. Optimism and confidence are the keynotes now.

Why this should be so is not so easy to explain. It cannot be that all was well with society. Unemployment, poverty, greed, disease and dirt are the dark blemishes on the fair face of Elizabethan England, but perhaps men had lived so long with these that they had come to accept them as part of the unchangeable face of nature. On the other hand the Englishmen of Elizabeth's day enjoyed far greater security, both as individuals and as a nation, than their fathers or grandfathers had ever known. To this factor of security we keep returning. Security bred confidence, confidence bred optimism, optimism left its mark on the literature of the age and coloured the image of it which the writers created and passed on to the generations that followed.

In the creation of the Elizabethan legend we must always acknowledge the importance of the rôle of the Queen herself. However much the preservation of England's independence and the build-up of England's strength in her reign may be due to factors, such as the continuing rivalry between France and Spain, the outbreak of rebellion in the Netherlands and of civil war in France, over which Elizabeth cannot herself have exercised more than marginal influence, there can be but little doubt that in the way in which she inspired the exertions of her subjects and won their loves and loyalties the Queen made a very vital personal contribution to the ultimate result.

If some of the members of her first Parliament may have thought that in the new Queen they had a comparatively young and inexperienced monarch whose policies could be moulded to their desires, Elizabeth was soon to show them how very wrong they were. In her own mind there was never any doubt but that she was mistress of her people, that she was born to command and they to obey. But the Queen knew better than to emphasise this perhaps unpalatable truth in her public pronouncements. Instead she took advantage of her sex in a still almost exclusively masculine age to win her subjects' affection, to gain their confidence and inspire their devotion. She knew how to handle men, and the possession of that ancient feminine skill was the foundation of her success and of the mythology which even her own generation began to weave about her person.

The course which Elizabeth chose to steer was a difficult one; in religion between the fervour of the puritans and the traditionalism of the conservatives; in diplomacy between the belligerence of a Walsingham and the caution of a Burghley; in economic policy between encouraging the enterprise of the pioneer and protecting the welfare of the people as a whole; in government between the attractions of autocracy and the need to secure the co-operation of her subjects; in finance between the needs of government and the capacity of the tax-payer. In every respect she succeeded, and though at times her success may have been achieved only at the cost of apparent weakness and vacillation, she deserves all credit for it.

Extensive though her powers as monarch were, Elizabeth was never one to flaunt them before her people without at the same time making clear her conviction that monarchy was a trust and not a right. The authority which she possessed was vested in her for the good of her subjects, and for the manner in which she used that authority she was answerable to God. Her own words, in her famous "golden speech" to a deputation from her last Parliament in 1601, sum up her view of her own responsibilities in a manner that can hardly be bettered, and give us at the same time a taste of that gracious eloquence with which she was wont to charm away all opposition in the great crises of her reign.

> I have ever used to set the Last-Judgment Day before mine eyes, and so to rule as I shall be judged to answer before a higher Judge, to whose judgment seat I do appeal, that never thought was cherished in my heart that tended not unto my people's good . . .
> I know the title of a King is a glorious title; but assure yourself that the shining glory of princely authority hath not so dazzled the eyes of our understanding, but that we well know and remember that we also are to yield an account of our actions before the great Judge . . .
> I was never so much enticed with the glorious name of a

King or royal authority of a Queen as delighted that God has made me His instrument to maintain His truth and glory and to defend this Kingdom from peril, dishonour, tyranny and oppression.

There will never Queen sit in my seat with more zeal to my country, care for my subjects, and that will sooner with willingness venture her life for your good and safety than myself. For it is my desire to live nor reign no longer than my life and reign shall be for your good. And though you have had and may have many princes more mighty and wise sitting in this seat, yet you never had nor shall have any that will be more careful and loving.

# APPENDIX A

# *Biographical Notes*

A DISADVANTAGE INHERENT in the topical approach to the Tudor period which has been followed throughout this book is that it results of necessity in a severe restriction of the space devoted to individual personalities, and, in some cases, in a scattering of references to one person through the pages of a number of chapters. To make amends in some measure for this depersonalisation of the narrative, brief summaries of the lives and careers of a selection of Tudor men and women are set out below. The selection of persons for inclusion in this section has not been entirely arbitrary. Some of them are there because they are obvious "big names" of the period. Others, perhaps not so famous, have earned a place as representatives of the many who shared their attitudes and beliefs.

## ALLEN

*William Allen, Cardinal* (1532-94), Catholic exile.

The third son of John Allen of Rossall Grange, Lancashire, he entered Oriel College, Oxford, in 1547, and proceeded M.A. in 1554. He became principal of St Mary's Hall in 1556, but terminated a promising university career by refusing to accept the Elizabethan Act of Supremacy. He resigned his principalship in 1560 and left Oxford for exile in Louvain in the following year. Shortly afterwards he returned for a time to his native Lancashire, but was continuously in exile from 1565. At Douai in 1568 he founded the English college to train Catholic priests for missionary work in England, and the first of these began their work in 1574. He was consulted by Pope Gregory XIII about the foundation of a

imilar English college at Rome. Though he was made a
ardinal in 1587 in recognition of his work for the English
mission, Allen lost credit with many English Catholics by his
upport of Philip II's plans for the invasion of England. He
lied in Rome.

Chief work: *A Defence of English Catholics* (1584).
Life by Martin Haile, Pitman.
See also *The Letters and Memorials of William Cardinal
Allen,* edited with historical introduction, by T. F. Knox
and others.

# BURGHLEY

*William Cecil, Lord Burghley* (1520-98) Elizabethan
statesman.

The only son of Richard Cecil of Burghley, he was edu-
ated at Stamford and Grantham grammar schools, St John's
College, Cambridge, and Gray's Inn. Connected by marriage
with two of the foremost scholars of his day, Sir John Cheke
and Sir Anthony Cooke, Cecil would probably have made a
brilliant legal career for himself had he not been attracted to
politics by the patronage of Protector Somerset. Though he
suffered a short imprisonment at the time of his patron's
fall, his talents were so valuable to those in power that he was
soon released and shortly afterwards (1550) made Secretary
of State and admitted to the Privy Council. He resigned the
Secretaryship in 1553 in protest against Northumberland's
scheme to make Jane Grey queen, but set his signature to it
under protest. Served Mary, though in a less prominent position. He was appointed Secretary of State by Elizabeth upon
her accession and served her continuously until the day of his
death. His influence upon Elizabeth's government and policy
was so profound that it is scarcely possible to distinguish "his"
policies from "those of the Queen". Generally speaking he was
in favour of firmness at home and moderation abroad, and
so incurred the special hatred of the oppressed recusants and
the contempt of the more belligerent of Elizabeth's councillors
who wanted to force a showdown with Spain. He survived all
his contemporaries and rivals and died in office. Knighted in
1551, created Baron Burghley in 1571, he resigned the Secre-

taryship upon his appointment as Lord Treasurer in 1572. He lavished considerable sums upon the building of Burghley House near Stamford which is still in the hands of his direct descendants.

> Life by Conyers Read in two volumes: (i) *Mr Secretary Cecil and Queen Elizabeth,* Jonathan Cape; (ii) *Lord Burghley and Queen Elizabeth,* Jonathan Cape.

# CARTWRIGHT

*Thomas Cartwright* (1535-1603), Elizabethan puritan.

Educated at Clare Hall and St John's College, Cambridge, he had to leave the university during Mary's reign because of his known and marked Protestant sympathies. He returned to his studies at Elizabeth's accession and became a fellow of St John's in 1560, moving to a fellowship at Trinity two years later. In 1565-7 he was in Ireland as chaplain to Adam Loftus, Archbishop of Armagh. He then returned to Cambridge and in 1569 became Lady Margaret professor there. From early in his career he had criticised the Elizabethan church settlement from a puritan point of view. From 1569 onwards his views were heard more publicly, in his lectures and sermons. He made a particular point of attacking, as unscriptural, the manner in which the clergy were appointed, and the ranks and degrees into which they were divided, arguing that all ministers ought to be equal in authority and be chosen by the congregation they were to serve. The established hierarchy was defended by John Whitgift and a major dispute developed which resulted in Cartwright being deprived of his professorship in 1570. He then retired to Geneva, but returned to England in time to engage in a second and more public controversy with Whitgift, the pamphlet warfare which began with the puritan *Admonition to the Parliament* in 1572. To avoid arrest he had to go into exile again, this time to Antwerp where he became minister to the English congregation. He returned to England in 1585 and secured the patronage of the Earl of Leicester who put him in charge of his almshouses in Warwick. Though he continued to criticise the establishment he never became a separatist and had no symathy with those who did. He was in trouble with the High Commission in 1590 because of his association with the presbyterian "classical" movement, but was protected then and in his closing years by the patronage of Burghley and King James of Scotland.

Chief works: *A Second Admonition to the Parliament* (1572); *A Reply to an Answer of . . . Whitgift against the Admonition.*
Life by A. F. Scott Pearson, *Thomas Cartwright and Elizabethan Puritanism,* Cambridge University Press.

# CRANMER

*Thomas Cranmer, Archbishop of Canterbury* (1489-1556), Henrician reformer.

Born at Aslockton, Notts., Cranmer entered Cambridge in 1503, graduated B.A. in 1512, M.A. in 1515, became a fellow of Jesus College, took his D.D. and received an appointment as lecturer in divinity. Apparently embarked upon a purely academic career, he came to the King's notice in 1529 when, in conversation with his former Cambridge colleagues Stephen Gardiner and Edward Fox, he suggested that an appeal to the universities of Europe would produce a learned public opinion in support of Henry's case. On the King's recommendation he was taken into the service of the Earl of Wiltshire (Anne Boleyn's father) and travelled with him on his embassy to the Pope and Emperor at Bologna in 1530. He was sent again as an ambassador to Charles V in 1532, but was recalled to be promoted, quite unexpectedly, to the now vacant see of Canterbury. In 1533, after the passage of the Act in Restraint of Appeals, he presided over the court which found the King's marriage to Catherine of Aragon to be invalid, and that with Anne Boleyn to be sound. A friend of the German reformers whom he met on his travels (and indeed married to the niece of one of them), and from early in his career an advocate of ecclesiastical reform, Cranmer did what he could in the lifetime of Henry VIII to further the reformation of the English church. However the respect in which he held the authority of the King was so great as to make it impossible for him at any time to act against Henry's

wishes, and so, despite his tenure of the highest office in the
church, he was not able to make much headway while Henry
lived, his chief successes being the authorisation of the English Bible and the publication of an English version of the
Litany. Cranmer was never ambitious for himself, and enjoyed, as none of his contemporaries ever did, the affection
and confidence of the King who refused to countenance any
of his enemies' attempts to pull him down. On the other
hand Cranmer's own merciful temperament is well evidenced
by his attempts to secure mercy for a diverse list of Henry's
victims, More, Fisher, Anne Boleyn, Cromwell and Catherine
Howard.

Upon the death of Henry VIII Cranmer, in company with
the Lord Protector Somerset, was able at last to give effect to
some of the plans for church reform he had been maturing
for some considerable time. The fruit of his labours is to be
seen in the destruction of images, the abolition of ceremonies
and the two prayer books of 1549 and 1552. He also
invited prominent continental reformers to visit him at
Lambeth, and tried to lay the foundations of a united
Protestant church. The accession of Mary and the restoration
of catholicism put Cranmer in a quandary. He had always
preached and believed in the necessity of obedience to legitimate authority, and now, by that legitimate authority, there
was restored in England a church whose teaching he had
come to believe was in error on certain vital points. His loyalty
to the Crown and his loyalty to what he believed to be the
truth were acutely in conflict. The many recantations and
declarations of his last days were the products of his earnest
endeavours to resolve this conflict of loyalties and to find a
formula that would satisfy the authorities without violating
his conscience, and not of a timorous attempt to escape the
stake. In the end his loyalty to his beliefs won the day. He
denounced his recantations and died a heretic's death.

Chief works: *The Book of Common Prayer* (1549, 1552);
   *A Defence of the True and Catholic Doctrine of the
   Sacrament* (1550).
Lives by G. W. Bromiley, *Thomas Cranmer, Archbishop and
   Martyr*, Lutterworth Press; A. F. Pollard, *Thomas Cranmer
   and the English Reformation*, Putnam; J. Ridley, *Thomas
   Cranmer*, Clarendon Press.

See also his *Works* edited by J. E. Cox, Parker Society, Vols. 12 and 24, Cambridge University Press; and J. Strype, *Memorials of Cranmer*, Oxford University Press.

# CROMWELL

*Thomas Cromwell, Earl of Essex* (1485?-1540), Henrician statesman.

After some years abroad as a soldier and merchant in Italy and the Netherlands, Cromwell returned to England in about 1512. Here, while continuing to engage in trade, he turned to the law and built up a considerable practice. He was a member of the House of Commons in the Parliament of 1523, and shortly afterwards entered the service of Cardinal Wolsey. On behalf of his new master he supervised the dissolution of more than a score of small monasteries whose revenues were to be applied to the maintenance of the Cardinal's college at Oxford and his school at Ipswich. When Wolsey fell from favour in 1529 Cromwell transferred himself to the King's service, entered Parliament under the patronage of the Duke of Norfolk, and, by 1531, had become a member of the King's council. From then on he rose steadily in power and influence until by 1532, when his chief rival, Stephen Gardiner, fell temporarily into disfavour, he had become the foremost of the King's ministers. It is generally accepted that his skill as a parliamentary manager was of invaluable assistance to Henry VIII in carrying through his "reformation" measures, the details of which were themselves in all probability planned by Cromwell from 1532 onwards. As the King's Vicar-general in spiritual matters from 1535 onwards he was intimately associated with the dissolution of the monasteries, the attack upon relics and pilgrimages, and the project for an English translation of the Bible. He also assisted the promotion of "reformist" bishops and preachers, and took the initiative in trying to secure a "Protestant" alliance for England abroad. Losing the King's favour over these latter two points, he was attacked by his political rivals, and arrested, attainted and executed on charges of treason and heresy in 1540. Pictured by Merriman as a ruthless, selfish and unprincipled man, his character has been partly rehabilitated by Elton who presents him as an administrative reformer, and Dickens who sees in him a patron of protestantism.

> Lives by R. B. Merriman, *The Life and Letters of Thomas Cromwell,* Clarendon Press; A. G. Dickens, *Thomas Cromwell and the English Reformation,* English Universities Press.
> See also G. R. Elton, *The Tudor Revolution in Government,* Cambridge University Press.

# DRAKE

*Sir Francis Drake* (1540?-96), Elizabethan seaman.

Born near Tavistock in Devon. The history of Drake's early years is obscure and the subject of much conjecture, though it is generally agreed that he came of a seafaring family and himself took early to the sea. He served, for instance, on voyages to the West African coast in 1565 and 1566. In 1567-8 he joined Hawkins' third expedition to the West Indies which met with disaster at San Juan de Ulloa. Thereafter, with the exception of two spells of comparative inactivity between 1580 and 1585 and between 1590 and 1595, and a period of service in Ireland in 1574-6, Drake was almost continuously at sea, engaged in bold, courageous, usually successful, but not easily justified attacks upon Spanish ships and colonial ports. His share of the booty must have been considerable. His most noteworthy exploits were his circumnavigation of the globe in the years 1577-80 and his attack upon Cadiz in 1587. The former followed in the track of earlier Spanish enterprise and made little contribution to the development of English trading links with the Far East. The latter did most effectively postpone the sailing of the great Armada for a year. In the fight against the Armada Drake commanded a division of the English fleet. He died of disease during the course of a raid on the isthmus of Panama in 1596. His skill and daring won him great renown in his own day, and ever since, and his reputation has as a consequence tended to overshadow those of men like Hawkins, Gilbert and Frobisher whose contribution to the maritime expansion of England was considerably more valuable.

Life by J. A. Williamson, *The Age of Drake*, A. and C. Black.
See also J. S. Corbett, *Drake and the Tudor Navy*, Longmans.


# FOXE

*John Foxe* (1516-87), Protestant martyrologist.

Born in Boston, Lincs., Foxe entered Oxford in about 1532.
He proceeded B.A. in 1537, became a fellow of Magdalen
College in 1539 and took his M.A. in 1543. Because he dis-
agreed fundamentally with the religious beliefs and practices
of his college he resigned his fellowship in 1545. Three years
later he was appointed tutor to the orphaned children of
Henry Howard, Earl of Surrey. This appointment was terminated at the beginning of Mary's reign when the children's
grandfather, the Duke of Norfolk, was released from his long
detention in the Tower. In 1554 Foxe, who had already made
public his opposition to the restoration of catholicism, retired
into exile, first at Strassburg and then at Frankfort. In this
latter city he soon became involved in the famous controversy
over the form of worship to be used by the exiled English
congregation. Foxe sided with John Knox and those who
favoured some amendment of the 1552 book against Richard
Cox and the party of "no change". In 1555 he removed to
Basle where he worked on the first (Latin) version of his
*Book of Martyrs* which was published in 1559. Foxe then
returned to England, secured the patronage of his former
pupil, now Duke of Norfolk, and set about revising and translating into English his great work which appeared under the
title *Acts and Monuments* in 1563. To meet criticism of in-
accuracy a second and revised edition followed in 1570, and
this was ordered by convocation to be purchased by every
bishop, cathedral chapter and archdeacon. Foxe's account of
the persecution of Mary's reign attained an immediate and
widespread popularity, and had a profound effect upon the
religious views of many generations of Englishmen. The
reliability of parts of his work has often been questioned and
is still a matter of debate.

Chief work: *Acts and Monuments* (The Book of Martyrs),
1563.

Life by J. F. Mozley, *John Foxe and his Book*, S.P.C.K.
See also J. M. Stone, "John Foxe's Book of Errors", in *The Month*, vol. XCV.

## GARDINER

*Stephen Gardiner, Bishop of Winchester* (1497?-1555), Henrician conservative.

Born at Bury St Edmunds, Gardiner was educated at Trinity Hall, Cambridge, where he became a fellow and eventually Master. He took his doctorate in Civil Law in 1521 and in Canon Law the following year, and entered the service of Cardinal Wolsey in 1524. In 1528, and again in 1529, he was employed on diplomatic missions to Rome in the furtherance of the King's marriage case, and won royal approval for his skilful conduct of the negotiations. In July 1529 he became King's Secretary and began to rise in political influence as Wolsey fell, becoming Bishop of Winchester in 1531 in succession to his former master. Though he was prepared to accept the royal supremacy his influence was at all times exerted in opposition to any further ecclesiastical innovations. His defence of the powers of convocation in 1532 incurred the royal displeasure, but his authorship of a full-length defence of the royal headship (his *De Vera Obedientia* of 1535) restored his political fortunes. In 1534 he was displaced in the Secretaryship by his great rival Cromwell. From 1535-8 he was ambassador to the French Court. On his return to England Gardiner, in concert with the Duke of Norfolk, worked for the overthrow of Cromwell and his policies. This was not achieved until 1540. For the next few years Gardiner's influence was dominant in the King's council, but before the end of Henry's reign his position was being threatened by the rise of Hertford and Lisle. For resisting the Edwardian reforms he was deprived of his bishopric and imprisoned. Restored in Mary's reign and made Lord Chancellor, he welcomed the restoration of the papal supremacy as a bulwark against protestantism.

Chief work: *De Vera Obedientia* (1535), available in translation in P. Janelle, *Obedience in Church and State*, Cambridge University Press.

Life by J. A. Muller, *Stephen Gardiner and the Tudor Reaction,* S.P.C.K.

See also J. A. Muller, *The Letters of Stephen Gardiner,* Cambridge University Press; L. B. Smith, *Tudor Prelates and Politics,* Princeton University Press.

# GILBERT

*Sir Humphrey Gilbert* (1539?-83), Elizabethan soldier and colonist.

The second son of Otho Gilbert of Compton, Devon, and a stepbrother of Sir Walter Raleigh, Gilbert was educated at Eton and Oxford and embarked upon a military career. He saw service under the Earl of Warwick at Le Havre in 1562-3, and with Sir Henry Sidney in Ireland in 1566, 1567 and 1569. Meanwhile he had already interested himself in overseas exploration, and in 1566 had presented his first petition to the Queen, seeking authorisation for an attempt to discover the North-west passage. After a brief appearance as a Member of Parliament in 1571 when he made a speech upholding the Queen's prerogative and was rebuked by Peter Wentworth, he commanded a small and very unsuccessful expedition to the Netherlands in 1572. In retirement from public life after this failure he composed his *Discourse for a Discovery of a New Passage to Cataia* which was published in 1576. Two years later he at last obtained the long coveted royal charter authorising him to plant a colony in the New World. His first attempt, in 1578, to put his schemes into effect was a complete failure, the ships getting no farther than Cape Verde. Thereafter, after another short spell of service in Ireland, he devoted his energies to raising funds for a second attempt. This materialised in 1583. After landing in Newfoundland and taking possession of it in the name of the Queen, Gilbert found it impossible to maintain discipline over his would-be colonists. The colony was abandoned, and Gilbert perished when the ship he was in foundered on the return voyage.

Chief work: *A Discourse for a Discovery of a New Passage to Cataia* (1576).

Life by W. G. Gosling, Constable.

See also D. B. Quinn, *The Voyages and Colonising Enterprises of Sir Humphrey Gilbert* (Hakluyt Society, 2nd series, vols. LXXXIII and LXXXIV).

# GREY

*Lady Jane Grey* (1537-54), Queen.

Dorset, and Frances, daughter of Charles Brandon, Duke of Suffolk and Mary, younger sister of King Henry VIII, her relationship to the royal family (see genealogical table No. 2) brought her into public prominence and made her the victim of the schemes of others. Brought up in the household of The eldest surviving daughter of Henry Grey, Marquis of Henry VIII's last Queen, Catherine Parr, she later became the ward of Lord Thomas Seymour (the brother of Protector Somerset) who had married Queen Catherine after Henry's death. Lord Thomas tried to arrange the marriage of Jane to King Edward VI, but Somerset wanted her as a bride for his own son. Finally, John Dudley, Duke of Northumberland, when King Edward was dying, saw in Jane a chance to preserve his own political power. He married her to his own son Guildford Dudley, persuaded Edward to bequeath his crown to her and prevailed upon most of the chief men in the kingdom to put their signatures to his scheme. On Edward's death Jane was duly proclaimed Queen, but the country rejected Northumberland's plan and rallied to Mary Tudor. Jane and her husband were imprisoned in the Tower. Condemned of high treason, she might have been reprieved but for the outbreak of Wyatt's rebellion in 1554 which so alarmed the government that it was thought safer to execute this potentially dangerous rival to the reigning Queen. Though only sixteen years old at her death Jane had already become famous for her learning, her piety and her good looks.

Life by P. R. B. Davey, *The Nine Days' Queen*, Methuen.
See also J. G. Nichols, *The Chronicle of Queen Jane and of Two Years of Queen Mary* (Camden Society, vol. XLVIII).

# HAWKINS

*Sir John Hawkins* (1532-95), Elizabethan seaman.

Born in Plymouth, the second son of a notable seafaring father, William Hawkins, John was bred to the sea and as a young man had already made several voyages to the Canaries before, in 1562, he fitted out the first of his own expeditions. This sailed to West Africa to pick up a cargo of Negro slaves who were then taken across the Atlantic and traded for the tropical products of Spain's Caribbean colonies. A considerable profit was made on the round trip, but this breach of their colonial monopoly so angered the Spanish authorities that when Hawkins tried to repeat his exploit in 1564 he found the Spanish colonists much less willing to do business with him. In 1567 when he tried for a third time he met with even stiffer resistance, and his fleet was all but destroyed when caught in the harbour of San Juan de Ulloa by a superior Spanish force. His reputation as a seaman and his marriage to the daughter of a former treasurer of the navy secured for Hawkins that office which he held until his death. This post was no sinecure to him and he devoted his very considerable energies to improving the design of the Queen's ships and to keeping them in constant readiness. In the fight against the Armada Hawkins commanded a section of the fleet and was knighted for his services. He served also on an unsuccessful expedition to the Portuguese coast in 1590, and died at sea during the course of a raiding expedition to the Caribbean five years later. It was on this same ill-fated expedition that Drake met his death. Often accused of having lined his own pockets at the expense of the government, Hawkins was the founder of a hospital at Chatham.

Life by J. A. Williamson, A. and C. Black.
See also C. R. Markham, *The Hawkins' Voyages* (Hakluyt Society, vol. LVII).


# KILDARE

*Gerald Fitzgerald, eighth Earl of Kildare* (d. 1513), Anglo-Irish magnate.

Son of Thomas Fitzgerald, seventh earl, he succeeded, upon his father's death in 1477, not only to the earldom, but also to the office of Lord Deputy of Ireland to which the council in Dublin elected him. Edward IV's attempts to appoint his own Lord Deputy were unsuccessful and the English King had in the end to accept as Deputy the man chosen by the Irish council. From then until his death in 1513, with one short intermission, Kildare was virtually uncrowned King of Ireland. Attracted to the Yorkist side by the confidence displayed in him by Richard III, Kildare was ready in 1487 to accept Lambert Simnel as "Edward VI" and to arrange for and witness his coronation in Dublin. After the defeat of Simnel at Stoke Kildare was more cautious. In 1494 Henry VII removed him from office, and sent him to imprisonment in the Tower while Sir Edward Poynings was sent to govern Ireland. Two years later, the English King, finding the expense of supporting Poynings' government too great, restored Kildare to the Deputyship which he retained until his death. Possessed of great power and estates by virtue of his earldom, Kildare also allied himself by marriage with many of the principal gaelic and Anglo-Irish lords. His personal power was so great that it was said that "all Ireland could not rule him". Consequently Henry VII found it expedient to let Kildare "rule all Ireland". His son, and successor in the Deputyship, was the ninth earl who was to be the last of his line, or of any Anglo-Irish house, to enjoy such extensive and independent power.

Life by D. Bryan, *The Great Earl of Kildare*, Talbot Press.


# KNOX

*John Knox* (1505-72), Scottish Reformer.

Born and educated at Haddington, Knox spent some time at the university of Glasgow and may have been also to St Andrews, though he is not recorded as a graduate of either place. That he studied theology is evidenced by his later writings, that he also studied law by the fact that his earliest recorded employment was as a notary in his native town. Later he abandoned the law and took employment as a private tutor. During the 1540s he became acquainted with the Protestant preacher George Wishart, and through his influence became a convert to protestantism. In 1547 he was chosen as their preacher by the Protestant congregation at St Andrews. For his support of the murderers of Cardinal Beaton, who were besieged in St Andrews castle, Knox, after the fall of the castle, was sent as a prisoner to France in one of the French galleys which had assisted in the siege. Released in 1549 he came to England and received official patronage, being appointed one of the King's chaplains and sent as preacher first to Berwick and later to Newcastle. Early in Mary's reign Knox, like so many of his fellow Protestants, found it advisable to withdraw to the Continent, where he travelled extensively until called to be minister to the English congregation at Frankfort. After his defeat in the celebrated controversy with Richard Cox over the form of prayer to be used by the English exiles there Knox had to leave Frankfort and seek refuge in Geneva. He returned thence to Scotland in 1555 and spent about nine months in travelling and preaching with considerable success. He returned to Geneva voluntarily in 1556, but was tried as a heretic and burnt in effigy in his absence by the Scottish bishops. In 1558 he wrote and published several strongly worded pamphlets, including his *First Blast of the Trumpet against the Monstrous Regiment of Women* which argued that the exercise of political power by women was contrary to nature, and which was inspired by the experiences of contemporary Protestants under Mary of Guise in Scotland and Mary Tudor in England. On his second return to Scotland in 1559 his preaching provoked a religious riot in Perth which became the signal for a revolt which overthrew the government of the Regent and the old order in the church. This triumph of the national and Protestant causes was the climax of Knox's career. His later years were spent in laying the foundations of the Scottish reformed church, and in defending it against the counter-attack of the Scottish Catholics who were inspired to greater effort by the return to Scotland of Mary Stuart in 1561. Knox died in 1572, having continued to the last to preach with his customary vehemence in support of the cause to which he had devoted so much of his life.

Chief works: *The First Blast of the Trumpet against the Monstrous Regiment of Women* (1558); *The History of the Reformation in Scotland* (1587).
Lives by P. H. Brown, A. and C. Black; A. Lang, Longmans.

See also D. Laing, *The Works of John Knox*, Bannatyne Club, Edinburgh; and G. Donaldson, *The Scottish Reformation*, Cambridge University Press.


# MARY

*Mary Stuart* (1542-87), Queen of Scotland.

Third and only surviving legitimate child of James V, Mary was born only six days before her father's death, and was therefore Queen of Scotland almost from birth. Her father's mother was Margaret Tudor, the elder sister of Henry VIII, and so Mary stood next to that King's children in succession to the English throne (see genealogical table No. 2). The attempt by Henry VIII in 1543 to unite the kingdoms of England and Scotland by marrying Mary to his only son Edward was frustrated by the pro-French party in Scotland who arranged an alternative match for her with the eldest son of the French King, and sent her for safety into France in August 1548. There she was brought up and educated as one of the French royal family, and married to the Dauphin, Francis, in 1558. On the death of Mary Tudor a few months later, Mary Stuart, who was already Queen of Scotland and dauphiness of France, laid claim to the throne of England, arguing that Elizabeth was the illegitimate offspring of a bigamous marriage and incapable of inheriting. The French Court supported her claim which accorded well with French ambitions. In July 1559, upon the death of his father, Mary's husband became King of France as Francis II, and Mary reached the summit of her career, being now Queen-Regnant of Scotland, Queen-Consort of France and Queen-claimant of England. But, by the terms of the treaty of Edinburgh of July 1560, Mary was obliged to abandon her claim to England. In December 1560 Francis II died, depriving his young widow of any authority in France, and Mary was left as Queen of Scotland alone, with an unacknowledged claim to be heir to Elizabeth. In 1561 Mary returned to Scotland, and for four years succeeded very well in retaining the loyalties and affections of her subjects during the particularly difficult times which followed the triumph of Knox and the Scottish Protestants in 1560. While maintaining stoutly her own right to worship in the Catholic fashion she did not attempt to coerce the Protestants.

Mary's marriage to her cousin Henry Stuart, Lord Darnley, in 1565 was the beginning of her undoing. A political match which was intended to strengthen Mary's claim to the English throne by binding in marriage two of the nearest heirs, this union brought to the Scottish Court an ambitious, wilful, selfish and unstable young man who soon provoked the jealousy of many influential persons including Mary's half-brother James Stuart, Earl of Moray, who had hitherto enjoyed the chief place in the Queen's confidence and felt himself ousted by the new arrival. Moray's rebellion, Darnley's treachery, the murder of Mary's secretary Rizzio, the murder of Darnley and Mary's marriage to Bothwell all followed in quick succession, produced by a complex of jealousies and rivalries which are not easy to disentangle, and resulted in a widespread reaction against the Queen whose part in all these intrigues did her little credit. She was obliged to abdicate, and imprisoned, but escaped and fled to England in 1568. It was during this turbulent period of her life, in June 1566, that her only child, the later James VI, was born, the son of Darnley.

From 1568 to the day of her death Mary was kept under restraint in England. To Elizabeth she was dangerous (more especially after the issue of the papal bull of excommunication against the English Queen in 1570) as the person who was recognised by Catholics as rightful Queen of England. Yet Mary was legitimate and crowned sovereign of Scotland, and Elizabeth would never assist the designs of those who wished any harm to an anointed ruler. For her own safety Elizabeth had to keep Mary under constraint. For the sake of the reputation of royalty she had to protect her from harm. The Scottish nobles who had forced Mary to abdicate were anxious to put her on trial for her part in the murder of Darnley. Mary would not be safe in Scotland. At liberty abroad she would be the centre of intrigues against Elizabeth much more dangerous than those which were hatched around her in her imprisonment in England. It is hard to see what other course was open to Elizabeth but to keep Mary a prisoner, once she had tried, and failed, to restore her to her Scottish throne under guarantees which the Scottish lords were not prepared to give.

In the end it was Elizabeth's subjects, anxious for the personal safety of their Queen and the security of their country, who obliged her to consent to Mary's execution as a party to the Babington conspiracy of 1586. The Act for the Queen's Safety of 1585 left Elizabeth no alternative but to put Mary on trial, and the evidence produced by Walsingham was more than enough to convict her. Yet even then Elizabeth hesitated and only with extreme reluctance, and under pressure from her councillors, signed the warrant for Mary's death.

Mary's personal charms which won so many champions to her side in her own day still exercise their magic upon many of her biographers who present her as the tragic victim of circumstances and the selfish intrigues of Elizabeth. Others hold that Mary's own wilfulness and obstinacy earned their own reward.

Lives by T. F. Henderson, Hutchinson; and D. H. Fleming, Hodder and Stoughton.

# MORE

*Sir Thomas More* (1478-1535), Henrician humanist.

The only surviving son of Sir John More, lawyer and later judge, Thomas was educated in London at St Anthony's school in Threadneedle street. In 1491 he entered the service of John Morton, Lord Chancellor and Archbishop of Canterbury, and later cardinal, where his alertness and ready intellect early made a very favourable impression. In 1492, probably at Morton's suggestion, he entered Oxford where he made the acquaintance of such renowned scholars as Thomas Linacre and William Grocyn, and was attracted to the "new learning" of the Renaissance humanists. Two years later he took up the study of the law, first at New Inn and then at Lincoln's Inn. Never wholly devoted to the law, More always found time for literary works. He met Erasmus for the first time in 1497 and formed a lasting friendship with him which was based upon their mutual respect for each other's scholarship and a mutual interest in classical studies. For a time, about 1500, More seriously considered entering the priesthood, but did not in the end proceed with this intention. As a Member of Parliament in 1504 More played an important part in successfully opposing the financial demands of Henry VII. In the following decade he built up for himself a highly successful legal practice in London. In 1515 he was first employed in the royal service on an embassy to the Netherlands. While there he commenced work upon his *Utopia* which was published in the following year. Thereafter he increasingly attracted the attention of the King and Wolsey by his efficient handling of all matters committed to him, and in 1518 he was admitted to the royal council. In the Parliament of 1523 he was Speaker, and played an important part in the negotiations over the subsidy. In 1527 when the opinions and writings of the Lutherans were being extensively circulated in England, More was called upon by Bishop Tunstall of London to write a defence of orthodox doctrine and practice, and produced his *Dialogue* which led to a controversy with William Tyndale. In 1529 More was appointed Lord Chancellor in succession to Wolsey, but he resigned his office in protest against the King's ecclesiastical measures. His refusal to deny the spiritual authority of the Pope (though he was quite prepared to profess his loyalty to the King and to accept his marriage with Anne Boleyn) brought upon him the full penalties of the law, and led to his execution in 1535. More enjoyed a European-wide reputation as a scholar and a writer, and his execution came as a shock to most people outside England.

Chief works: *The History of King Richard III* (1513); *Utopia* (1516); *The Dialogue* (1528); *The Supplication of Souls* (1529); *A discourse of Comfort* (1534).

Lives by R. W. Chambers, *Thomas More*, Jonathan Cape; E. M. G. Routh, *Sir Thomas More and his Friends*, Oxford University Press; T. Maynard, *Humanist as Hero*, Macmillan.

See also his *Works* edited by W. E. Campbell and A. W. Reed, Eyre and Spottiswoode; and William Roper's *Life of More* (Early English Text Society, vol. CXCVII).


# MOUNTJOY

*Charles Blount, Lord Mountjoy, Earl of Devonshire* (1563-1606), Elizabethan adventurer.

The second son of James, sixth Lord Mountjoy, Charles was educated at Oxford and the Inner Temple. Determined to restore the waning fortunes of his family he made his way to Court in about 1583, and soon attracted the attention of the Queen. Though he early fought a duel with Essex, who saw in him a rival, the two men later became friends. From 1586, when he was knighted, Blount was constantly seeking military renown, in the Netherlands, or in Brittany. He also provided his own ships for service against the Armada. On the death of his elder brother in 1594 he became the eighth Lord Mountjoy. The opportunity he had so long awaited came at last when Essex failed to suppress the Tyrone rebellion in Ireland and became involved in a treasonable conspiracy against the Queen. Although Mountjoy had been involved in Essex's schemes, the Queen gave him a chance to redeem himself and sent him as Lord Deputy to Ireland in 1600. There his policy of planting garrisons in rebel territories and laying waste the countryside eventually had its effect. The defeat at Kinsale of the Spanish force sent to help the rebels sealed the fate of the latter, and Tyrone surrendered to Mountjoy in 1603. In the following year Mountjoy, now Earl of Devonshire, was one of the commissioners who negotiated the Anglo-Spanish peace. This was the climax of his career. His marriage in 1605 to Penelope, the divorced wife of Lord Rich, lost him favour at Court, and he died shortly afterwards.

Life by C. Falls, *Mountjoy, Elizabethan General*, Odhams Press.
See also C. Falls, *Elizabeth's Irish Wars*, Methuen.

# NORFOLK

*Thomas Howard, Earl of Surrey and Duke of Norfolk* (1473-1554), Henrician soldier.

The grandson of John Howard, first Duke of Norfolk, and staunch supporter of Richard III, who was killed at Bosworth, Thomas, as a youth, shared in the political downfall of his family. However the military abilities of the Howards, and their willingness to display their loyalty to the new royal house, soon restored their fortunes. In 1498 Howard served with his father on the northern borders. In 1512 he was a subordinate commander of the ill-fated expedition to Spain, and in the following year he and his father defeated a Scottish invasion at Flodden. By now the Howards were fully restored to favour. The father recovered the Dukedom of Norfolk in 1514 and the son became Earl of Surrey, eventually succeeding to his father's dukedom in 1524. Proud of his noble ancestry, allied by his second marriage to the house of Buckingham and ambitious for political power, the younger Howard soon came into conflict with first Wolsey and then Cromwell. Though his services as a soldier and as a naval commander were often in demand in the 1520s and 1530s when his military reputation stood high, Norfolk never quite attained the political eminence he so much desired. Though he attempted to profit from Wolsey's fall, he soon found himself supplanted by Cromwell, and thereafter he is to be found doing his best to oppose the reforming policies of the new secretary. After Cromwell's fall in 1540 the way at last seemed clear for Norfolk's ambition, but his triumph was brief. The wars of the 1540s advanced the military reputation and political fortunes of the younger men at Court, and the foolish extravagances of his son, the poet Surrey, involved the house of Howard in a second downfall. Though condemned of treason in 1547 Norfolk was saved from execution by the death of Henry VIII. He remained in prison throughout the reign of Edward VI, was released and restored to favour by Mary, but died in the following year.

# NORTHUMBERLAND

*John Dudley, Earl of Warwick and Duke of Northumberland,* Edwardian politician.

The eldest son of Edmund Dudley, councillor to Henry VII, John was admitted to the Inner Temple in 1511, but did not complete his legal education, turning instead to the profession of arms. He served in France in 1523 and was knighted in the same year. Created Viscount Lisle and Lord Admiral in 1543, he was joint leader of Henry VIII's great assault upon Scotland in 1544, and in the following year commanded the English channel fleet against the French. A rising star at

Court at the end of Henry's reign, he was one of the councillors who were appointed by the terms of that King's will to carry on the government during the minority of his son Edward. Initially Dudley supported Somerset's protectorate, and was created Earl of Warwick at the outset of the new reign. Personally ambitious, he later led the opposition to Somerset's social policies, was responsible for the suppression of Kett's rebellion in 1549 and engineered the downfall of the Lord Protector in the same year. Predominant in the council from then to the end of the reign, he secured for himself the dukedom of Northumberland, supported the radical wing of the reformers in the church and encouraged commercial expansion abroad. On the death of Edward VI he tried to perpetuate his power by excluding the Princess Mary from the throne in favour of Jane Grey to whom he married his son Guildford Dudley. His plot failing, he was executed for treason. He was the father of Robert and Ambrose Dudley, earls of Leicester and Warwick respectively in the reign of Elizabeth I.

Life by P. Lindsay, *The Queenmaker,* Williams and Norgate.

# PARKER

*Matthew Parker, Archbishop of Canterbury* (1504-75), Elizabethan theologian.

Parker was born at Norwich and educated at Corpus Christi College, Cambridge, taking his B.A. in 1525. Two years later he was ordained priest and made a fellow of his college. In 1528 he took his M.A. and declined Wolsey's invitation to become a foundation fellow of his new Cardinal College at Oxford. Steering clear of politics and devoting himself to his studies he took his B.D. in 1535 and his D.D. in 1538, becoming Master of his college in 1544 and Vice-Chancellor of the university in 1545. At the same time he had attracted the attention of the Court and was appointed chaplain to Anne Boleyn in 1535 and to Henry VIII in 1537. After Henry's death Parker married Margaret Harlestone who came of a family connected with the reformers. He also at this time became a close friend of Martin Bucer during the latter's sojourn in Cambridge. Because of his marriage and his as sociation with the reformers, Parker was, on Mary's accession, deprived of all his preferments. He did not go into exile though he found it advisable to go into hiding. Selected by Elizabeth to fill the see of Canterbury left vacant by the death of Cardinal Pole, Parker was extremely reluctant to accept the position and would very much have preferred to remain at Cambridge. After his elevation to the primacy it was Parker's influence which was predominant in shaping the Elizabethan church. While energetic in maintaining England's independence of Rome, Parker was also active in combating the extremer demands of the puritans, and by his insistence upon the retention of many customs and practices of the traditional church incurred their bitter hostility. Always primarily a scholar and only secondarily an archbishop, Parker helped to produce the ~~Bishops' Bible~~ and to remodel the statutes of Cambridge university. It was to Corpus Christi that he bequeathed his invaluable collection of manuscripts.

Life by V. J. K. Brook, Clarendon Press.
See also J. Strype, *The Life and Acts of Matthew Parker,* Clarendon Press.


# POLE

*Reginald Pole, Cardinal and Archbishop of Canterbury* (1500-58), Marian archbishop.

Through his mother, Margaret, Countess of Salisbury, Pole was closely connected with the house of York, being a great-nephew of both Edward IV and Richard III. Always intended for the church, he was given his schooling in the Charterhouse at Sheen, and entered Magdalen College, Oxford, in 1513. Here he came under the guidance of Thomas Linacre and showed great promise as a scholar. He took his B.A. in 1515. Patronised by his second cousin, King Henry VIII, Pole seemed to be embarked upon an uneventful yet distinguished career. From 1521-7 he studied in Italy. In 1529 he went abroad again, this time to Paris, to avoid being involved in the King's matrimonial proceedings. He was, however, unable to escape entirely and was obliged to help Edward Fox to obtain from the university of Paris opinions in Henry's favour.

From July 1530 to January 1532 he was back in England, but being unable to approve of the King's proceedings he retired once more to Italy where he gathered round him in Padua a distinguished circle of scholars. Though for a while he retained the good opinion of the King, this was irretrievably destroyed by the publication of his *Pro Ecclesiasticae Unitatis Defensione* in 1536 and by his appointment as a cardinal in the same year. Thereafter Pole was committed to the papal side, and the wrath of the King was visited upon his family in 1538. During the years of his exile Pole set an example in virtue and scholarship which made a considerable contribution to the reform of the papacy and the college of cardinals. Upon the accession of Mary he came to England as papal legate to supervise the return of the English church to the Roman obedience, becoming Archbishop of Canterbury in succession to the deprived Cranmer. It was a great disappointment to Pole that the Marian restoration was not complete. He died a few hours after Mary.

Chief work: *Pro Ecclesiasticae Unitatis Defensione* (1536). Life by W. Schenk, Longmans.

# RALEIGH

*Sir Walter Raleigh* (1552?-1618), Elizabethan writer and colonist.

Raleigh's earlier career was very similar to that of his elder half-brother Sir Humphrey Gilbert, and included military service in France in 1569-72, in the Netherlands in 1577-8 and in Ireland in 1580-1. Attracting the Queen's attention by his good looks and his bold spirit he rose rapidly in royal favour in the 1580s, receiving, among other favours, the grant of a substantial estate in Munster. After Gilbert's death in 1583 Raleigh took upon himself the continuation of his half-brother's interest in colonisation. In 1584 he sent ot an expedition to explore the North American coast. This took possession of a vast tract of land which was later called Virginia in the Queen's honour, and selected Roanoke Island in Pamlico sound as a suitable site for the plantation of a colony. The first attempt at a settlement there was made in

1585, but the colonists returned home with Drake in the following year. In 1587 Raleigh tried again. This time the necessary relief force was delayed by the outbreak of the Spanish war and did not reach Roanoke until 1589 when no trace of the settlers could be found. In the 1590s Raleigh switched his interest from North to South America, and from colonial promotion to the search for "Eldorado" the city of gold that was believed to stand upon the upper waters of the River Orinoco, but his exploratory journey in 1595 produced no fruit. Suspected of opposing the accession of James of Scotland he was tried and condemned in 1603 but reprieved and remained a prisoner in the Tower until 1616. During his imprisonment he devoted himself to literary and scientific pursuits and wrote a *History of the World*. He eventually secured his release in order that he might search once more for "Eldorado", but his expedition was a failure, and upon his return to England he was executed to appease the wrath of Spain. Though he was probably not the first man to introduce tobacco to England he was certainly the first eminent Englishman to acquire the habit of smoking.

Chief work: *The History of the World.*
Lives by D. B. Quinn, *Raleigh and the British Empire,* English Universities Press; E. Thompson, *Sir Walter Raleigh, the Last of the Elizabethans,* Macmillan.
See also E. C. Strathmann, *Sir Walter Raleigh, a Study in Elizabethan Skepticism,* Columbia University Press.

# SIDNEY

*Sir Philip Sidney* (1554-86), Elizabethan poet and soldier.

The eldest son of Sir Henry Sidney and Mary, daughter of John Dudley, Duke of Northumberland, Sidney was educated at Shrewsbury and Christ Church, Oxford. Though, in common with many of the young men of his class, he left the university without taking his degree, he had early won the admiration of his elders by both his character and his abilities. From 1572 to 1575 he made an extended tour abroad, sojourning in France, Austria and Italy, and visiting Hungary, Bohemia and many parts of Germany. On his return to England he secured an entry to the Court circle through the influence of his uncle, the Earl of Leicester. In 1576 he went to Ireland to visit his father who was then Lord Deputy. In this same year Sidney probably first met Penelope Devereux who was to inspire so many of his verses. Her marriage to Lord Rich in 1581 did not interrupt the flow of verses, though Sidney's own marriage to Frances Walsingham two years later did. Sidney's interest in literature gathered about him a considerable circle of writers which included Edmund Spenser. Yet Sidney was not only a poet and found physical inactivity irksome especially when the cause of protestantism, which was very dear to him, seemed to be faring so ill in Europe. The chance for activity came in 1585 when Leicester was sent with an English force to assist the Netherlanders, and took his nephew with him. Sidney died of a wound received in battle at Zutphen in the following year and was widely mourned.

    Chief works: Sonnets (1575-83); *Apologie for Poetrie* (1579); *Arcadia* (1580).

    Lives by F. S. Boas, Staples Press; M. W. Wallace, Cambridge University Press; H. R. Fox Bourne, Chapman and Hall.

    See also Fulke Greville, *The Life of the Renowned Sir Philip Sidney,* Clarendon Press.


## SOMERSET

*Edward Seymour, Earl of Hertford and Duke of Somerset* (1506?-52), Lord Protector.

The eldest son of Sir John Seymour of Wolf Hall, Wiltshire, Edward entered the service of Henry VIII's sister Mary in 1514. He saw his first military service under her husband, the Duke of Suffolk, in France in 1523. He entered the King's service in the following year, and had risen to the rank of gentleman of the privy chamber by 1536. In that year the marriage of his sister Jane to the King laid the real foundation of his fortune, and was followed very shortly by his elevation to the peerage as Viscount Beauchamp. The birth of Prince Edward in the following year was the occasion for the further promotion of Seymour to the earldom of Hertford. The death of Queen Jane caused but a temporary setback to her brother's career. His military abilities, employed against

ne Scots and the French in 1544 and 1545, won him con-
iderable renown, and his influence at Court began to eclipse
nat of the older men such as Norfolk. The fall of the
Iowards (Norfolk and his son) in 1546 left the way clear for
iertford at Henry's death to assume control of the govern-
nent as Lord Protector for his young nephew the new King,
vho made his uncle Duke of Somerset. Somerset then em-
arked upon a policy of moderate religious and social reform,
ut his ecclesiastical measures touched off revolt in the south-
vest, and his social policies were held by his contemporaries
o have contributed to the outbreak of rebellion in East Anglia.
Ie was therefore unseated from his protectorship in 1549
y a conspiracy of councillors led by John Dudley, Earl of
Varwick, and soon to be Duke of Northumberland. Though,
fter a short imprisonment, Somerset was permitted to resume
is seat on the council, he never regained his lost authority,
nd was eventually executed on a charge of treason trumped
p by his personal enemies in 1552. Known as "The Good
)uke" because of his humanitarian interest in the condition
f the poor, Somerset was personally as rapacious as any of
is contemporaries and enjoyed a substantial share in the
poils of the church.

See A. F. Pollard, *England under Protector Somerset*, Kegan
    Paul.

# TYNDALE

*William Tyndale* (1494?-1536), Translator and contro-
ersialist.

Born in Gloucestershire, Tyndale was educated at Oxford
Magdalen Hall), taking his B.A. in 1512 and M.A. in 1515.
urning to the study of theology he later removed to Cam-
ridge where he remained until about 1521. He then secured
ppointment as tutor to the children of a Gloucestershire
entleman, and spent much of his spare time preaching in the
illages round about his employer's home. His vigorous ser-
nons often provoked heated controversy, and led Tyndale to
ntertain a poor opinion of the Biblical knowledge of his
pponents. In order to assist the spread of the knowledge and

understanding of scripture Tyndale resolved to make the provision of an English version of the Bible his life work. He travelled to London, but failed to secure the assistance which he had hoped for from the scholarly Bishop Tunstall. Instead he found a patron in Humphrey Monmouth, a cloth merchant with whose assistance he took up residence in Germany in 1524, out of reach of the English ecclesiastical authorities. The remaining twelve years of Tyndale's life were spent in exile in Germany and the Netherlands, working upon his translation. His version of the New Testament first appeared in England in 1526, his translation of the first part of the Old in 1530. He also wrote several controversial pamphlets in which he criticised the contemporary church and upheld the authority of the secular power. His *Obedience of a Christian Man*, in which he enlarged upon the authority of princes, met with Henry VIII's approval and led to an invitation to him to return to England, but the attack upon the King's matrimonial proceedings which he included in his *Practice of Prelates* brought the negotiations for his return to an abrupt close. He was betrayed to the Netherlands' authorities in 1535 and burnt as a heretic in 1536.

Chief works: *Parable of the Wicked Mammon* (1528); *The Obedience of a Christian Man* (1528); *The Practice of Prelates* (1530); *An Answer to Sir Thomas More's Dialogue* (1530).

Lives by R. Demaus, The Religious Tract Society, London; J. F. Mozley, S.P.C.K.

See also *Works,* ed. by H. Walter (Parker Society, 1848-50).

## TYRONE

*Hugh O'Neil, Earl of Tyrone* (1550-1616), Irish rebel.

Grandson of Conn Bacach O'Neil who was created first Earl of Tyrone in 1542. After the death of his grandfather Hugh was removed to England to save him from the enmity of his uncle, Shane O'Neil, who was recognised by the O'Neils as chief. Brought up in the household of Sir Henry Sidney, the father of the more famous Sir Philip who was only a few years younger than he, Hugh should have succeeded, in English law, to his grandfather's title when his elder brother

Brian was killed in 1562. He was allowed to return to Ireland in 1568, and remained loyal, but was not recognised as earl until 1585. Accepted by the O'Neils as chief in succession to his cousin Turloch in 1595, he became involved in the rebellion of Maguire and O'Donnel in the same year, and built up, with their assistance, a formidable coalition of gaelic powers. He was eventually defeated by and surrendered to Mountjoy in 1603. Pardoned, and restored by James I, he fled abroad in 1607 and died in Rome.

Life by Sean O'Faolain, Longmans.
See also C. Falls, *Elizabeth's Irish Wars*, Methuen, and *Mountjoy, Elizabethan General*, Odhams Press.

# WALSINGHAM

*Sir Francis Walsingham* (1530?-90), Elizabethan statesman.

The only son of a prominent London lawyer, Francis entered King's College, Cambridge, in 1548 and resided there until 1550 though he did not take any degree. He next embarked upon a legal career by entering Gray's Inn in 1552, but his strong Protestant leanings drove him into voluntary exile during Mary's reign. These five years abroad shaped his later career, for he devoted them to the serious study of the languages, laws and policies of the principal states of Europe, and to the making of personal contacts which were to be of great service to him later. Upon Elizabeth's accession he returned to England and sat in Parliament as one of the members for Banbury. He early recommended himself to Cecil by the ease with which he could obtain secret intelligence from his many contacts abroad, yet Walsingham did not receive any official appointment until 1570 when he became ambassador to France and helped to negotiate the Anglo-French treaty of Blois (1572). In 1573 he returned to England and was made Secretary of State. Foreign affairs were his special concern. He took a thoroughly "Protestant" view of the contemporary diplomatic scene and constantly endeavoured to encourage the Queen to pursue a more active policy in support of the Netherlands' revolt and in defence of the Huguenots in France. Equally constantly he was disappointed by Elizabeth's vacillation which was due in large measure to the more cautious advice of Burghley. Walsingham also built up an extensive network of secret agents whose information enabled him to expose Mary Stuart's implication in the Babington conspiracy, and to forecast accurately the size and armament of the great Armada. Walsingham also displayed considerable interest in the exploits of English navigators. His daughter Frances married successively Sir Philip Sidney and Robert Devereux, Earl of Essex.

Life by C. Read, *Mr Secretary Walsingham and the Policy of Queen Elizabeth*, Clarendon Press.
See also *Journal of Sir Francis Walsingham*, ed. C. T. Martin (Camden Society, 1871).

## WENTWORTH

*Peter Wentworth* (1524?-96), Elizabethan parliamentarian.

The eldest son of Sir Nicholas Wentworth of Lillingstone Lovell in Buckinghamshire, little is known about his early life. His second marriage, which took place before 1557, was to Elizabeth, the sister of Sir Francis Walsingham, and brought him into contact with persons of prominence. Wentworth's parliamentary career began in 1571 when he became member for Barnstaple. His younger brother, Paul, had already sat in the Parliaments of 1563 and 1566, and had made a name for himself by his outspokenness on behalf of parliamentary freedom of speech. Peter soon outstripped his brother as an energetic defender of what he conceived to be the privileges of Parliament. He sat in nearly every Parliament between 1571 and 1593. In 1571 he attacked Sir Humphrey Gilbert for attempting to overawe the House with threats of royal displeasure, and joined in support of the puritan campaign for a revision of the prayer book. In 1576 he made a noteworthy speech in defence of the liberties of the House of Commons but was, out of respect for the Queen, stopped by the House itself which then committed him to custody. After a short imprisonment in the Tower he was released at the request of the Queen. In 1587 he returned to the attack and, by proposing a series of questions to the House, attempted to secure a closer definition of the privileges of the Commons. Once again he was imprisoned, but this time at the command of the Queen. Elizabeth, however, was sufficiently careful of Parliament's susceptibilities to make it clear that this imprisonment was the consequence of things said and done outside the House and not therefore covered by parliamentary privilege. Wentworth's third imprisonment came in 1593 when his reopening of the succession question caused the Queen considerable offence. This time quite a strong party in the Commons regarded his detention as a breach of privilege and sought his release. Though Wentworth's constant campaigning won no significant concessions from the Queen, he and his associates did teach the House of Commons the arts of opposition which they put to such good use in the following reigns.

See W. L. Rutton, *Three Branches of the Family of Wentworth,* London, 1891; and J. E. Neale, "Peter Wentworth", in *English Historical Review,* vol. XXXIX.

# WHITGIFT

*John Whitgift* (1530?-1604), Elizabethan Archbishop.

The eldest son of a prosperous Grimsby merchant, Whitgift was educated at St Anthony's school, London, and Pembroke Hall, Cambridge, where he came under the Protestant influence of the Master, Nicholas Ridley, and his tutor, John Bradford. He took his B.A. in 1554 and M.A. in 1557, and for the next twenty years followed the academic profession with considerable success. Fellow of Peterhouse in 1555; B.D. and Lady Margaret Professor of Divinity in 1563; Master of Pembroke Hall and D.D. in April 1567; Master of Trinity and Regius Professor of Divinity later in the same year; he reached the summit of his university career when he became Vice-Chancellor in 1570. Already engaged in a dispute over church government with Thomas Cartwright, Whitgift was now able to secure the latter's eviction, first from the Lady Margaret chair, and later from his fellowship at Trinity. Two years later Cartwright returned to the attack by writing a reply to Whitgift's *Answer to the Admonition to the Parlia-*

*ment* and engaged his rival in a second and more public controversy. Meanwhile Whitgift's abilities as a preacher and a disciplinarian had recommended him to the Queen, who in 1577 made him Bishop of Worcester. In 1583 he succeeded Edmund Grindal as Archbishop of Canterbury and devoted the rest of his days to maintaining the episcopal government and the ceremonial of the church against the attacks of the puritans. His insistence upon a more vigorous discipline of the clergy, enforced with the aid of the Court of High Commission, led to the ejection or resignation of a considerable number of puritan clergy, and made him the direct object of some of the more outspoken criticisms of the anonymous "Martin Marprelate" in 1588–9. Whitgift lived to crown James I, but died shortly after the close of the Hampton Court conference.

> Lives by V. J. K. Brook, *Whitgift and the English Church*, English Universities Press; P. M. Dawley, *John Whitgift and the Reformation*, A. and C. Black.
> See also his *Works*, ed. by J. Ayre (Parker Society 1851-3); and J. Strype, *The Life and Acts of John Whitgift*, Clarendon Press.

## WOLSEY

*Thomas Wolsey, Cardinal and Archbishop of York* (1475?-1530), Henrician statesman.

Wolsey was born in Ipswich and educated at Magdalen College, Oxford, where he became a fellow in 1497, and soon afterwards Master of Magdalen College School. After resigning his college offices he served for a time as chaplain to the governor of Calais and entered the King's service in 1507. Employed by Henry VII on diplomatic missions, he rose rapidly in royal favour during the early years of the reign of Henry VIII, and by 1512 was foremost in importance of the King's councillors. From then until his fall from favour in 1529 the history of England and the life story of Wolsey are virtually inseparable. He planned the campaigns against France in 1512 and 1513, and had a controlling voice in the conduct of English diplomacy from then onwards. His services to the King were rewarded in the customary manner of the day by promotion in the church. Already possessed of a plurality of lesser livings before the accession of Henry VIII, he received many more from the new King. Early in 1514 he received the bishopric of Lincoln, and was translated to the archbishopric of York later in the same year. This latter see he held until his death. In 1518 he acquired the bishopric of Bath and Wells, which he exchanged in 1523 for that of Durham. Durham he likewise resigned when he was appointed to Winchester in 1529, so that at no time did he hold more than two English bishoprics. In 1515 he replaced William Warham as Lord Chancellor, and was in the same year made Cardinal. In 1518 he became papal legate *a latere,* an appointment which was renewed from time to time and conferred on him for life in 1524. The possession by one man of power so extensive in both church and state naturally aroused the jealousy of those who felt themselves excluded, and made for Wolsey many enemies who were quick to pull him down when his failure to secure for the King a separation from Catherine of Aragon lost him the royal favour. His sometimes high-handed methods of government made him very unpopular, and he found it almost impossible to secure the co-operation of Parliament in his schemes. In the 1520s he secured permission to dissolve a number of monasteries out of whose revenues he proposed to endow a school in Ipswich and a college in Oxford. The latter has survived as Christ Church. As Lord Chancellor he made of Star Chamber a very effective instrument for the suppression of petty tyrannies. Condemned, but pardoned, for a breach of *Praemunire* in 1529, he was on his way to London to face a further charge of treason when he died at Leicester in 1530.

Lives by M. Creighton, Macmillan; and A. F. Pollard, Long-
    mans.
See also G. Cavendish, *The Life of Cardinal Wolsey,* ed.
    R. S. Sylvester, Early English Text Society, vol. CCXLIII.

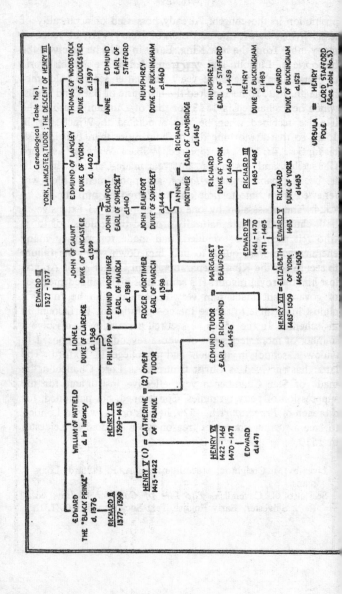

Genealogical Table No.1.

YORK, LANCASTER, TUDOR; THE DESCENT OF HENRY VII

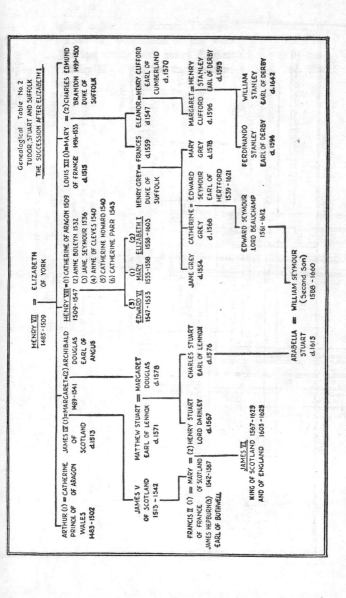

Genealogical Table No. 2
TUDOR, STUART AND SUFFOLK
THE SUCCESSION AFTER ELIZABETH I

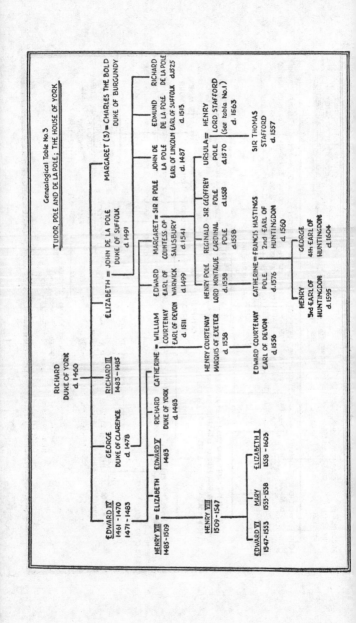

Genealogical Table No 3

TUDOR, POLE AND DE LA POLE; THE HOUSE OF YORK

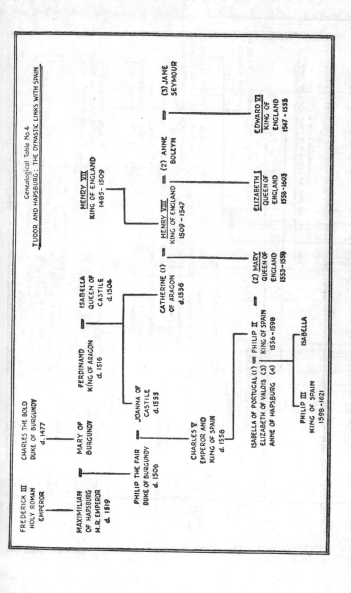

Genealogical Table No.4

TUDOR AND HAPSBURG : THE DYNASTIC LINKS WITH SPAIN

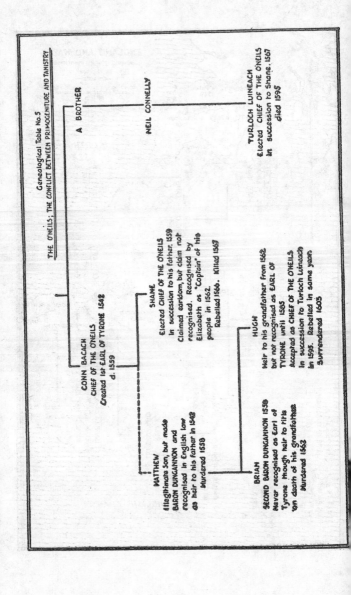

Genealogical Table No. 5

THE ONEILS; THE CONFLICT BETWEEN PRIMOGENITURE AND TANISTRY

**A BROTHER**

**NEIL CONNELLY**

**TURLOCH LUINEACH**
Elected Chief of the Oneils
in succession to Shane. 1567
died 1595

**CONN BACACH**
CHIEF OF THE ONEILS
Created 1st EARL OF TYRONE 1542
d. 1559

**SHANE**
Elected Chief of the Oneils
in succession to his father. 1559
Claimed earldom, but claim not
recognised. Recognised by
Elizabeth as "Captain" of his
people in 1562.
Rebelled 1566. Killed 1567

**MATTHEW**
Illegitimate son, but made
BARON DUNGANNON and
recognised in English law
as heir to his father in 1542
Murdered 1558

**HUGH**
Heir to his grandfather from 1562
but not recognised as EARL OF
TYRONE until 1585
Accepted as CHIEF OF THE ONEILS
in succession to Turloch Luineach
in 1595. Rebelled in same year.
Surrendered 1603

**BRIAN**
SECOND BARON DUNGANNON 1558
Never recognised as Earl of
Tyrone though heir to title
'on death of his grandfather 1563
Murdered 1563

ENGLAND AND WALES
Showing places mentioned
in the text

20 10 0      20    40    60
Miles

SCOTLAND

Edinburgh ✕ Pinkie
1549
• Ayton
Berwick
R. Tweed
✕ Flodden
1513

Solway
Moss
1542
R. Tyne

NORTH
SEA

R. Eden

IRISH SEA

York

WALES

R. Dee

WELSH MARCHES

R. Severn

Lichfield

Coventry

Bosworth
✕ 1485

East
Stoke
1487

R. Trent

Walsingham

R. Yare

Peterborough

R. Ouse

Cambridge
Ipswich

R. Wye

Gloucester

Oxford

Colchester

Llandaff

Bristol

Westminster
Reading

London
Greenwich

R. Thames

Glastonbury

Canterbury
Dover

R. Exe

ENGLISH CHANNEL

IRELAND

0 10 20 30 40 50
Miles

ATLANTIC
OCEAN

ULSTER

TYRONE

CLANDEBOYE

ARDS

Dundalk

Drogheda

CONNACHT

MEATH & THE PALE

R Shannon

OFFALY

Dublin

KILDARE

LEINSTER

LEIX

IRISH SEA

MUNSTER

Kinsale

ATLANTIC OCEAN

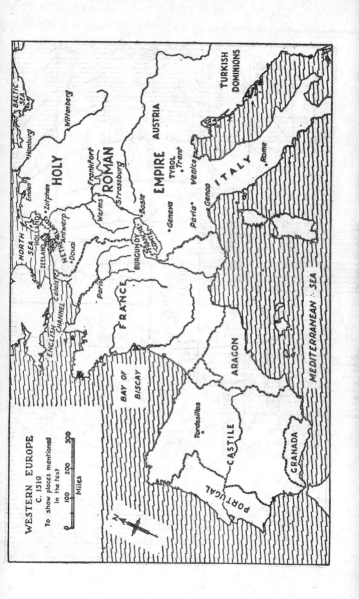

WESTERN EUROPE
C. 1519
To show places mentioned
in the text

0  100  200  300
Miles

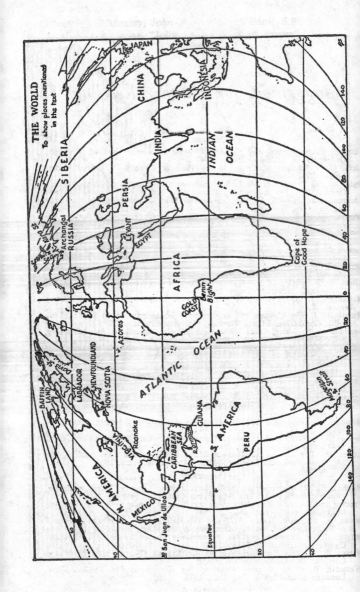

THE WORLD
To show places mentioned
in the text

# Suggestions for Further Reading

## CHAPTER 2

Caspari, F. *Humanism and the Social Order in Tudor England.* Chicago: University of Chicago Press, 1954.

Firth, C. B. "Benefit of Clergy in the Time of Edward IV," *English Historical Review,* XXXII.

Ogle, A. *The Tragedy of the Lollards' Tower* (The Case of Richard Hunne). Oxford: The Pen-in-Hand Publishing Co., Ltd., 1949.

Thompson, A. H. *The English Clergy and Their Organization in the Later Middle Ages.* New York and London: Oxford University Press, 1947.

Waugh, W. T. "The Great Statute of Praemunire," *English Historical Review,* XXXVII.

## CHAPTER 3

Beard, C. A. *The Office of Justice of the Peace in England.* New York: Columbia University Press, 1904.

Dunham, W. H. *Lord Hastings' Indentured Retainers, 1461–1483.* New Haven, Conn.: Yale University Press, 1955.

Elton, G. R. *The Tudor Revolution in Government.* New York and London: Cambridge University Press, 1959.

Habakkuk, H. J. "The Market for Monastic Property," *Economic History Review,* X.

Hurstfield, J. *The Queen's Wards.* London: Longmans, Green & Co., Ltd., 1958; Cambridge, Mass.: Harvard University Press, 1959.

Leadam, I. S. *Select Cases Before the King's Council in Star Chamber,* Selden Society, vols. 16 and 25.

Reid, R. R. *The King's Council in the North.* London: Longmans, Green & Co., Ltd., 1921.

## CHAPTER 4

Elton, G. R. *The Tudor Constitution.* New York and London: Cambridge University Press, 1960.

Fortescue, J. *De Laudibus Legum Angliae.* Edited, in translation by S. B. Chrimes. New York: The Macmillan Company; London: Cambridge University Press, 1942.

Neale, J. E. *Elizabeth I and Her Parliaments.* London: Jonathan Cape, Ltd., 1953.

———. *The Elizabethan House of Commons.* London: Jonathan Cape, Ltd., 1949; New Haven, Conn.: Yale University Press, 1950.

Roper, W. *The Life of Sir Thomas More,* Early English Text Society, vol. 197. New York and London: Oxford University Press, 1935.

## CHAPTER 5

Hughes, P. *The Reformation in England.* 3 vols. London: Hollis & Carter, 1950–54; New York: The Macmillan Company, 1951–54.

Proctor and Frere. *A New History of the Book of Common Prayer.* London: Macmillan & Co., Ltd.

Smith, H. Maynard. *Henry VIII and the Reformation.* New York: Russell & Russell, Inc., London: Macmillan & Co., Ltd., 1962.

Smyth, C. H. *Cranmer and the Reformation Under Edward VI.* London: Cambridge University Press, 1926.

Usher, R. G. *The Reconstruction of the English Church.* New York and London: D. Appleton & Co., 1910.

Westcott, B. F. *A General View of the History of the English Bible.* London: Macmillan & Co., Ltd., 1872.

## CHAPTER 6

Baskerville, G. *English Monks and the Suppression of the Monasteries.* London: Jonathan Cape, Ltd., 1940.

Habakkuk, H. J. "The Market for Monastic Property," *Economic Histor* *Review,* X.

Hill, J. E. C. *The Economic Problems of the Church.* New York and Lor don: Oxford University Press, 1956.

Knowles, D. *The Religious Orders in England,* III. New York and London Cambridge University Press, 1959.

Youings, J. "The Terms of the Disposal of the Devon Monastic Lands, *English Historical Review,* LXIX.

CHAPTER 7

Colinson, P. *The Letters of Thomas Wood, Puritan.* London: The Athlor Press.

Dawley, P. M. *John Whitgift and the Reformation.* New York: Charle Scribner's Sons, 1954; London: A. & C. Black, Ltd., 1955.

Dickens, A. G. *Lollards and Protestants in the Diocese of York, 1509 1558.* New York and London: Oxford University Press, 1959.

Garret, C. H. *The Marian Exiles.* London: Cambridge University Press.

Hopf, C. *Martin Bucer and the English Reformation.* Oxford: Basil Black well & Mott, Ltd., 1946; New York: The Macmillan Company, 1947.

Knappen, M. M. *Tudor Puritanism.* Chicago: University of Chicago Pres 1939.

Marchant, R. A. *Puritans and the Church Courts in the Diocese of Yor 1560–1642.* London: Longmans, Green & Co., Ltd., 1960.

CHAPTER 8

Bayne, C. G. *Anglo-Roman Relations, 1558-1565.* London: Oxford Universi Press, 1913.

Gerard, J. *The Autobiography of John Gerard, an Elizabethan.* Trans. Caraman. London: Longmans, Green & Co., Ltd., 1955.

Hughes, P. *The Reformation in England, III.* New York: The Macmilla Company; London: Hollis and Carter, 1954.

Pollen, J. H. *The English Catholics in the Reign of Queen Elizabeth.* Lor don: Longmans, Green & Co., Ltd.

Simpson, R. *Edmund Campion.* London: Hodge & Co., Ltd.

Smith, L. B. *Tudor Prelates and Politics.* Princeton, N.J.: Princeton Un versity Press, 1953.

CHAPTER 9

Brown, P. H. *John Knox.* London: A. & C. Black, Ltd., 1895.

Bryan, D. *Gerald Fitzgerald, the Great Earl of Kildare.* Dublin: The Talbe Press, Ltd., 1933.

Curtis, E. *A History of Ireland.* New York: Barnes & Noble, Inc.; Londor Methuen & Co., Ltd., 1961.

Donaldson, G. *The Scottish Reformation.* New York and London: Can bridge University Press, 1960.

Dunlop, R. The Plantation of Leix and Offaly, *English Historical Review,* V

Edwards, R. D. *Church and State in Tudor Ireland.* London: Longman Green & Co., Ltd., 1935.

Falls, C. *Elizabeth's Irish Wars.* London: Methuen & Co., Ltd., 1951; Ne York: Hillary House Publishers, Ltd., 1959.

Henderson, T. F. *Mary Queen of Scots.* London: Hutchinson & Co., Ltd 1905.

Mackenzie, A. M. *The Rise of the Stewarts.* London: Oliver & Boyd, Ltd 1957.

———. *The Scotland of Queen Mary and the Religious Wars, 1513–163 London: Oliver & Boyd, Ltd., 1957.

Wilson, P. *The Beginnings of Modern Ireland.* Dublin: Maunsel & Co., Ltd 1912.

CHAPTER 10

Corbett, J. S. *Drake and the Tudor Navy.* London and New York: Lon mans, Green & Co., Ltd., 1898.

Geyl, P. *The Revolt of the Netherlands.* London: Williams and Norgat Ltd., 1932; New York: Barnes & Noble, Inc., 1958.

Mattingly, G. *The Spanish Armada.* Boston, Mass.: Houghton Mifflin Con pany; London: Jonathan Cape, Ltd., 1959.

Pollard, A. F. *Wolsey.* New York and London: Longmans, Green & Co Inc., 1953.

Read, C. *Mr. Secretary Walsingham and the Policy of Queen Elizabet Cambridge, Mass.: Harvard University Press; London: Oxford Universi Press, 1925.

CHAPTER 11

Fisher, F. J. "Commercial Trends and Policy in Sixteenth-Century England," *Economic History Review*, X.
——. "The Development of the London Food Market, 1540–1640." *Economic History Review*, V.
Nef, J. U. "Prices and Industrial Capitalism, 1540–1640," *Economic History Review*, VII.
Stone, L. "State Control in Sixteenth-Century England," *Economic History Review*, XVII.
Tawney, R. H. *The Agrarian Problem in the Sixteenth Century*. London: Longmans, Green & Co., Ltd., 1912; New York: Longmans, Green & Co., Inc., 1913.
——. *Religion and the Rise of Capitalism*. New York: Harcourt, Brace & Company, Inc., 1926; London: John Murray, 1927; New York: The New American Library (Mentor Books), 1947.
Thirsk, J. *Tudor Enclosures* (Historical Association pamphlet No. G. 41).

CHAPTER 12

Gosling, W. G. *The Life of Sir Humphrey Gilbert*. London: Constable & Co., Ltd., 1911.
Quinn, D. B. *Raleigh and the British Empire*. London: English Universities Press, Ltd., 1947; New York: The Macmillan Company, 1949.
Ramsay, G. D. *English Overseas Trade During the Centuries of Emergence*. New York: St. Martin's Press; London: Macmillan & Co., Ltd., 1957.
Williamson, J. A. *Maritime Enterprise, 1485–1558*. New York and London: Oxford University Press, 1913.
——. *Sir John Hawkins*. New York and London: Oxford University Press, 1927.
——. *The Voyages of the Cabots*. London: Argonaut Press, 1929.

CHAPTER 13

Baker, C. H. C. and Constable, W. G. *English Painting of the Sixteenth and Seventeenth Centuries*. New York: Harcourt, Brace & Company, Inc., 1930.
Barley, M. W. *The English Farmhouse and Cottage*. London: Routledge and Kegan Paul, Ltd., 1961; New York: Hillary House, Inc., 1962.
Chambers, E. K. *The Elizabethan Stage*. 4 vols. New York and London: Oxford University Press, 1923.
Einstein, L. D. *The Italian Renaissance in England*. New York: Columbia University Press, 1927.
Garner, T. and Stratton, A. *The Domestic Architecture of England During the Tudor Period*. London: B. T. Batsford, Ltd., 1914.
Gotch, J. A. *Early Renaissance Architecture in England*. New York: Charles Scribner's Sons, 1914.
Walker, E. *A History of Music in England*. New York and London: Oxford University Press, 1952.

# Index

244